Edexcel Economics

and Edexcel International

TARGET B-A*

Year 12 & 13 Microeconomics

Ian Marcousé

A-Z Business Training Ltd

Contents

Section 3.1: Business Growth

Section 3.2: Business Objectives

Section 3.3: Business Objectives

Section 3.4: Market Structure

Thinking like an economist

Grade C. What is it?

Edexcel suggests that 'thinking like an economist' equates to developing models based on assumptions. This is important, but it is clear that there are other key factors in thinking like an economist. Economists like to base arguments on objective rather than subjective evidence. And they usually make two assumptions that are rarely stated: that the key human motivation is self-interest; and the key business motivation is profit maximisation.

Do absorb the logic of building models, including abstract ones such as perfect competition. It's easy to fight against the unrealistic nature of this theory – but it's better to accept that it's an interesting, illuminating theory, even if it rarely applies in the real world.

Grade B (i) Where's the beef?

The beef lies in how an examiner expects students to tackle any economic problem/question. If you are able to frame the problem using economic theory, your answer will be hugely more acceptable. Your supporting arguments must never be anecdotal or personal/subjective – they should be based on objective evidence such as latest government data.

Grade B (ii) Why it matters

It matters because every academic subject needs a core of academic thinking. In economics there's a desire to build models and to turn the underlying algebra into diagrams that can be used to illustrate constant and changing situations. The assumptions underpinning such models should always be stated.

Don't worry about critiquing the models you're using. Some – such as the Phillips curve and the Laffer curve – have always had as many critics as supporters.

Grade A The other side

There is a risk that 'thinking like an economist' suggests that all economists think in the same way. They don't. After the unforecast recession of 2009, students at Manchester University formed the *Post-Crash Economics Society* and wrote a book ('Econocracy') that criticised the narrow curriculum taught as Economics around the world. Furthermore, behavioural economists use research into actual human behaviour rather than relying on theoretical models. So 'thinking like an economist' can be broader than the exam board's definition (as the examiners know perfectly well).

Exam tip: at A Level, the most obvious sign of thinking like an economist is to seize every opportunity to frame your analysis of a problem through the prism of a diagram. Well-labelled and well integrated into the text – diagrams ooze marks.

Grade A* The critical perspective

When evaluating any theory, the most important thing is to show mastery of that theory. That earns you the right to question its underlying assumptions (are they realistic? Do they contain an inherent political bias?) or to critique the way the theory is being used in practice. The starting point, though, is to master the theory, so be prepared to ask questions about how the model works – and the circumstances in which it may fail to work effectively.

Thinking like an economist: transmission mechanism (to top response level)

Chain 1. If the housing market is in a mess an economist would want to build an accurate model of supply and demand (1) … and use it to analyse the problems (2). This would be done using objective evidence (3) ... in the hope of using the model to make predictions (4) … to help offer solutions to the problem. (5)

Chain 2. Models, like laws, are made to be broken (1). This is because every model is a simplification of the real world's complexities (2) ... and therefore should be evaluated, not worshipped (3) Some models such as the Laffer Curve can be questioned for being politics, not economics (4)… and others might be questioned for their predictive accuracy in the real world (5).

Ceteris paribus and building models

Grade C. What is it?

Ceteris paribus is Latin for 'all other things being equal'. The reality of markets (micro-economics) and economies (macro-economics) is that they are in a state of constant flux. The real world has a huge number of variables that make it near-impossible to identify cause and effect for any individual variable. So ceteris paribus means assuming that every variable stays constant apart from the one you're looking at. It may be unrealistic, but it's used widely in economic analysis.

Grade B (i) Where's the beef?

The beef lies in the idea of model-building. Economics is founded in theory which models real-world behaviour – almost always in ways that place ceteris paribus at the centre. This makes the models correct in their own terms – based on their own assumptions – but without necessarily meaning that the models provide much insight into the real world. So the subject goes on treating certain things as true that are disproved by evidence from the real world (which is very strange).

Grade B (ii) Why it matters

This topic matters because economics has a huge effect on political decisions. Economists persist in warning governments that setting a national minimum wage will cause unemployment – even though this has not been generally true in the many countries that have brought in this legislation (including the UK). The ceteris paribus assumption allow economists to assume away the demand-side benefits from higher minimum wages, while focusing on the supply-side analysis.

Grade A The counter-argument

Even though it slows down the analysis, it's essential that every assumption should be stated. It's lazy to assume that the reader knows the assumptions that underpin your arguments. Models such as *perfect* competition are a critical part of thinking like an economist, but require key assumptions to be stated as well as understood.

Grade A* The critical perspective

The strongest arguments are based on solid economic models such as types of market or types of business behaviour. It is important to think critically from within the theory rather than outside it. But having shown the solidity of your understanding of the model, be bold in questioning whether the theory is outgunned by counter-theory, or whether the theory holds up in the real world, especially in whether it holds up beyond the assumption of ceteris paribus. And <u>always</u> state your assumptions.

Do remember that economics is a social science, not a 'real' (or physical) one. Models are based on assumptions about human behaviour – but that behaviour changes over time due to new trends, ideas and attitudes. So the assumptions must be stated.

Don't forget to state 'ceteris paribus' every time you're analysing a situation with several variables. It shows that you understand the problem of drawing real-world conclusions from your arguments.

Exam tip: examiners are quite tolerant of students who fail to state assumptions, but to get the highest response levels it is vital to show the examiner your grasp of theory – especially the ceteris paribus assumption.

Ceteris paribus and models: transmission mechanism (to top response level)

Chain 1. The best models are based on a limited number of assumptions (1) … that are clearly stated and remembered (2) … and have a general impact on understanding and decision-making (3). Yet there are exceptions to every theory (4) … and a risk the theory encourages over-simplification. (5)

Chain 2. With more than 5 million firms in the UK it's invaluable to have an overall theory containing category models such as perfect competition (1) … which help allow each firm to be assessed (2). But with big, broad theories it's easy to forget the assumptions underpinning individual parts such as monopoly or monopolistic competition (3) ... creating the threat of simplistic conclusions being drawn (4)… such as that perfect competition represents the base reality of most small firms (5).

Positive and normative statements

Grade C. What is it?

A positive statement is one that is definite enough to be checked or verified. It doesn't have to be 'positive' in the sense of having an optimistic outlook. So an example of a positive statement is the very negative-sounding: 'this company is going to lose £1 million this year'. At the end of the year this statement can be checked, so it's positive. A normative statement is a matter of opinion that cannot easily be verified, such as 'Ed Sheeran is a better singer than Sam Smith'. Examiners of economics like positive statements but are wary of normative ones.

Do reflect on some of the statements made in the 'Brexit' debate. The bus-side claim of £350 million a week for the NHS was a positive statement – but also a lie. Perhaps Andrea Leadsom's promise of Brexit's 'sunlit uplands' was preferable, though clearly normative.

Grade B (i) Where's the beef?

The beef lies with your ability to distinguish clearly between the two types of statement. You need to spot the difference when reading the exam stimulus materials, and know when you're using one approach or the other. Sometimes it's absolutely right to be normative. If the exam text tells you about immoral business practices in developing countries, you have every right to sound angry or condemning. But do explain the reasoning behind your opinion.

Grade B (ii) Why it matters

It matters because an academic crime is *opinion stated as fact*. In other words you must know when your arguments are based on your opinions, not on objective evidence. Having opinions is a wonderful thing – and can make you a better economist – but you must know when your writing is normative – and make it clear that you know.

Don't shy away from opinion. The Laffer Curve may or may not be accurate, but there's no doubt about its political purpose – to cut income taxes on the rich. It's fair to have an opinion on that.

Grade A The counter-argument

The counter-argument is based on scepticism of factually-based, supposedly objective writing. In recent years populist politicians have even claimed that 'people are fed up with experts', implying that the electorate now wants normative views rather than positive arguments. Most economists would reject the idea that the electorate's opinions matter in this particular way. People may be fed up with facts, but economists should always prefer fact to normative fiction.

Grade A* The critical perspective

Despite economists' faith in objective argument, there are a worrying number of cases where social scientists have built persuasive cases on apparent evidence that has crumbled under scrutiny. As many as half of all social science research proves impossible to replicate – implying that the first study was flawed. Objective argument based on evidence is a fine thing; but harder to achieve than you'd think.

Exam tip: if you spot a normative statement within a broadly objective argument (in the exam text), pick it out and try to find a way to use it to answer a question or two. The examiner will admire your analytic skills.

Positive and normative: transmission mechanism (to the top response level)

Chain 1. If a positive statement is backed by evidence (1) … it can only be countered by finding other evidence that refutes the original (2) … or by finding flaws within the evidence (3). In law they have a great way to describe real truth: it must be 'the truth, the whole truth and nothing but the truth' (4). Any economist that meets that test deserves our serious attention.

Chain 2. A normative statement may be a matter of opinion (1) … but the value of that opinion is worth considering (2) … because wisdom can grow with experience as well as academic excellence (3)… meaning that the opinion of a great expert may be worth more than the opinion of a recent graduate (4) .. especially if that normative statement is backed by unstated but high quality analysis. (5)

Value judgements in decision-making

Grade C. What is it?

Collins English Dictionary says that 'If you make a value judgement on something, you form an opinion about it based on your principles and beliefs and not on facts that can be checked or proved'. In other words it is a normative process, not a positive one. But this may be overstated. Often, firms and governments make value judgements on what to do based on partial evidence, perhaps supplemented by principles and beliefs. Each year the Chancellor of the Exchequer's Budget is based on a series of value judgements, such as the 'right' income tax rate.

Grade B (i) Where's the beef?

The beef lies in evaluating the factors influencing the value judgement. In some cases the main factor may seem to be political conviction (the push for Brexit, perhaps) and in others an economic philosophy, such as the privatisation of the probation service. A further possibility is that the value judgement is made after gathering evidence – perhaps based on regional trials of the policy – in which case the judgement is as close to an objective decision as it's possible to achieve.

Grade B (ii) Why it matters

It matters because A Level Economics is based on the view that objective, evidence-based analysis and evaluation is the ideal. So although value judgements are inevitably required by economists and politicians alike, they should be as close to objectivity as possible. In the past, huge decisions (such as the multi-£billion 'Free Schools' programme) have been made with no proper trialling or testing. This is anti-economic in its approach. Proper value judgements need evidence.

Grade A The other side

A minority of economists see pure theory as a justification for decisions. That theory may be from the political right (free-market economics) or political left (a Marxist approach). Such convictions may lead to a view of a 'hard' Brexit as the start of a new, glorious era for Britain; or may want the nationalisation of the banks as the start of a new socialist era.

Grade A* The critical perspective

A sceptic would see other worries in an economist's value judgements. Several supposed 'think-tanks' refuse to state where their funding comes from. Those funded by tobacco companies, oil companies or right-wing U.S. billionaires have a vested interest in making the 'right' value judgements – right, that is, to serve their masters' interests. When viewing economic arguments, there's a lot to think about

Do accept that value judgements are inevitable, because there is rarely a full set of facts and figures pointing in a clear direction. So the issues are how much effort was made to get objective evidence? And what may have been the other factors influencing the decision made?

Don't fall into the trap of questioning the motives only of those you disagree with. Also accept that politicians will make economic decisions with an eye on the politics, e.g. the next election date.

Exam tip: it works hugely well to spot a value judgement in the evidence presented by the exam board – or in the questions you are being asked. Don't condemn, but do ask whether the judgement is fair.

Value judgements: transmission mechanism (to the top response level)

Chain 1. If economic analysis includes a value judgement it's vital to acknowledge it (1) … probably by explaining the need for it (2) … perhaps due to the absence of clear evidence (3) ... or because judgement has become inevitable (4) ... as when a firm such as Apple must respond to inflationary pressures by either pushing prices up or by acting to cut production costs.

Chain 2. An exam 'crime' is to treat a value judgement as if it's factually based (1) … which usually occurs when the student doesn't know there's another side to the argument (2) … and therefore assumes that their own opinion is shared by everyone (3)… or indeed that their opinion is a fact (4). Your politics are not a problem unless you fail to realise that they are influencing your economics. (5)

The economic problem

Grade C. What is it?

According to Edexcel, *the* economic problem is scarcity, i.e. human beings have unlimited wants on a planet with limited (finite) resources. The implication is that the most important economic task is to encourage the creation of more products and services to reduce the scarcity. In effect, to stimulate more economic growth. This desire is complicated by the fact that not all resources are renewable. The existence of non-renewable resources such as oil must eventually hinder growth.

Grade B (i) Where's the beef?

One beefy issue is whether economic analysis takes seriously the question of renewables and non-renewables – and therefore the sustainability of growth. Environmentalists believe that sustainability ('the health of the planet') is so important that governments should no longer aim to maximise economic growth. Most economists ignore sustainability within their analysis, but mention it as an extra issue within their conclusion – almost as an afterthought.

Grade B (ii) Why it matters

It matters because it affects the politics underpinning the economic argument. Scarcity and economic growth are comfortable areas for free market economists and for businesspeople. Inequality is a more difficult topic for those on the political right, but comfortable for those who value government intervention. By ignoring inequality as part of the economic problem, a political choice is being made.

Grade A The other side

The counter-argument is to question the initial assumption. Who says that scarcity is 'the' economic problem? We live in a world with plenty of food (with something like 40% of food being wasted in the UK) and plenty of clean water (we flush our toilets with perfect drinking water). The problem is one of allocation. Westerners have more than they can use/need, while much of the world goes hungry. Scarcity may be an economic problem, but distribution/inequality is every bit as important.

Grade A* The critical perspective

Assumptions are an essential building block of theory. But they should always be stated explicitly. Calling scarcity 'the economic problem' is no more than an assumption. From that assumption flows a chain of logic that makes economic growth seem all-important. In politics this would be called 'framing an argument', meaning getting people thinking and talking about what you want them to think. Good economists question the assumptions underlying every theory.

Do master the logic of the economic problem. Unlimited wants mean that the demand side of economic growth will always be moving ahead. And finite resources mean that it's critical to maximise supply through highly efficient resource allocation.

Don't shy away from criticism. Examiners want students to understand economic theory, but also have the grasp and confidence to construct and evaluate an economic debate.

Exam tip: environmentalists focus on scarcity of (the earth's) physical resources In fact, day by day, scarcity of labour with the right skills proves a bigger constraint – both in developed and (especially) in developing countries.

The economic problem: transmission mechanism (to the top response level)

Chain 1. If resources such as oil are in short supply (1) … the price mechanism will create the incentives to achieve an efficient re-allocation (2) … perhaps including households switching to electric cars to avoid the high cost of petrol (3). The invisible hand of the market will achieve this (4) ... without any government intervention. (5)

Chain 2. For a UK household fed from a food bank (1) … hearing of Britain's high levels of food waste is chilling (2) … as it confirms the unfairness of food distribution in Britain today. (3) Few would doubt that the cause is income inequality (4) ... which may lead to inequality of opportunity. (5)

Renewable and non-renewable resources

Grade C. What is it?

Renewable resources should never run out. They include wind and solar power, where the consumption has no effect on future supply. By contrast fossil fuels such as coal, oil and gas could all run out if consumption levels are too high. They are non-renewable. A famous investor maxim is 'buy land; they're not making it any more'.

Grade B (i) Where's the beef?

The beef comes from the tension between conventional and green/environmental economics. Most economists view scarcity as a reason to push for faster economic growth. If the country had a higher GDP, fewer people would be in absolute poverty. Environmentalists relate scarcity to non-renewable resources – and push for slower economic growth to stop so many resources being consumed. There is no right and wrong here – only argument & counter-argument (perfect for exams).

Grade B (ii) Why it matters

The topic matters in relation to the long-term future of the planet and its inhabitants. Environmentalists worry that key resources will run out, leaving the economy and ecology unbalanced. They might take this further, relating it to global warming. Trees are renewable, but in regions like the Amazon, rain forests may be destroyed to provide land for agriculture. Trees absorb CO2, so their depletion may hasten global warming.

Grade A The other side

Many free market economists are sceptical of this apocalyptic view, suggesting that market forces (the price mechanism) will stop people over-purchasing items in ever-more limited supply. So, as non-renewables start to run out, the restricted supply pushes prices up – cutting demand. And the high prices act as a signal to encourage firms to develop innovative substitutes for the resources concerned.

Grade A* The critical perspective

A common critique is to question the priorities and motives of those focused on the relatively distant ecological future. Have they not noticed that hundreds of millions have no running water and no proper sanitation? Or, less far away, have they not noticed the massive rise in the use of food banks in the UK? Are these not more urgent problems, requiring an energetic, perhaps angry, response? Today's problems may be being kicked into the long grass while people focus their energies on problems that may yet be solved by innovative, unexpected solutions.

Do keep your exam answers focused on economic arguments. You may have touched on renewables/non-renewables in Geography or Chemistry – but you must keep thinking as an economist.

Don't forget firms have incentives to act in environmentally friendly ways. In the short term toilet-roll producers want to boost their image by saying 'we plant two trees for every one we use'. In the long term they want to ensure continuity of supply of new trees to cut down.

Exam tip: avoid being too 'preachy' on environmental matters. Keep your analysis cool and two-sided. Leave judgements about what's right and wrong to your conclusion – and make sure to back your views with clear arguments.

Renewable & non-renewables: transmission mechanism (to top response level)

Chain 1. Fossil fuels such as oil and gas are non-renewable (1) … and therefore could be hit with a carbon tax (2) ... to help firms adjust today to the internal cost pressures (3) ... that would otherwise only hit them when supply runs out (4). Pain today would help avoid shock tomorrow (and the carbon tax would discourage consumption, making existing supplies last longer (5).

Chain 2. Renewables also have environmental impacts (1) … such as cows munching their grass in a field – but apparently creating a great deal of CO2 (2). So there is an equal case for taxing 'exhaust emissions' from cows (3) … on the grounds of taxing negative externalities. (4) There is no reason to ignore environmental hazards just because they come from renewable sources. (5)

Opportunity cost

Grade C. What is it?

Opportunity cost is the cost of missing out on the next best alternative when making a decision. This may be measurable, such as the interest payments foregone when capital is invested. Or it may literally be immeasurable, such as the loss to Tesco of its focus on building Tesco USA when it should have focused on its weakening position in UK grocery. The direct cost was the £2 billion loss made by Tesco UK. The opportunity cost was far, far higher.

Grade B (i) Where's the beef?

The beef comes from the attempt to quantify the costs. After all, opportunity costs are hypothetical, not real. Some can be quantified, such as the rate of interest, but many can only be estimated, such as the potential profits from a firm you've decided *not* to buy. They *may* be quantified with the benefits of hindsight, but that can be unfair on the decision-makers.

Grade B (ii) Why it matters

It matters because decisions by firms, consumers and governments all involve choices – and that involves deciding what to do and what *not* to do. The opportunity cost (missing out on what you've decided *not* to do) can come back to bite the decision-maker. Huge recent rises in state pension provision may have been at the cost of younger families, especially those with disabilities. Evaluating opportunity cost may require moral as well as economic considerations.

Grade A The other side

The counter-argument is to question the value of opportunity cost considerations and calculations, especially hypothetical ones. There are two risks involved. One is the risk of being overwhelmed by the choices/options and therefore struggling to decide. The second is that the attempt to quantify all options may be manipulated – leading to poor decision making. There are many who believe the government decision to build high-speed railway HS2 has been political rather than economic.

Grade A* The critical perspective

It is important to be able to question and critique the way in which opportunity cost is used by firms or government. Nevertheless, opportunity cost is a vital part of the way economists think. So important, in fact, that it often forms the heart of the analysis of key decisions such as take-over bids, deciding whether to open new markets in country A or B, or in government spending programmes. And opportunity cost is at the heart of macro as well as micro decision making.

Do try to give relevant examples of opportunity cost. It feels a bit lazy that every student wants to compare government spending to the NHS. The opportunity cost of higher pay for teachers might be fewer textbooks purchased. So try to give highly relevant examples.

Don't forget opportunity cost applies to consumers as well as firms. In the attempt to maximise utility, consumers face the standard problem: how to value the next best alternatives

Exam tip: avoid shorthand examples of opportunity cost, such as 'e.g. current interest rates'. The opportunity cost of a decision is almost always worth a paragraph of analysis.

Opportunity cost: transmission mechanism (to the top response level)

Chain 1. If a firm invests heavily in one factor of production (perhaps capital in the form of robotics) (1) ... the opportunity cost may be borne by the other factors (2). Labour may be hard hit with a cut in budgets due to the higher investment in capital (3). This may become a worry if the opportunity cost of the capital investment proves to be a fall in staff motivation (4) .. which may hit productivity (5)

Chain 2. For almost every UK household opportunity cost is a central (if unknown) concept (1) ... because of the need to keep spending down to the level of income. (2) A decision to go for a birthday meal may mean subtle cutbacks later in the week (3) .. and thereby avoid digging into savings or getting into debt. (4) For households, firms and government, every decision involves opportunity cost. (5)

Capital and consumer goods

Grade C. What is it?

Capital goods can be used over and over again and are therefore investments into the future of a firm or household. Typically a capital good is a piece of machinery, such as a robot or a washing machine. Households may buy a new car or a firm may buy a new truck. Both are capital goods.

Consumer goods are consumed or used once only, such as a bottle of wine or a train ticket. Capital goods are about the future, whereas consumer goods are about today's needs – like feeding the family.

Grade B (i) Where's the beef?

The key economic principle is the overlap between micro and macro. Many concepts are clearly one or the other, but capital and consumer goods are equally important in micro and macro analysis. The difference between the two matters in micro and macro exams, but especially in combined exams such as Edexcel's Paper 3.

Grade B (ii) Why it matters

Capital v consumer goods is an important distinction when looking at economic growth and development. In each year from 1990 to 2019 China invested more than 40% of its GDP into capital goods such as roads and railways – and was the world's fastest-growing economy. By contrast, slow-growing western countries such as the UK and Italy spend less than 20% of annual GDP on capital goods.

Grade A The other side

Free market economists discourage the separation of capital from consumer goods. They believe that 'investment' is a meaningless term. Their logic is to say that the only investment that creates economic value is profitable investment. In other words it's the profit that matters, and it's the profit that creates economic growth. They criticise China for excessive investment in unprofitable schemes such as their network of super-fast railways.

Grade A* The critical perspective

In economics there's a constant debate between the role of theory and the role of 'empirical' research. The latter means looking for statistical evidence, i.e. looking for the facts. In the case of the Chinese growth story, it's hard to argue against the correlation between high investment in capital goods and high GDP growth. But a) correlation doesn't prove causation and b) free market economists do not jettison theory in the face of contrary evidence.

Do remember that capital goods are one-off items, often involving large sums, e.g. buying a house or building a factory. Such spending hinges on confidence, so tends to be very cyclical. In good times spending on capital goods booms. In bad times it slumps.

Don't doubt the importance to free market economies of consumers and consumer goods. When times are tough consumers tend to dis-save, which keeps GDP relatively stable. Businesses can postpone capital spending, but can't avoid regular spending on consumption goods such as raw materials.

Exam tip: when reading the exam text, always consider whether the market/product is a capital or consumer good – and follow the analysis through.

Capital and consumer goods: transmission mechanism (to top response level)

Chain 1. Capital goods such as cars may be bought only once every 3-5 years by households (1) … making it a challenge to establish customer loyalty (2) … because it's hard to establish a habit (e.g. a diet Coke every lunchtime) (3). So producers can be especially tempted into cartel arrangements (4) … or into excessive spending on research & development. (5)

Chain 2. Consumer goods (especially *normal* goods) are a valuable stabiliser within market economies (1) … so although capital goods spending may fall by 15+% in a recession (2) … the stability of spending on weekly consumer items such as shampoo and socks (3) ... keeps the overall decline in GDP down to a manageable figure such as 5% (4). The 2019 Brexit crisis proved this to be true. (5).

Use of Production Possibility Frontiers (PPF)

Grade C. What is it?

The production possibility frontier (PPF) is a graph that shows a simplified version of an economy, assuming it consists of just two types of good/service. This might be capital goods and consumer goods, which would be a reasonable simplification. But sometimes (as below) the PPF graph uses an assumption such as that the economy consists just of cars and pizzas. This has the benefit of spelling out that this type of assumption is a massive simplification – perhaps too much so.

Grade B (i) Where's the beef?

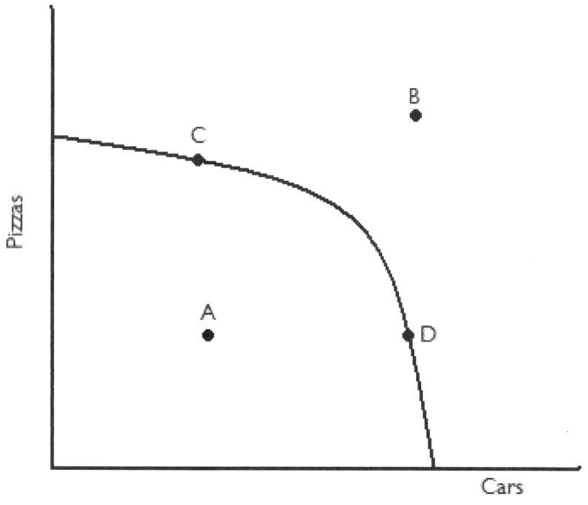

The big issue is opportunity cost, e.g. the trade-off between sales of cars and pizzas (see left). The PPF line suggests that more of one thing is inevitably at the cost of the other. This gives rise to an important macro-economic theory: 'crowding out'. If, on the graph to the left, it showed state sector on one axis and private sector on the other, a rise in state spending would 'crowd out' the private sector.

Grade B (ii) Why it matters

PPF matters because 'crowding out' has a huge following on the political right. If a rise in state spending 'crowded out' private sector spending, there would be no point to it. All it would do is suck the life out of the private sector. Such a claim was made in 2010, when the Chancellor said that 'austerity' cutbacks in state spending would allow more room for private sector growth. It didn't happen.

Grade A The other side

A critic would point out that a) economies very rarely operate at maximum capacity, so the PPF theory is flawed and b) modern economies are dominated by services, and they don't really have a maximum capacity in the way goods do.

Grade A* The critical perspective

It can be useful to investigate an idealised theory such as the perfectly competitive market, but PPF surely goes too far. In a world where a large Tesco might stock 20,000 items, how much insight can really come from the assumption of only two?

Do note that B (in the graph to the left) is a theoretically impossible combination since it's beyond the PPF. A, by contrast, is possible, but suggests a significant under-utilisation of (maximum) capacity.

Don't worry about whether the PPF 'curve' is drawn as an arc (as here) or as a straight diagonal line. It makes no difference to answering exam questions.

Exam tip: the most confusing questions concern opportunity cost. These are about movements along the PPF. Remember that if there's a move to the right from point C, *that* means more C and less D. So the opportunity cost of more D is less C.

Use of PPF: transmission mechanism (to get the top response level)

Chain 1. A PPF showing capital goods and consumer goods on its two axes (1) … can provide a valid simulation of the UK economy (2). If the economy is at full capacity, extra capital spending would – in the short run – have to be at the expense of the consumer (3) … though in the longer term it could boost economic growth (4) … shifting the PPF to the right. (5)

Chain 2. The PPF operates like neo-classical theory about long-run aggregate supply (1) … in that both assume the economy is always at full capacity (2). This is why supply-side policies are so highly regarded (3) ... as they don't have to cost anything (4) but can still push macro capacity to the right. (5)

Movements and shifts in PPF curves

Grade C. What is it?

Movement along the PPF occurs when changes in consumption patterns lead to a reallocation of resources from one type of good to another. In the graph below, a movement from point Y to point U represents a switch away from capital goods towards consumer goods. In both cases the economy is operating at its maximum, but with a different mix of products wanted and sold. Shifts in the PPF either come from general economic growth (shifting the PPF to the right) or, as here, by an increase in the productivity of one good – in this case capital goods.

Do note that the increase in output of capital goods shown on the graph must be due to greater productivity, i.e an ability to get more output from the same number of inputs. This might be due to technological advances or other innovations.

Grade B Where's the beef?

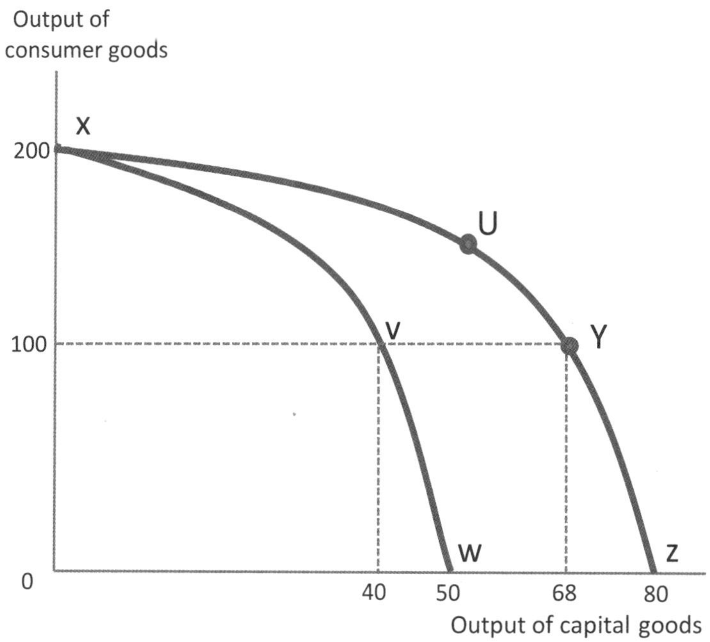

The diagram shows an economy with a PPF of XW, now operating at point V. Then the PPF moves to XZ, operating at point Y. Calculate the **original** and **new** opportunity costs of producing 100 units of consumer goods. Answer on the right below

Don't worry about where the economy is along the PPF curve; that's just a matter of consumer choice. The problem comes when actual output is to the left of the PPF.

Answer: the opportunity cost of producing consumer goods is measured in the foregone output of capital goods. Originally producing 100 consumer goods was at the cost of 50-40 = 10 capital goods. Now it's at the cost of 80-68 = 12 capital goods. So the opportunity cost of consumer goods has increased due to higher productivity on capital goods.

Grade A The counter-argument

It should be remembered that PPFs can shift leftwards, perhaps due to physical factors such as a severe earthquake or due to environmental factors such as global warming. In future, some economies near the equator may suffer permanent reductions in their ability to produce agricultural goods.

Grade A* The critical perspective

To a free market economist, perfection is when the economy operates on its PPF, with productive and allocative efficiencies maximised. This ignores social factors such as free healthcare & education, which improve equity and long-term growth.

Movement and shifts in PPF: transmission mechanism (to top response level)

Chain 1. The PPF is a simplified model assuming a closed economy (1) … but there are few of those in today's globalised world (2). If the model incorporated imports and exports, i.e. an open economy (3) it would effectively have injections & withdrawals (4) making it like the circular flow of income. (5)

Chain 2. If the economy operates to the right of the PPF (1) … there is effectively a positive output gap (2) ... with an over-stretched economy and strong inflationary pressures (3) ... derived from demand pull factors (4). To fix this the Chancellor needs to tighten fiscal and/or monetary policy. (5)

Specialisation and division of labour

Grade C. What is it?

Specialisation by individuals is called the division of labour. Instead of one person doing every aspect of a work process, the job is divided into many different actions, allowing those with different skills to specialise in one aspect of the job. One person measures the bride-to-be; another discusses fabrics and colours; another buys all the materials and fabrics; another cuts the material; another sews the dress together; another sews on buttons and cuffs.

Grade B (i) Where's the beef?

The key is that specialisation can boost efficiency and is therefore a core part of the early benefits of expansion to small firms. As firms expand they find more scope for specialisation in the form of division of labour, and therefore enjoy rising productivity and efficiency – allowing production costs per unit to fall.

Grade B (ii) Why it matters

Specialisation matters a lot because of its central role in Adam Smith's *The Wealth of Nations* (1776) which British and American economists see as the start of the subject. Smith wrote in detail about the division of labour used in the manufacture of pins. He estimated that one person might be able to make 20 pins in a day, but with division of labour a workforce of 10 could produce 48,000 pins a day. From 1776 to today, much of the world's economic growth has come from this insight.

Grade A The counter-argument

High division of labour can mean repetitive, deskilled work in which the role of the human being has been cut back to the equivalent of a robot. Sitting at a supermarket checkout all day (beep beep) might feel like that. In the early days of industrialisation there were ferocious fights between workers and bosses over the awfulness of the jobs people had to do. Even today people prove willing to do dull jobs as long as the pay is adequate. But having alienated staff on the look-out for a better job elsewhere can erode the productivity benefits of high division of labour. Good employers recognise this and try to balance specialisation with satisfaction.

Grade A* The critical perspective

Economics looks at issues in a rational way, such as identifying the right degree of specialisation to maximise productivity and profits. This is logical, but not necessarily right in the long term. Highly repetitive work gives rise to more problems of stress than does work that seems demanding, but actually gives people (such as managers) greater control over their working lives. So greed over today's profits can lead to problems down the line, as staff absenteeism rises.

Do be aware of the advantages of division of labour:
- enables staff to become highly skilled at a specific task
- makes it easy to develop machinery to help with tasks (or robots to replace staff)
- allows early-stage growth to boost productivity, efficiency & profit

Don't forget the disadvantages:
- excessive repetition may lead to high absenteeism and cause a rift between workers (us) and managers (them)
- this may affect production and service quality
- … which affects customer loyalty

Exam tip: remember Adam Smith's pins as a classic example of the benefits of high division of labour. And if you can, remember 20 pins for one person; 48,000 for 10 (240 times more productive)

Specialisation: transmission mechanism (to get to the top response level)

Chain 1. As a new firm grows from one-person business to employing dozens (1) … it can employ specialist staff to take on specific roles such as accounting or marketing (2). This means more expertise in the business which should boost productivity (3) ... and the development of even more expertise as people learn their job better (4) … boosting quality while bringing unit costs down. (5)

Chain 2. If a business over-simplifies tasks by high division of labour (1) … it may find that creeping alienation undermines efficiency (2) … with the best staff leaving for a more interesting job elsewhere (3)... and others showing lack of trust in their bosses (4) … perhaps leading to absences or strikes (5).

Functions of money

Grade C. What is it?

Money has four economic functions: as a medium of exchange (replacing barter), a measure of value (what's a service worth?), a store of value (under the bed or in a deposit account) and as a method of deferred payment. The latter is important because most business transactions take place using credit, meaning that a delivery of £10,000 worth of goods today may not result in payment for several months. Deferred payment was not possible many years' ago, when barter was the standard method of exchange.

Grade B (i) Where's the beef?

The beef comes from the potential that the multiple uses of money may conflict with each other. In its function as a medium of exchange, economies need enough money to create the liquidity to carry out as many transactions as are required. But a high level of supply of money may undermine its function as a store of value by creating inflation, with ever-rising prices cutting the value of household savings.

Grade B (ii) Why it matters

Money matters in many ways in a modern economy/society. In theory 'a measure of value' means valuing the goods and services being bought – helping firms to decide whether they can make a profit by producing them. But a different way of looking at 'a measure of value' is to see money as a measure of an individual's success. The annual Sunday Times rich list ranks the top 500 richest people in the UK – perhaps encouraging a view that money is the ultimate test of achievement.

Grade A The counter-argument

The role of money may have become overly central in the UK, but in developing countries it remains a key part of economic growth. A well-developed credit system helps firms to trade with confidence; and low inflation makes it possible for firms to save cash for when they need it to invest in their growth.

Grade A* The critical perspective

Many nurses, teachers and care workers wish for a higher income, but feel pride in doing a job they believe to be socially useful. The central role of money and wealth may make it hard for these workers to feel valued by a society that gives them relatively poor financial rewards. Despite this, the economic functions of money must be remembered. The invention of money enabled societies to benefit from specialisation and exchange, both locally and internationally. The risk today is that money becomes an end in itself rather than a means to an end.

Do remember the four functions of money. The most important in micro economics is 'as a measure of value'. This is because money is the means by which we place a value on market transactions, bringing buyers and sellers together.

Don't doubt the importance of money to modern economies. It is more obvious in bad times than good. In recessions 'lack of liquidity' becomes the great concern. That simply means enough money to oil the wheels of the economic system while it's struggling.

Exam tip: examiners love to see the analytic process of breaking something down into its component parts. Knowing the four functions of money achieves exactly this.

Functions of money: transmission mechanism (to top response level)

Chain 1. If a developing economy can create the financial system (and legal back-up) to allow transactions to take place on credit (1) … firms will find new ways to expand based on specialisation and exchange (2). Deferred payment helps in financing expansion (3) ... and growth gives opportunities for mechanisation (4) … which can boost quality and consistency while bringing unit costs down. (5)

Chain 2. 'Deferment' is important in economics because it means putting off paying (1) … which is crucial for firms to trade on credit (2) … and is also important for transactions such as hedging, which can be an important way to achieve stability (3). For example easyJet uses hedging to control its fuel costs for the coming year (4). Money makes it possible to value such transactions – and pay them. (5).

Free, mixed and command economies

Grade C. What is it?

A free market economy is based on Adam Smith's principle of 'the invisible hand', in which free consumer and producer decisions come together via the market mechanism. A command economy is based on government decisions that are supposedly in the best interests of the people. The government commands the economy by deciding on resource allocation, such as that 80,000 size 10 boots will be made. In a mixed economy, many markets operate freely, but the government commands others, e.g. the NHS, the education system and much of social care.

Grade B (i) Where's the beef?

The heart of this topic is understanding the dividing line between the private and public sector. Where does the remit of the government stop? A common mistake is to assume UK exports are affected directly by the UK government. In fact most exports are due to free decisions between overseas consumers and UK producers.

Grade B (ii) Why it matters

This topic matters because it's a perfect example of the tricky interface between economics and politics. Many on the right of the Conservative party are passionate about free market economics. Their zeal sometimes makes them lose sight of the important work done by the state (government), such as the national minimum wage. On the left of the Labour party are many whose instincts favour state action over the free market – making them sympathetic to command economies.

Grade A The counter-argument

The counter argument is that the lines drawn between free market and command economies may not be political or philosophical – they may simply reflect self-interest. Passion for free market economics correlates with the desire to keep government small and taxes low. Perhaps family wealth or high income creates a vested interest for low taxes. On the other side, desire for state solutions to economic problems may be influenced by careers in the civil service or the NHS.

Grade A* The critical perspective

Wisdom in this area tends to come from scepticism – about motives and about experience. Some of the most zealous political supporters of the free market and the command economies have no business experience at all. They went from school to university to politics. Do they really know enough to make decisions such as the disastrous privatisation of the probation service or – years' earlier – the equally disastrous decision to nationalise the UK's steel industry?

Do remember the key economists: **Smith** wrote in the 18th century about the power of the free market. **Marx** wrote 'The Communist Manifesto' in the 19th century – and can be seen as the father of command economies. **Hayek** was a 20th Century thinker on the need for a small state and the risks of big business linking with the state.

Don't shy away from pointing out the difficulties in disentangling the economics from politics and self-interest; especially with this topic

Exam tip: nearly every economy today is mixed. Typically this means there are sectors left to the free market, such as the market for flowers, and others dominated by the state. The arguments are about the dividing line.

Free, mixed and command: transmission mechanism (to top response level)

Chain 1. In a mixed economy it is hard to draw the right line between public and private sectors (1) ... with supporters of the free market wanting the involvement of private companies (2) ... while others believe government involvement is needed (3). In recent years there have been problems with privatisation and outsourcing (4)... proving there are no simple market solutions to every problem (5)

Chain 2. Between 1945 and 1989 Eastern Europe operated under communist command economies (1) ... which provided good education and high levels of social equality (2) ... but at the cost of consumer freedoms and choice (3)... including queueing for the limited supplies of consumer goods (4). Very few economists would support a return to a system based on command economies. (5)

Advantages/disads of free & command economies

Grade C. What is it?

The key economic arguments for the free market are to promote efficiency plus incentives to individual enterprise. In political terms the argument for the free market is that it's rooted in individual free choice. Set against those arguments are the desire for equality and for the social/common good rather than the triumph of the individual.

Grade B (i) Where's the beef?

In essence, it doesn't get beefier. The argument between free and command economies permeates much of the subject, for example privatisation versus nationalisation of the railways. Few today believe in a pure version of the command economy (even in Cuba this is being relaxed), because most people want individual choices to be reflected in the economy and in their lives. But the free market ideal (which has a huge sway over UK and US policy-making) should also be challenged. Yes, we all want to have choice, but most of us also care about society – especially a social safety net for those in medical or social difficulties.

Grade B (ii) Why it matters

You need to know the disadvantages of each system. The free market works wonderfully in many sectors, but is problematic with social necessities such as healthcare and education, and with natural monopolies such as water supply. And, of course, the free market has no incentive to provide public goods. With command economies, there is typically no problem with achieving productive efficiency, but a huge problem with allocative and dynamic efficiencies. This is why consumers have hugely more choice in a free market than a command system.

Grade A The counter-argument

A main counter-argument today would be from an environmental viewpoint. A 'green' economist might condemn command and free market economists for their obsession with economic growth. From that point of view, the wrong counter-point is being examined. It should be green versus other, not command v. free.

Grade A* The critical perspective

One can question the 'free v command' framing of the argument from another perspective. Globally, the pure command approach is virtually dead; the real battle of minds is between 'mixed' and free market economies. In mixed economies the government still has a significant role, as do markets; only in the minds of extreme free market purists is government (and taxation) a conspiracy against freedom.

Do remember the pros and cons of the free market. Pros: as long as competition is effective, costs should be minimised and consumer welfare maximised. In the words of Milton Friedman, there should be: 'Freedom to choose'. Cons: consumer choices may be ill-advised (Coke v carrots), and market failure may be frequent.

Don't forget the pros and cons of the command economy. Pros: even if output is not maximised, more equal distribution may leave the poor better off. Cons: failure to achieve allocative efficiency and therefore consumer utility is sub-optimal.

Exam tip: don't stay locked in the extremes; reach for the middle to consider the pros and cons of a mixed economy.

Ads/disads of free & command: transmission mechanism (to top response level)

Chain 1. In an idealised free market economy all firms are small price-takers (1) ... using resources such as labour that are in highly flexible supply (2) ... and all customers are small enough to lack monopsony power (3). In such a world consumers are sovereign ('Kings') (4) and companies have to respond to whatever the customer wants. (5)

Chain 2. The economies of Scandinavia are very mixed, with significant state sectors (1) ... yet with vibrant, innovative market sectors (2) ... and high levels of social equality (4) ... for example their Gini coefficients are remarkably low (4)... meaning that their version of a mixed economy may be a good balance between economic freedoms and economic equity. (5)

Role of the state in a mixed economy

Grade C. What is it?

Every economy on the planet is mixed. Each has some element of government involvement and some activity by private enterprise (even if it's informal, 'black market' activity). The big ideological battle is between those wanting 'big government' (with state spending amounting to 50%+ of GDP) and those advocating small government. Brexiteer economists talk fondly about Singapore, with a government spending 19% of GDP, while in France the figure is 56%. But do those economists hanker to be like the Philippines, with state spending at 18%?

Grade B (i) Where's the beef?

The beef comes in two parts: first, the political issue of the size of the state: minimal as in Singapore and the Philippines – or welfare state-ist as in Sweden and France. The UK is in the middle, though closer to France than the Philippines. The second is how the state sees its priorities. In the U.S. and Russia, military spending is a major item; in the UK transfer payments are huge (transferring income from workers to those in need of pensions, disability benefits or low-wage top-ups).

Grade B (ii) Why it matters

It matters hugely to understand where the role of the state starts and stops. In the UK, consumers predominantly make decisions about how and what to spend with no reference to the state. UK imports, for example, are a matter of a customer's personal preference for a German Mercedes over a British Jaguar. Such transactions are nothing to do with the British government. But households pay tax to help pay for roads, streetlights, the police, the army, schools and the whole National Health Service.

Grade A The counter-argument

In America, especially, there's a widespread hostility to the state in general and taxation in particular. It is suggested that taxation is theft. In fact countries such as Nigeria and India have virtually no tax on incomes, but the American critics seem reluctant to move there. In the UK, there's special pride in a free, state-run NHS.

Grade A* The critical perspective

The state plays a key part in every mixed economy, but it lacks the equivalent of the private sector's 'creative destruction' – the dynamic force that pushes loss-makers out of business, creating the space for dynamic newcomers. So the state is relatively good at permanent essentials such as healthcare and education, but very poor at competing in fluid, dynamic markets. That's for the private sector.

Do remember that free markets aren't good at everything. They have no incentive to supply public goods and no incentive to correct market failures. Only the state can do these things. True, they may prove incompetent, showing government failure, but that doesn't alter the state's role: to step in when the private sector has problems it cannot solve.

Don't forget that state-run organisations are prone to inefficiencies because they usually lack direct competitors. Year 13 economics has a name for this consequence of complacency: x-inefficiency.

Exam tip: do try to be balanced about the role of the state. It's important, though far from perfect (even without the politicians).

Role of the state: transmission mechanism (to top response level)

Chain 1. A key purpose of the state is to fill the gaps left by the private sector (1) ... such as housing in London and the south-east that is affordable to street-sweepers, security guards and teachers (2). In the private sector, demand is meaningless without the ability to pay (3) ... which is where the state steps in (4) ... to create a civilised society where ordinary people have healthcare and a home. (5)

Chain 2. Some free-market economists view the state with suspicion, even contempt (1) ... certain that every market works better without 'nanny state' interference (2). If they had been listened to, smoking would still be widespread and sugary drinks untaxed (3) ... which is hard to reconcile with the social good (4). Perhaps the state's role deserves a bit more respect. (5)

Rational decision making

Grade C. What is it?

Rational decision making means choosing an outcome based on logic and evidence, not hunch or guesswork. Rational decision making has to be based upon an underlying objective, such as to get a baby to sleep through the night, or to prevent accidents. In economics there are two underlying assumptions of rational decision making:

1. That consumers aim to maximise their utility (within the constraints of their income)

2. That firms aim to maximise profits

Grade B (i) Where's the beef?

These underlying assumptions of rationality help in predicting behaviour. For example a firm aiming to maximise its profit will produce at the output level where marginal cost = marginal revenue. And consumers aiming to maximise utility will (unconsciously) find the right mix in their rate of consumption of different items. You may want to spend your £5 lunch-money on crisps, sweets and cola; someone else might prefer a chicken salad sandwich and a mineral water. But both can feel equally satisfied (if not equally healthy) with their choices.

Grade B (ii) Why it matters

It matters because economics prides itself on being a true social science and therefore based on rationality. And the practical (and financial) value of the subject is based on forecasting the future – based on the predictability that comes from everybody doing things for the same reasons, e.g. maximising household utility.

Grade A The counter-argument

The counter-argument would rarely be based on Michael Gove's Brexit pronouncement that 'People in this country have had enough of experts'. The issue lies more in questions about the objectives chosen by individuals and firms. Are we all as one-dimensionally self-interested as the assumptions imply? Some people's rationality may be based on something else, such as environmentalism.

Grade A* The critical perspective

One approach to rationality would be to ask: if economists are equally rational, how come they draw such different conclusions from the same evidence? Can Marx, Keynes and Hayek all have been rational? The answer is yes, but raises questions about the Specification's approach. Assuming that consumers maximise utility and firms maximise profits may be over-simplifying life's complexities.

Do be willing to question the assumption of rationality. A close look at the UK and USA in the lead-up to the 1929 and 2009 crashes inevitably points more towards irrationality (way beyond 'animal spirits') than rational decision making. Theory should never assume away the way the world actually works.

Don't hold back from criticising and questioning in class and home-work. Gaining feedback will help you develop your thoughts in preparation for exam answers.

Exam tip: show the rationality of your own thinking by stating your assumptions and the evidence on which your arguments are based. And make sure to state every link in your logic chain.

Rational decision making: transmission mechanism (to the top response level)

Chain 1. The assumption is that consumers act rationally to maximise their utility (1) … and thereby achieve the best economic value from the resources they own or earn (2). But there are many exceptions to this, caused by market failures such as asymmetric information (3) ... or irrational preferences such as for high-priced brands (4) ... or for guaranteed loss-makers such as lottery tickets.

Chain 2. Among firms economists assume profit maximisation (1) … which is a good predictor of most firms most of the time (2). But some firms are altruistic and other business leaders seem set on self-aggrandisement (3)… meaning that ordinary assumptions of economic behaviour break down (4) … and calling 'rational decision-making' into question. (5)

Movements along - and shifts in - demand curves

Grade C. What is it?

Demand curves slope downwards due to income effects and substitution effects (see **Do** box, right). The downward slope reflects the natural inverse relationship between price and demand. The higher the price the lower the demand; the lower the price the higher the demand. If a firm cuts the price of its product, it effectively moves downwards along the demand curve. In the graph below, the price cut from £5 to £4 creates a movement from point A to B.

Grade B (i) Where's the beef?

The beef comes from distinguishing between situations in which there are movements along – and those where there are shifts in – the demand curve. In fact there are only two things that cause movement along the curve: 1. A decision to change price, whether by the firm or the government. 2. A shift in the supply curve, which will cause movement along the demand curve. In all other circumstances changes in demand factors will cause the demand curve to shift right or left.

Grade B (ii) Why it matters

It matters because supply, demand and equilibrium are at the heart of micro and macro-economics. Any gap in your understanding of demand threatens to undermine your mastery of 'market forces'. Below is a graph showing movement along a demand curve.

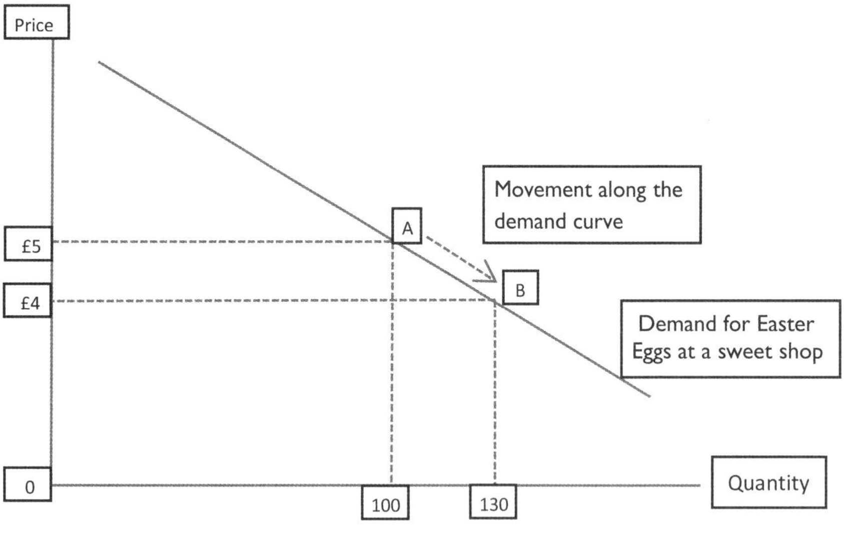

Grade A The other side

A critic of the demand curve shown above would question whether any business has certainty over the demand conditions it faces. The graph shows a clear linear relationship between price and demand. The real world may be more complex.

Grade A* The critical perspective

Possibly, just possibly, the downward-sloping demand curve may be a thing of the past. At the premium/celeb/money-no-object end of the market a higher price may make something 'worth' more to the consumer and therefore make demand rise.

Do remember the 2 reasons why the demand curve slopes downwards: 1. The income effect means that as the price of an item rises, fewer households can afford it (so sales fall). 2. The substitution effect means the higher the price of a good, the more customers will switch to cheaper rivals.

Don't forget that more and more firms are using 'dynamic pricing' methods that effectively mimic traditional commodity markets. When you buy an online hotel room or train ticket, the price you pay depends upon real-time levels of demand and supply.

Exam tip: make sure to spell out the precise reason for a change in price. Has the firm been hit by changes in external conditions? If so, the demand curve will have shifted. If the reasons are internal, such as a new boss has taken over, a price change will be due to movements along the curve.

Movements along - and shifts in - demand curves

Shifts in the demand curve – for Coca-Cola

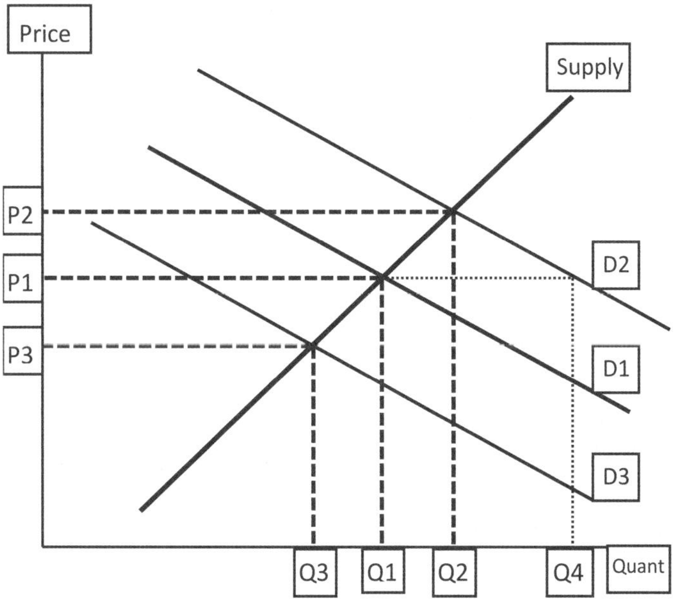

The graph shows demand for Coke at an equilibrium point of P1Q1. If a brilliant new advertising campaign boosts demand for Coke, the demand curve could shift rightwards, to D2. If the price stayed the same at P1, demand would rise to Q4. But actually price will rise to P2, with equilibrium at Q2.

Do remember the demand curve shows today's relationship between price and demand.

If the firm chooses to change price, this causes a slide along the demand curve, i.e. movement, not a shift.

Don't forget that demand conditions can change over time.

A brilliant advertising campaign might shift the demand curve rightwards, but also make it steeper due to its higher level of product differentiation.

Little or nothing in business stays the same for long.

Reasons for a shift in the demand curve

Demand will shift leftwards or rightwards in response to a wide number of outside factors: economic, social and competitive. On the graph above, a big price cut by Pepsi would push demand for Coca-Cola down from D1 to D3. A new scare story about health might do exactly the same.

Test yourself (answers in tiny print at the foot of the page)

1. State two factors that might cause Coke's demand curve to shift from D1 to D2

2. What would be the effect on Coke's demand curve of a decision by the company to increase the price by 5%?

3. Which way would the demand curve move if there was a price rise on a complementary good?

4. Which way would Coke's demand curve move if there was a dispute between Coca-Cola and Tesco, causing Tesco to withdraw the drink from its shelves?

Movement and shifts: transmission mechanism (to get the top response level)

Chain 1. A newly appointed Marketing Director may want to push the company's demand curve rightwards (1) … to boost sales volume and selling prices and thereby increase revenue (2) … and probably profit (3). To do this the Director could consider better or more advertising (4) … or perhaps switching resources from old-school media to digital, web-based promotion (5).

Chain 2. Some businesses have no control over their demand curve (1) … because the market itself determines the price, e.g. for raw cocoa beans (2). If Springtime hail-storms in Brazil and the Ivory Coast cut the available supply of cocoa (3) ... the price may shoot upwards (4) … by a sharp leftwards movement along the demand curve (5)

Answers: 1a) The launch of a new, Coca-Cola flavour 1b) A brilliant new advertising campaign for Coca-Cola 2. = *None*. There would simply be leftward movement up the demand curve. 3. Sales would fall from D1 to D3 4. A leftwards shift e.g. from D1 to D3

Causes of shifts in demand curves

Grade C. What is it?

Critical to exam success is to distinguish between determinants of demand and causes of shifts in demand. The factors that *determine* demand are static. For example the demand for rooms at the Premier Inn, Wimbledon is determined by competition locally, nearness to the station, price and so on. Causes of shifts in demand are dynamic, i.e. factors that have changed. And, to *shift* the demand curve, they must be factors other than a change in price and a change in supply.

Do remember the main causes of a rightward shift in the demand curve:
- higher spend on advertising
- a favourable change in fashion or consumer taste
- rising real household incomes
- the collapse of a direct competitor
- a price rise by a rival/substitute
- a price cut on a complementary good

Grade B (i) Where's the beef?

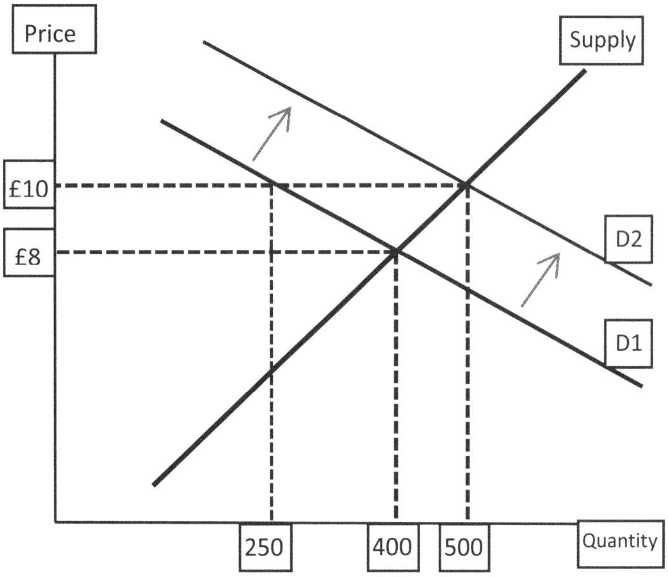

The big issue is to be expert at handling diagrams such as the one on the left. And then able to say why changes to demand cause a shift in the demand curve. The graph shows a firm in a stable position with its demand curve D1 and a price of £8. Then a factor such as a rival's bankruptcy shifts demand to D2.

Don't confuse shifts in from movement along the demand curve. Movement along only happens because of changes in supply conditions

Grade B (ii) Why it matters

Shifts in demand matter because of their huge implications for firms. In the diagram above, while demand = D1 if the firm charged £10 it would sell 250 units with a revenue of £2,500. If demand shifts to D2, £10 becomes the equilibrium price with a sales volume of 500 units – doubling revenue to £5,000.

Exam tip: don't get complacent about the 'easy stuff' on supply and demand. Examiners are quite clever at finding new ways to test whether you really understand shifts in – and movement along – these curves.

Grade A The counter-argument

Even sceptics about market economics accept the logic of shifts in demand curves – especially these days, when computer-controlled 'dynamic pricing' methods use demand theory to set ever-changing prices for flights, hotels and much else.

Grade A* The critical perspective

The moral doubts about demand curves relate to concern about allowing 'market forces' to control prices and therefore the amount people can afford. Recently the price of the health drug liothyronine was increased from 16p to £9.22 – 5,663% up

Shifts in demand: transmission mechanism (to get the top response level)

Chain 1. A big new product launch by a rival pushes your demand curve leftwards (1) … shifting your equilibrium price and sales to an unprofitable position (2). You could act quickly to cut your average costs (3) … or shift your demand curve back to the right (4) … by heavy spending on social media. (5)

Chain 2. A rightwards shift in demand may have come from rising consumer incomes (1) … providing your firm with a boost to sales and the price level (2). This is great, but should be treated warily (3) ... because it's just your good fortune (4) … and a change in the economy will shift the curve back left (5)

Diminishing marginal utility

Grade C. What is it?

Utility is the value individuals place on using or consuming a product or service. I love chocolate, so it has a high utility for me. In this case its utility could be measured as satisfaction or pleasure. I don't love cars, so the utility I gain from my Toyota is practical: it's convenient because it gets me from A to B reliably. Marginal utility is the utility I gain from one more unit of consumption. And diminishing marginal utility means that the second 200 gramme bar of Dairy Milk gives me less satisfaction than the first.

Grade B (i) Where's the beef?

The beef comes from two sources. First: diminishing marginal utility can be given as a high-level explanation of why demand curves are downward-sloping. The more Easter Eggs I eat the less utility I gain from the extra one. The second factor is opportunity cost: as utility diminishes, opportunity cost rises. As I eat my 3rd Easter Egg, I am missing out badly on the alternative of a piece of fruit.

Grade B (ii) Why it matters

What matters here is access to higher grades. The ordinary student knows that demand curves are downward-sloping. A good student says that's due to substitution and income effects. The top student explains that it's due to diminishing marginal utility. It's a more technical, more academic explanation.

Grade A The counter-argument

The counter argument is that diminishing marginal utility may be too simplifying an assumption. An addict may gain an equal amount of utility from every 'fix'. And my relationship with chocolate is complex. Sometimes I buy it casually, impulsively; on other occasions I'm desperate. So the utility I gain from consuming that first bar varies considerably; it's too simplifying to assume I always gain a utility of x with the first bar and x – 1 with the second. Sometimes that 1st bar is worth 4x to me.

Grade A* The critical perspective

On its own, marginal utility theory provides some useful insights. But theorists want to use it as part of a model for the economy as a whole – in which all consumers are seeking to maximise their utility. This paints a picture of perfect consumer rationality that is hard to square with the real world. Indeed modern behavioural economics is largely based on proving the irrationality of much consumer decision-making. I've been in a queue where someone bought twenty lottery tickets. Presumably the 20th gave him as much (irrational) utility as the 1st.

Do appreciate that marginal utility theory has a long lineage, going back to great 19th and early 20th century economists such as Alfred Marshall and Joan Robinson. It was originally considered a left-wing piece of theory pointing to the desirability of income equality. Today it's a key part of right-wing, free market economics.

Don't treat theory as fact. A theory such as diminishing marginal utility is perfect for debate, critique and doubt.

Exam tip: there are often exam questions on allocative efficiency. This efficiency can only occur if households maximise their utility in the decisions they make. So allocative efficiency relies on diminishing marginal utility.

Diminishing marginal utility: transmission mechanism (to top response level)

Chain 1. No-one suggests that consumer purchases are knowingly made on the basis of diminishing marginal utility (1). People may be shopping with small kids in tow – and making lots of irrational purchases (2). But underpinning these decisions is diminishing marginal utility (3) ... as people buy two packs of crisps but not three (4)… and try to get good value for money from their weekly shop. (5)

Chain 2. Rational consumers attempt to maximise the total utility they gain from their income/spending (1) … partly by switching consumption to other goods/services (2) … once diminishing marginal utility has set in (3). This model of consumer behaviour assumes that people have perfect knowledge of alternative products (4)… and that markets are perfectly competitive. (5)

Price elasticity of demand (PED)

Grade C. What is it?

PED measures the extent to which a price change on a good or service causes a change in its demand. It is measured proportionately, by use of this formula:

$$PED = \frac{\%\ \text{change in quantity (demand)}}{\%\ \text{change in price}}$$

The answer will always be negative, because a price change has an inverse effect on demand, i.e. price up, demand down and price down, demand up.

Grade B (i) Where's the beef?

The beef lies with the calculation – especially the ability to reorganise the PED formula. With 20% of A Level marks going for calculations, examiners need elasticity questions, but also need to be creative about asking them. Make sure to tackle the questions on the right.

Grade B (ii) Why it matters

Micro-economics uses a lot of models that assume (explicitly or implicitly) freely competitive markets with high (or infinite) levels of price elasticity. In the real world, every business does all it can to avoid such a situation – because there's so little scope for making big profits. Firms use design and marketing to differentiate their products and therefore reduce PED. Those with the lowest PED (think Apple iPhones and Chanel perfumes) gain the highest profit margins.

Grade A The other side

The counter-argument to the above comes from free market purists. They believe competition is such a powerful force that it overcomes temporary differentiation and restores perfectly competitive markets. Of course, even if price elasticity is near-infinity (in a state of perfect competition) it is still measurable – but they trust that as long as the state doesn't intervene, competition will eat away at differentiation. Therefore the super-normal profits of an Apple or a Chanel get eaten away.

Grade A* The critical perspective

In reality, PED is easy to talk about, but hard to measure. Many different factors affect every brand's sales so it can be hard to disentangle price changes from the many variables. So measuring today's PED is very difficult. Then a further factor is timescale; just because PED was -0.8 the last time it was measured doesn't mean the same is true today. PEDs change over time as competitive forces change, so a new pricing decision may prove to be wrong, because it's based on the wrong data

Do learn to be comfortable with terms such as *price elastic* (PED is high, i.e. between -1.0 and infinity) and *price inelastic* (PED is low, between -0.01 and -0.99). Examiners also like the term *unitary elasticity*, meaning a PED of around -1.0. In this case a price change has no effect on revenue, because the % change in price is cancelled out by an opposite change in demand.

Don't be scared of estimating a PED. If the text tells you about a great brand, you can assume that the PED is likely to be low.

Exam tip: students often get the PED formula the wrong way round. Remember that with *all* elasticities, quantity goes on top.

Price elasticity: transmission mechanism (to the top response level)

Chain 1. Even though it seems attractive for a firm to cut prices if its products have a high PED (1) ... and thereby make such gains in sales volume that revenue rises (2) ... it's almost impossible for this plan to work in isolation (3). If firm A cuts its prices and demand shoots up, the losers are competitors B and C (4)... who will have to react by cutting their prices – which loses firm A its advantage. (5)

Chain 2. If a business can reduce its PED to below -1.0 (1) ... it can boost its revenue and profit by pushing its prices up (2). To achieve this it needs to differentiate its products (or services) from its rivals (3)... by better design, cleverer marketing and branding or outstanding customer service (4) ... making customers buy the brand and forget about its price tag. (5)

Worked examples (with answers)

Grade C question:

Q1. Firm A sells 500 units a week at £8 each. Then it puts its price up to £9 and sales fall to 470 units.

a) Calculate the price elasticity of demand.

b) State whether the goods are price elastic or price inelastic.

ANSWER

1a) PED = % change in quantity / % change in price

1a) % change in quantity = *minus* 6%

1a) % change in price = *plus* 12.5%

1a) ANS = -6 / +12.5 = -0.48

1b) Price inelastic

Grade A/A* question:

Q2. An online fashion clothing site has monthly revenues of £12,000 from the sale of 240 items. Its PED is -2.0. At 'Black Friday' it cuts its price by 20%.

2a) Calculate its new sales revenue

2b) Explain what assumptions you've made.

ANSWER

2a) Its original price was £50 per unit (£12,000/240), so a 20% cut is to £40.

2a) The 20% price cut should boost demand by 40% if the PED is -2, i.e. to 336 units

2a) 336 units x £40 = £13,440

2b) Assuming PED is unchanged since the last time it was measured/estimated. And assuming no rival responds with their own price cut (starting a price war)

Economic calculations: test yourself; answers in back of book

Grade C question:

Q1. For each of the following, state whether the good is price elastic, price inelastic or has unitary price elasticity

a) Price elasticity is – 2.5

b) A10% price cut boosts demand by 8%

Grade B/A questions:

Q2. Marmite has a price elasticity of demand of -0.2. At a price of £4 per large jar it sells 200 units a week at Morrison's Wimbledon. Calculate the effect on Marmite sales revenue of a 15% price rise.

Q3. At Morrison's Wimbledon, small bars of Cadbury's Dairy Milk (CDM) and Mars Galaxy are both priced at 60p. The daily rate of sale is 120 CDM and 80 Galaxy. Then Galaxy cuts its price to 54p. Sales of Galaxy rise to 112 bars and sales of CDM slip to 108.

a) Calculate Galaxy's price elasticity of demand

b) Calculate the change in Galaxy daily revenue.

Grade A/A* question:

Q4. A manager has been set the task of boosting sales from 40,000 to 50,000 units a month. The product is priced at £2 each and is believed to have a PED of – 0.625.

a) Calculate the new price that must be set to achieve the sales target.

b) Explain why, when the price is changed, the PED may prove higher than – 0.625.

For answers see back pages

Income elasticity of demand (YED)

Grade C. What is it?

YED measures the extent to which a change in consumers' real income causes a change in demand for a good or service. It is measured proportionately, by use of this formula:

$$YED = \frac{\%\ \text{change in quantity (demand)}}{\%\ \text{change in real income}}$$

The answer will usually be positive, because demand for most goods increases when we're better off, giving a positive correlation between income and demand. But some goods have negative YED, with consumers abandoning them when they are better off, returning in tough times, e.g. a recession. These are inferior goods.

Do learn the terminology of income elasticity. **Normal** goods have moderately +ive YED, e.g. +0.5 whereas **luxury** goods have strongly +ive YED such as +4. **Inferior** goods have –ive YED, e.g. -1.5, so if income rise by 3%, sales will fall by 3% x 1.5 = 4.5%.

Grade B (i) Where's the beef?

Students find YED much harder to answer questions on than PED. Above all else, they confuse the two. So the beef lies in disentangling the two types of elasticity. Both measure correlation, but are quite separate. PED is the correlation between price changes and demand changes, while YED measures the correlation between incomes and demand. These are two quite separate causal factors.

Don't underestimate the importance to firms of forecasting sales. Estimating your YED is an important part of that process.

Grade B (ii) Why it matters

It matters because of the importance of YED to sales forecasting. Firms need to anticipate the future, e.g. to know how many graduate trainees to hire. If a firm knows that its YED is +2.5, it can use a Bank of England economic forecast of 3% growth next year to anticipate a 7.5% jump in sales. That's invaluable.

Grade A The counter-argument

Some might argue that YED is less important than PED because a business makes decisions based directly on price elasticity, but no business can control the economy. Therefore YED may be interesting, but it's not important. In fact there are many decisions that can be based on YED, most obviously a decision to diversify, and therefore be influenced less by things the firm can't control.

Exam tip: stop yourself ever writing about 'elasticity'. It's always price elasticity of demand/supply or income elasticity. In exams students muddle them up. That robs them of quite easy marks.

Grade A* The critical perspective

With PED, it's easy to see the goal: to minimise the figure and therefore maximise power over pricing and profit. With YED it's harder because you could argue for as low a figure as possible, to minimise the impact on demand of a boom or recession. Or, because economies grow over time, there's a case for having a strongly positive YED, so that economic good times become your great times.

Income elasticity: transmission mechanism (to the top response level)

Chain 1. When a recession next hits, producers of luxury goods will be hit hardest (1) … as their strongly positive YEDs (say, +4) give a positive correlation with falling incomes and GDP (2) … so a YED of +4 correlates with a 5% *fall* in real incomes (3) ... to give a sales *decline* of -5% x +4 = 20% (4). In previous recessions many luxury firms such as sports car producers have gone under. (5)

Chain 2. If it's difficult for a luxury producer to survive a recession (1) … because of the impact on demand caused by high positive YED (2) ... firms see value in merging to create a more diversified business (3)… with a balance of normal, luxury and even inferior goods (4). Volkswagen owns the Skoda and Seat brands, but also Audi, Porsche, Rolls Royce and Lamborghini. (5)

Cross-price elasticity (XED)

Grade C. What is it?

Cross-price elasticity (XED) measures how a % price change in one good affects the demand for other goods. In most cases the goods will be unrelated so there's no effect at all. But rival and complementary goods will have a measurable level of XED.

Formula for XED = $\frac{\text{\% change in demand for Good B}}{\text{\% change in price of Good A}}$

With rivals XED will be positive, for example rival Good A's price increase cuts its demand, with customers switching from high-price Good A to Good B. With complementary goods XED will be negative.

Do learn the terminology of cross-price elasticity. **Complementary** goods have negative XED, because a price rise by Good A hits demand for that good, but also complementary goods such as Good B. **Substitute** goods have +ive YED, as sales benefit from their rival's price increase.

Grade B (i) Where's the beef?

The beef lies in the calculation, which is easy to get wrong. It's often hard to disentangle what the question wants and therefore a challenge to decide what should be plugged into XED formula. With the formula, remember that demand always goes at the top.

Grade B (ii) Why it matters

XED matters because firms want as much certainty as possible about their future, because certainty breeds confidence. Ideally, then, a firm's products would have very low XEDs. So a price cut by a rival or a price rise by a complementary good would have little or no effect. If your product's XED is high, your sales volumes are worryingly affected by decisions made by the bosses of other companies.

Don't forget that most goods are **unrelated**, e.g. a banana and a BMW. In this case the XED will be zero.

Grade A The counter-argument

On the other hand you could follow the views of free market economists, who would be delighted at a situation in which every business feels insecure and therefore has to try its hardest to survive. High XED = high pressure and therefore constant work to maximise efficiency – to the benefit of customers.

Grade A* The critical perspective

It's easy for economists to place efficiency on a pedestal from the comfort of their salaried jobs and nice offices. Often it's efficiency based on flexibility, as in hiring extra staff this week but firing them next week. For company bosses and especially their staff, a degree of security is a fine thing, creating the potential to invest in the future, perhaps by increasing spending on R&D and on robotic machinery. Low XEDs provide a sounder basis for long-term success.

Exam tip: it's easy to freeze over this formula. It all seems too much. But just remember two things: demand always goes on top and because the causal factor is the price change, at the bottom will go Good A.

Cross-price elasticity: transmission mechanism (to the top response level)

Chain 1. When Cadbury puts the price up on Dairy Milk (1) … there's a modest fall in sales as people switch to alternatives such as Galaxy (2) … so XED has kicked in, with price up on Cadbury (Good A) causing a sales increase for Galaxy (Good B) (3) ... meaning that the XED between these rivals is positive (4). With XED, rivals have positive XEDs while complements have negative XEDs. (5)

Chain 2. To minimise XED you want your product to be irresistible (1) … so that people choose it without thinking or caring about the price of rivals (2). This seemed to be true when Nespresso first came out, promoted by film star George Clooney (3). Customers ignored cheaper rivals and ignored the overpriced Nespresso pods (the complimentary good) (4). Nestle made a fortune. (5)

Numerical questions on XED and YED

Grade B/C questions (answers on the right)

1. An 8% price rise in Good A causes sales of Good B to move from 2,400 units a week to 2,520.

1a) Calculate the cross-price elasticity between Good A and Good B.

1b) State whether Good B is a complement or substitute to Good A.

2. Sales of Ferraris rose by 12% in the UK last year, when the UK's real GDP rose by 1.6%.

2a) What is the implicit income elasticity of Ferraris in the UK?

2b) Why may this figure be misleading?

Grade A questions

3. The price of Artiflex was cut from £1.30 to £1.17p. This caused sales of Artiflex to rise from 650,000 units a month to 689,000 and sales of rival Struflex to fall from 240,000 to 235,200. Struflex kept its price constant at £1.35.

3a) Calculate the cross-price elasticity between Artiflex and Struflex.

3b) Calculate Struflex's loss of revenue per month.

4. Last year £45million of Cadbury Crème Eggs were sold at an average price of 50p. This year Cadbury expects volume sales to be 92.25 million eggs. Their forecast is based on economic estimates that wages will rise 2.9% in 2019, while inflation will average 1.9%.

4a) Calculate the implicit income elasticity of Crème Eggs in the UK.

4b) Briefly explain why the income elasticity of Crème Eggs might rise in the future.

Grade A* questions

	Good A	Good B	Good C
Price elasticity	-1.2	-	-
Income elasticity	+2.5	-	-
Cross-price elasticity	-	-0.2	+0.4

Good A sells 10,000 units a month at £5 each in a crowded market that's been growing due to steady 2% a year rises in real GDP. The firm has decided to straight away cut the price of Good A by 10%.

5. Calculate: 5a) Good A's probable monthly unit sales in the coming year

5b) Ignoring the YED factor, calculate the % impact on demand for Good C as a result of Good A's price change.

5c) State whether Goods B and C are complements or substitutes for Good A.

5d) Identify two actions Good C could take to reduce its cross-price elasticity in relation to Good A

Answers:

1a <u>% Q of Good B</u>
% P of Good A
=
+5%/+8%=+0.625

1b B is complement

2a) <u>% Q of Ferrari</u>
% ch in incomes
= +12%/+1.6%
=+7.5

2b) Other factors may have boosted last year's demand, e.g. extra ad spend

3a) <u>% Q of GoodB</u>
% P of Good A
= -2%/-10% = -0.2.

3b) Struflex lost 4,800 x £1.35 = £6,480 a month.

4a) <u>% ch Q of Eggs</u>
% ch in incomes
= +2.5%/1% =+2.5

4b) If Cadbury market them as more special than rivals, their luxury status may rise.

Answers (Q5)

5a) Without a price increase sales would grow by 2% x +2.5 = 5% to 10,500. A 10% price cut would add -10% x -1.2 = 12% more demand. So the total monthly sales should be 10,500 X 1.12 = 11,760 units

5b) Good will take a -12% x 0.4 = 4.8% hit to its sales volume.

5c) As proven by Q5b) Good C is a substitute for A, whereas Good B is a complementary good

5d) Differentiate more clearly, by a USP or branding.

Significance of price elasticity of demand

Grade C. What is it?

Price elasticity matters to governments when making policy decisions, notably on indirect taxes or subsidies. In 2018 the government brought in a 20% tax on added-sugar soft drinks such as Coca-Cola and Red Bull. The decision to make it a 20% rate of tax would have been influenced by the estimated price elasticity of demand for these drinks. The higher their price elasticity, the lower the rate of tax needed to achieve a targeted effect on consumption. See box on the right.

Do remember the calculations involved. If the government wants to cut sugary drink consumption by 20%, a 20% tax increase works if the price elasticity is -1. If the PED of these drinks is -0.5, prices must rise by 40% to get the desired fall in sales of 40% x -0.5 = 20%. If PED is -4, a 5% price rise would achieve the sales target of *minus* 20%.

Grade B (i) Where's the beef?

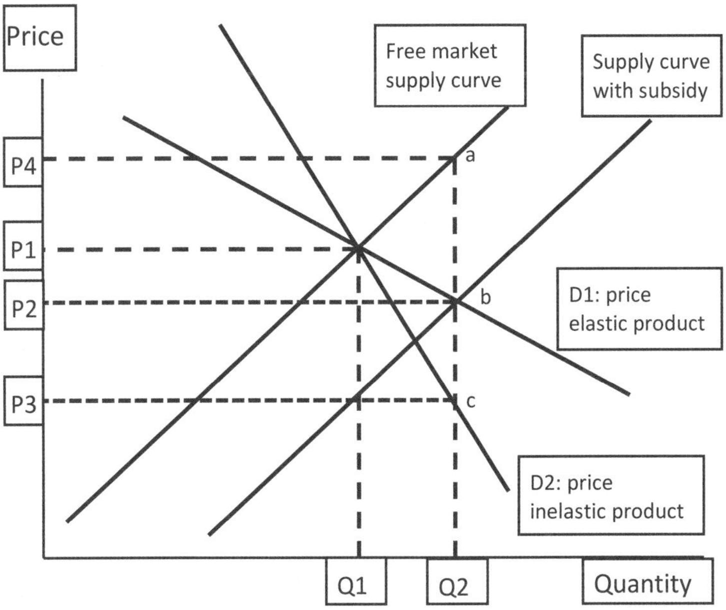

With this subsidy diagram, to push demand for a merit good up from Q1 to Q2, a subsidy of a – b is needed for price elastic D1. For price inelastic D2 a higher subsidy of a – c is required.

Don't forget the difference between what the consumer pays and the producer receives. For D2, the consumer pays P3, the producer receives P4 and the government/ Taypayer pays the difference.

Grade B (ii) Why it matters

Government spending and revenue-raising are important issues. Careful use of price elasticities could help government minimise the spending tied up in subsidies, e.g. for green energy. This could help achieve the right level of carbon reduction at the lowest possible cost (and opportunity cost, avoiding cutbacks elsewhere).

Exam tip: graphs like the one shown are hard to explain unless they are very well labelled. To do that in an exam it's vital to draw your graph on a big scale – especially if you have big handwriting.

Grade A The counter-argument

There will always be critics of any form of tax or subsidy, but no-one would criticise the attempt to spend as efficiently as possible, using price elasticities.

Grade A* The critical perspective

Evidence shows many indirect taxes and subsidies are poorly targeted. Price elasticities are hard to calculate/estimate, making the theory even tougher in practice.

Significance of PED: transmission mechanism (to get the top response level)

Chain 1. If the government wants to boost sales of electric cars it might set a target such as +50% (1). It should then get an estimate of the price elasticity of demand for electric cars, e.g. -2.0 (2) ... and calculate the price cut needed to hit the target (3) … e.g. ? x -2.0 = +50% (4) .. so subsidy is 25%. (5)

Chain 2. A cash-strapped government might want to cut its subsidy bill (1) … such as the subsidies for nuclear power (2). If a 30% subsidy is scrapped suppliers' output and jobs will be hit (3). If the PED is -0.5, scrapping a subsidy will cut demand by 15% (4). The higher the PED the bigger the effect.(5)

Movements along - and shifts in - supply curves

Grade C. What is it?

Supply curves slope upwards for the simple reason that the higher the market price, the more enthusiastic suppliers are to supply (see **Do** box, right). The upward slope reflects the natural positive relationship between price and supply. The higher the price the higher the willing level of supply; the lower the price the fewer the number of suppliers who can make a profit at such low prices. If the market price of a product declines, there would be a downward movement along the supply curve. In the graph below, the price cut from £5 to £4 creates a movement from point X to Y.

Grade B (i) Where's the beef?

The beef comes from distinguishing between situations in which there are movements along – and those where there are shifts in – the supply curve. In fact there are only two things that cause movement along the curve: 1. A decision to change price, whether by the firm or the government. 2. A shift in the demand curve, which will cause movement along the supply curve. In all other circumstances changes in supply factors will cause the supply curve to shift right or left.

Grade B (ii) Why it matters

It matters because supply, demand and equilibrium are at the heart of micro and macro-economics. Any gap in your understanding of supply threatens to undermine your mastery of 'market forces'. Below is a graph showing movement along a supply curve.

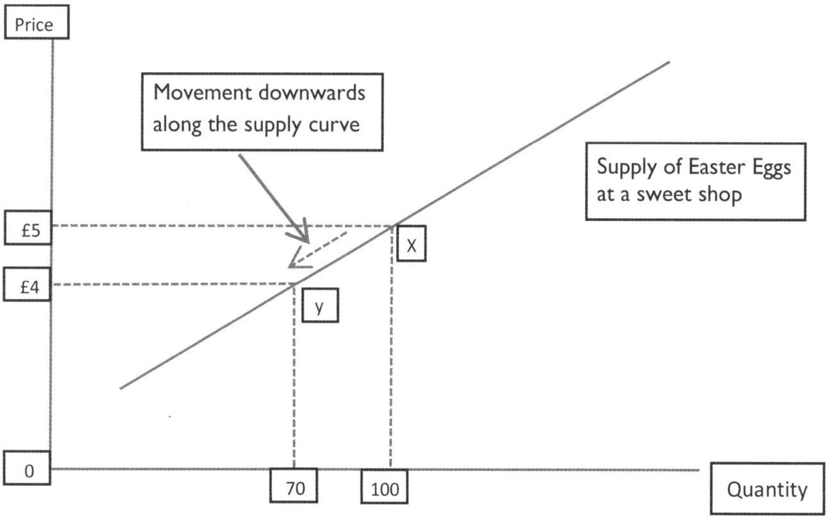

Grade A The other side

A critic of the supply curve shown above would question whether any business has certainty over the supply conditions it faces. The graph shows a clear linear relationship between price and supply. The real world may be more complex.

Grade A* The critical perspective

Business managers might be puzzled at this way of showing supply. They would focus more on issues of speed, reliability and quality of supply. But although micro-economics can be criticised for being abstract, it provides its own insights.

Do remember the 2 reasons why the supply curve slopes upwards:
1. The higher the price the happier existing suppliers are to push up their production levels 2. Higher prices make it possible for high-cost producers to supply. These may not be inefficient, they may just suffer high costs such as wages and property costs.

Don't forget the global nature of modern business. If market prices for posh shoes are high in Hong Kong, UK producers (among others) will be attracted to supply to this market. So the higher prices attract higher supply levels (and the UK gets some export business.

Exam tip: make sure to show understanding about why some firms have high supply costs. One may have particularly high ethical standards; another may make everything by hand. High costs of supply are not always an indication of inefficiency or incompetence.

Movements along - and shifts in - supply curves

Shifts in the supply curve – for Coca-Cola

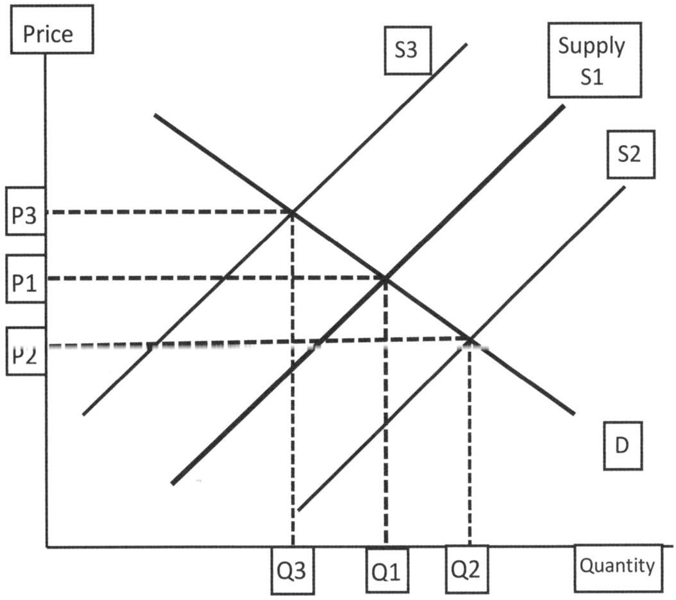

The graph shows supply of Coke at an equilibrium point of P1Q1. If an innovative productivity breakthrough cuts unit costs, the supply curve will shift rightwards, to S2. Alternatively, if a rise in labour costs increased unit costs, the supply curve would move to the left, to S3, with equilibrium at P3Q3.

Do remember the supply curve shows today's relationship between price and supply.

If the firm chooses to change price, this causes a slide along the supply curve, i.e. movement, not a shift.

Don't forget that supply conditions can change over time. A new vegan restaurant may find it easy to get organic, plant-based ingredients until it opens a few more outlets – and its suppliers can't keep up.

Supply may dry up from that source, forcing them to purchase from more expensive rivals.

Reasons for a shift in the supply curve

Supply will shift leftwards or rightwards in response to cost factors or to physical factors such as floods or – in the longer term – global warming. On the graph above, an increase in the world oil price would push up the price of plastic (bottle) packaging, pushing Coca-Cola's supply curve to the left from S1 to S3.

Test yourself (answers in tiny print at the foot of the page)

1. State two factors that might cause Coke's supply curve to shift from S1 to S2

2. What would be the effect on Coke's supply curve of a decision by the company to increase the price by 5%?

3. Which way would the supply curve shift if a new entrant burst onto the UK market for cola?

4. Which way would the supply curve move if there was a bust-up between Coca-Cola and Tesco, causing Tesco to withdraw the drink from its shelves.

Movement and shifts: transmission mechanism (to get the top response level)

Chain 1. A newly appointed Marketing Director may want to push the company's supply curve rightwards (1) … to boost the company's ability to make profits even in difficult market conditions (2) … with low market prices (3). To do this the Director must get costs down (4) … perhaps by moving production to a factory in an area with lower property and labour costs (5).

Chain 2. There are factors affecting the supply curve that businesses have no control over (1) … because the ingredients are market-determined such as raw cocoa beans in producing chocolate (2). If the pound falls against other currencies the UK cost of cocoa will rise (3) ... pushing up production costs for chocolate (4) … and therefore shifting the supply curve to the left (5).

Answers: 1. A cost reduction, e.g. rise in £ cuts the price Coca-Cola pays Head Office for the secret syrup Coke is made from. 2 = productivity improvements. 2. None at all, causes movement not a shift 3+4 same answer: It wouldn't; *demand* would be affected.

Causes of shifts in supply curves

Grade C. What is it?

Critical to exam success is to distinguish between determinants of supply and causes of shifts in supply. The factors that *determine* supply are static in the short run. For example the supply of rooms at Premier Inn, Wimbledon is determined by the size of the building minus any rooms currently out of action, e.g. being redecorated. Causes of shifts in supply are dynamic and longer-term, i.e. factors that have changed. To *shift* the supply curve, there must be factors that change the costs, e.g. an increase in staff pay or higher variable costs such as laundry.

Do remember the main causes of a rightward shift in the supply curve:
- a productivity breakthrough that cuts costs per unit
- a fall in the world commodity price of ingredients
- a fall in the cost of imported materials due to a rise in the £,
- a fall in labour costs, possibly because of a recession

Grade B (i) Where's the beef?

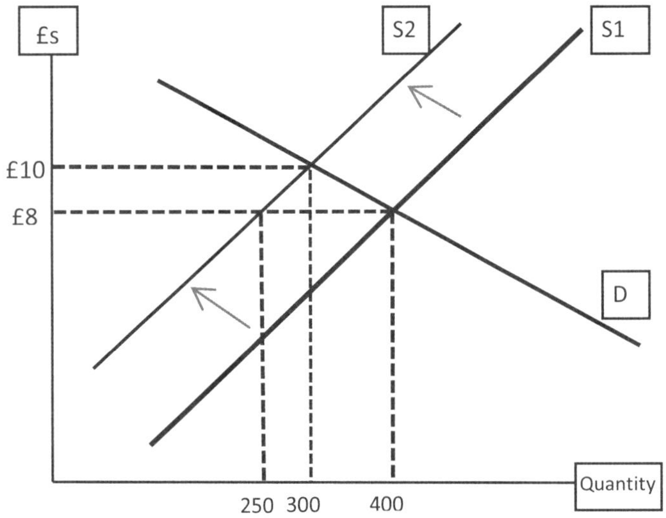

The key is to be expert at handling diagrams such as the one on the left. And able to say why changes to supply cause a shift in the supply curve. The graph shows a firm in a stable position with its supply curve S1 and a price of £8. Then a factor such as the bankruptcy of a supplier shifts supply to S2.

Don't confuse shifts in from movement along the supply curve. Movement along only happens because of changes in demand conditions.

Grade B (ii) Why it matters

Shifts in supply matter because of their huge implications for firms' profits. In the diagram above, while supply = S1, at the market price of £8 it would be happy to sell 400 units with a revenue of £3,200. If supply shifts to S2, at £8 the firm only wants to supply 250 units, potentially generating £2,000.

Exam tip: don't get muddled between supply and demand factors. Changes in demand *will* affect supply, but not the supply curve. When examiners ask about the effects of changes in supply (or demand) they mean the immediate, direct effect.

Grade A The counter-argument

In recent years, with fiercely competitive retail markets, left-shifting cost curves have caused different outcomes from back in the day. Years' ago, rising costs caused rising prices. Today they can cause 'shrinkflation', i.e. firms pull their cost curves back to their original (rightwards) position by cutting the weight/pack size.

Grade A* The critical perspective

There's a risk that supply curves present too simplified a view of business life. Some costs that may rise (such as interest charges on loans) won't affect firms' behaviour because they are fixed in the short term. So the theory simplifies reality.

Shifts in supply: transmission mechanism (to get the top response level)

Chain 1. A robot with artificial intelligence replaces 4 staff members (1) … cutting production costs per unit by 10% (2). This pushes the supply curve to the right (3) … allowing your firm to undercut rivals' prices (4) … boosting demand, revenue and profits – at your competitors' expense. (5)

Chain 2. A 10% rise in the cost of raw cocoa threatens a leftward shift in Cadbury's supply curve (1) … and therefore damage to the firm's profits (2). So a decision is made to cut the pack size by 10% (3) ... which stops the supply curve shifting (4) … and allows its equilibrium position to be unchanged (5)

Price elasticity of supply (PES)

Grade C. What is it?

Price elasticity of supply (PES) measures the responsiveness of suppliers to a change in the market price. We know that higher prices attract higher supply, but by how much and within what timescale? If a market has a high PES, producers are willing and able to respond quickly and near-limitlessly to rising prices.

$$\text{PES formula} = \frac{\%\ \text{change in quantity supplied}}{\%\ \text{change in the market price}}$$

Because supply curves slope upwards as suppliers respond positively to higher prices, PES figures are always positive.

Grade B (i) Where's the beef?

The beef is in the scope for confusion between price elasticity of supply (PES) and of demand (PED). Questions on PES are among the least well answered in the subject. You have to keep clearly in mind that this is about ease or difficulty in changing output – and then distinguish between the short and long-term factors.

Grade B (ii) Why it matters

It matters because it has a huge effect on prices. The world oil price jumps around month by month not because of big changes in demand, but due to erratic supply made worse by relatively low price elasticity of supply. After all, if supply could respond quickly to rising demand, prices would settle down equally quickly. In markets where PES is high, prices will be more stable.

Grade A The counter-argument

Although most economists favour high, responsive price elasticities of supply, others may see PES as a factor to be treated with caution. They see a high PES as a possible sign of excessive flexibility, perhaps reflecting a 'gig economy' with too few protections for staff and suppliers. After all, the only way a business can respond instantly to new, higher demand is by having staff on call day and night. Mrs Bloggs having a heart attack and needing an ambulance at 3AM is one thing; Mrs Bloggs wanting a Flat White delivered at 3AM is perhaps another.

Grade A* The critical perspective

A standard A Level answer on PES emphasises the short-term difficulties and long-term possibilities. It draws upon the view that in the long run all factors of production are variable. But economics fudges the difficulty of separating the short and long run in an ever-changing world. As there's no clear dividing line between the short and long run, PES values may remain quite low even in the long run.

Do remember that PES is largely within the control of the supplier. Currently the NHS has almost no elasticity of supply because of previous government decisions to cut the number of hospital beds. Well-run firms hate to turn customers away, so keep PES high.

Don't ignore the rights of staff to stable earnings; how else will they ever get a mortgage? When economics forgets about people, it reverts to its famous name: 'the dismal science'.

Exam tip: let the word 'elasticity' ring a bell in your brain: 'is this PED or PES?' For every 100 answers to a question on PES, 40+ students are wasting their time (and grade) writing about PED.

Price elasticity of supply: transmission mechanism (to the top response level)

Chain 1. If a lurch in fashion brings demand flooding towards a firm (1) … it needs to have a high enough PES to be able to respond well (2). Only if it had a PES of +1 would it be able to respond instantly to any jump in demand (3) ... but as long as its PES is in the range +0.5 to +0.75 it should be able to keep customers happy (4) ... with only a modest queue arising and perhaps a small price rise (5)

Chain 2. Some firms face constantly erratic demand, such as an ice cream parlour (1) … where sales one week can be 4 times higher than the week before (2). This makes it vital to have highly flexible production system (3)… and therefore a high PES (4) ... and happy customers on hot days (5).

Calculating & interpreting price elasticity of supply

Grade C. What is it?

Price elasticity of supply (PES) is easy to calculate but hard to interpret. The formula places *% change in quantity supplied* at the top and *% change in price* at the bottom (see right hand page). The hard thing is to interpret the result. The PES will always be positive but may vary considerably depending on circumstances. In August a seaside hotel may be fully booked and have an upward PES of +0; that same hotel in February may have 2 rooms booked out of 120 and an upward PES of +100 or more.

Grade B (i) Where's the beef?

Much of the beef comes from analysing the difference between short-term PES and long-term PES. This is covered in the entry that follows. The other important issue is being able to label correctly the numerical values of PES. These range from +0 (perfectly inelastic supply) to + ∞ (perfectly elastic supply) via relatively inelastic (+0.01 to +0.99) and relatively elastic (+1.01 but less than ∞). So a PES of +0.5 is relatively supply inelastic and a PES of +1.5 is relatively supply elastic.

Grade B (ii) Why it matters

It matters because it's easy to see how consumers respond to price signals, but much harder to understand the problems firms have in adjusting supply to meet demand. As I write, Airbus (airplane manufacturer) has an order book worth €500 billion but annual sales turnover of €60bn. At that rate it might take 8 years to deliver all the planes on order. *That's* the effect of supply price inelasticity.

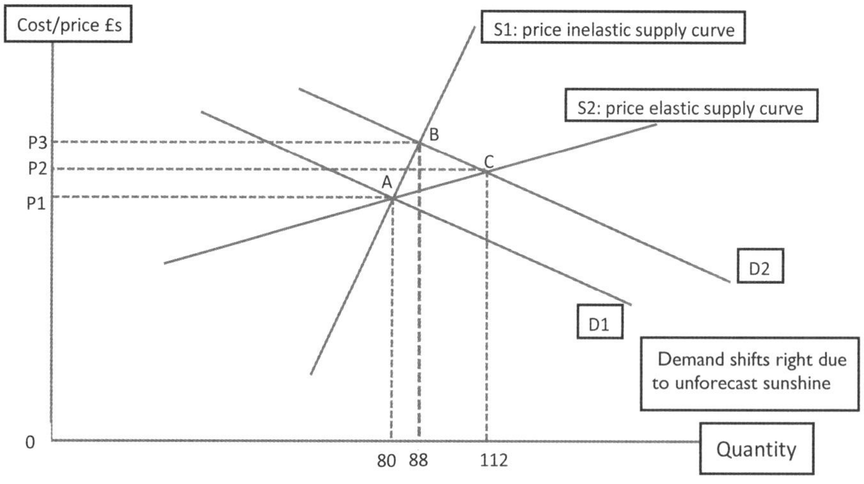

Grade A The counter-argument

The maths of PES are often put forward sloppily, with too little use of 'ceteris paribus'. The maths work only because of assumptions about the constancy of supply responses to price change. True supply curves are likely to be more erratic – upward-sloping, yes, but more bumpy, with inconstant price elasticities of supply.

Grade A* The critical perspective

Some economists might question whether supply elasticity is as price-sensitive as is implied by the term PES. There may be so many physical and other constraints on supply that responsiveness to price may be hard to measure and to prove.

Do practise graphs like the one on the left. This shows that when demand shifts rightwards, the firm with price inelastic supply manages to get supply up by 10%, from 80 to 88 units. Whereas the business with price elastic supply gets its production up 40% from 80 to 112 units. If this is the grocery business, in the future supermarkets will all want to deal with the firm with price elastic supply.

Don't forget that the ideal supply elasticity is infinite. In other words firms would love to be able to double or quad-ruple production instantly if demand was buoyant enough.

Exam tip: show the examiner you understand how to make production more flexible and therefore more elastic. It would be great to have flexible labour, willing to work 2 hours one day; ten hours the next; also good might be robots that can work through the night when needed.

Worked examples (with answers)

Grade C question:

Q1. When the market price is £6, firm A produces 500 units a week. When the market price rises to £7.20 it works frantically but successfully to get production up to 650 units a week.

a) Calculate the price elasticity of supply.

b) State whether the goods are relatively supply price elastic or price inelastic.

ANSWER

1a) PES = $\frac{\text{\% change in quantity supplied}}{\text{\% change in price}}$

1a) % change in quantity supplied = +30%

1a) % change in price = + 20%

1a) ANS = +30% /+20% = +1.5

1b) Relatively supply price elastic

Grade A/A* question:

Q2. Two years ago, when the market price for 4 toilet rolls fell from £1.50 to £1.20, Firm B responded by dropping out of the market altogether. Last month, when the price rose from £1.40 to £1.54, it increased its supplies from 50,000 to 70,000 packs.

2a) Calculate its PES last month

2b) Explain why it stopped producing two years ago.

ANSWER

2a) PES is +40%/+10% = +4

2b) Firm B enjoys highly price elastic supply conditions, with great supply flexibility. So just as it could respond last month by upping production by 40%, two years' ago it had the flexibility to stop production while prices were too low to be profitable.

Economic calculations: test yourself; answers in back of book

Grade C question:

Q1. For each of the following, state whether the good is supply price elastic, price inelastic or has unitary supply price elasticity

a) Supply price elasticity is 2.5

b) A10% price increase encourages a firm to boost supply by 6%

c) A 6% fall in the market price leads Firm C to reduce supply from 450 to 423 units

Grade B/A question:

Q2. Using the supply curve below, calculate the price elasticity of supply as:

a) Price rises from £4 to £6

b) Price rises from £8 to £12

c) Price rises from £12 to £14

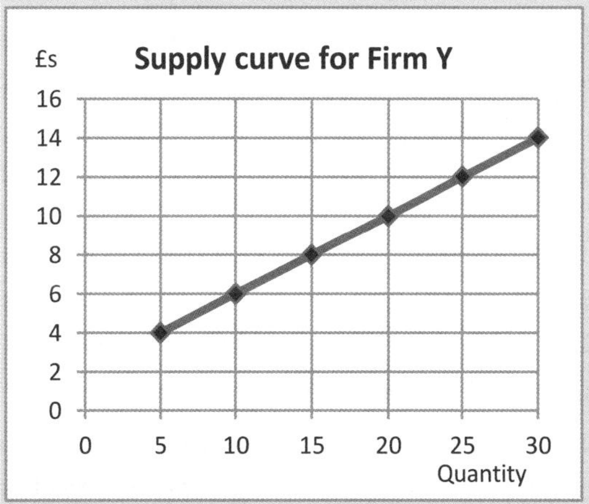

d) Briefly explain the implication of your findings

Grade A/A* question:

Q3. Explain how the arrival of production robots with artificial intelligence (A.I.) might affect the price elasticity of supply of grocery products such as chilled ready-meals.

For answers see back pages

Short and long-run price elasticity of supply

Grade C. What is it?

The price elasticity of supply (PES) of every item will be different in the long-term compared with the short. Economists define the short-term as the period within which fixed factors are unalterable, creating an inevitable limit to PES. For instance short-term supplies of Tesla cars may be limited by the size of the Tesla factory. In the long-term, of course, Tesla can build a bigger or another factory – relaxing the constraint and therefore making PES more elastic.

Grade B (i) Where's the beef?

The beef lies in your ability to understand which supply factors are fixed or variable in the short term. For a small bakery ingredients such as flour and yeast should be variable, as they can quickly obtain extra from their suppliers. But if the bakery advertises bread made from organic flour bought from local farmers, it may be impossible to obtain extra in the short-term if the local farmers have run out.

Grade B (ii) Why it matters

It matters because it has a huge effect on the market mechanism. Ideally a change in consumer tastes (and therefore demand conditions) yields a quick response by changes in supply. So a new equilibrium point is reached, perhaps at the same price level as before. But if supply elasticities are low in the short-term, a market may remain in disequilibrium for some time – with customers perhaps unable to get the Chanel bag they want, or with prices jumping upwards.

Grade A The counter-argument

There's no doubt that, in a world dominated by manufacturing, there was once a clear-cut division between short and long-term supply. Arguably it's different today, with the service sector accounting for 80% of GDP and with the rise of 'weightless' online businesses. If your online system is operating through the cloud and your fulfilment and delivery system is outsourced to manufacturers, your short-term PES may be as high as your long-term PES. As ever, it's risky to generalise; each firm works in its own unique way, facing unique constraints.

Grade A* The critical perspective

These days, most companies boast of their efficient Just In Time (JIT) systems. So it was interesting that when an apparent Brexit date loomed in early 2019, many suppliers spent heavily on extra warehouse space to hold extra inventory (stocks). Even today, the simplest way to achieve high price elasticity of supply is to hold large stocks of finished product - and respond instantly to new opportunities.

Do remember the fixed factors that will make short-term PES relatively price inelastic – or even perfectly price inelastic. They include:
- physical factors such as size of factory or storage depots
- whether the item is highly perishable and therefore can't be stockpiled
- staff so skilled and specialised that recruiting and training new ones might take years.

Don't forget that – short term or long term – price elasticities of supply are always positive.

Exam tip: seize opportunities to emphasise the difference between short and long-term price elasticities of supply. It's reasonable to suggest that in the long run, virtually every product's PES must be close to infinity.

Short and long-run PES: transmission mechanism (to the top response level)

Chain 1. In the short-term a jump in the market price of your product may be hard to react to (1) ... because you can't quickly find new staff and the training takes many months (2). You increase supply slightly by offering overtime to existing staff (3) ... but you have to pay double-time so it adds significantly to your unit costs (4) ... and is only affordable if the market price has risen significantly (5).

Chain 2. In the long run you can expand capacity by opening a bigger factory (1) .. thereby raising the ceiling on your maximum production level (2). At the same time you might want to increase flexibility (3)... and therefore raise the PES (4) ... perhaps by putting more staff on zero-hours contracts (5).

Equilibrium price and quantity

Grade C. What is it?

Equilibrium is at the heart of micro-economics. It provides the reassuring idea that – left alone – supply and demand will naturally converge at the equilibrium point. In effect, this mechanism is what Adam Smith called the 'invisible hand'. In economics, things don't get any more famous than that.

Do be clear about the logic of equilibrium. It is the point where supply and demand are equal and therefore it is inherently stable. If nothing changes, sales volume and the selling price will remain constant at that equilibrium level.

Grade B (i) Where's the beef?

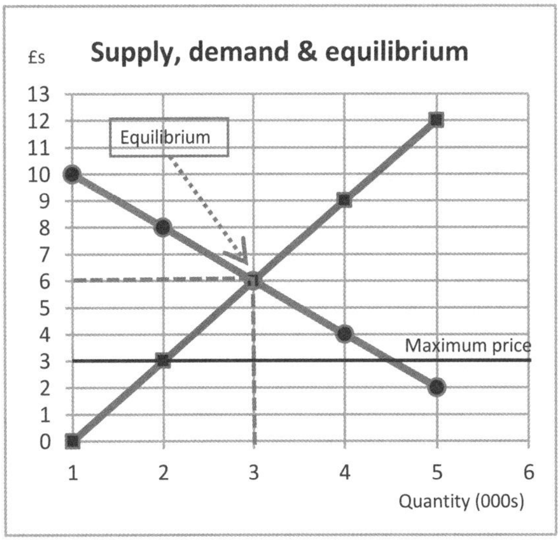

The big issue here is graphical analysis. If the government chose to place a maximum price of £3 on this product, this would pull the market away from the £6/3,000 unit equilibrium. At £3, customers want to buy 4,500 units, but suppliers only want to produce 2,000. So there will be a 2,500 shortfall. Shops will run out, so people will come early and queue to get hold of their favourite item. Just as in Britain during World War 2.

Don't doubt the pull of the equilibrium. If supply is too high prices will fall and suppliers will cut back. The only question mark is about how long the process will take.

Grade B (ii) Why it matters

In the 19th century Karl Marx said that capitalism would implode under the weight of its own contradictions. The answer, by neo-classical economists was to emphasise the benign effects of doing nothing, thanks to the tendency for dislocated economies or markets to revert to equilibrium and therefore stability. So equilibrium is a concept at the heart of economic and political debate/dispute.

Exam tip: it's important to label the equilibrium point clearly, as on the graph to the left. And when you've drawn a graph, make sure to refer to it extensively in your written analysis. That usually pushes your mark straight up to top-level analysis.

Grade A The other side

The equilibrium is the free market *and* social optimum only if there is no market failure. But in 2019 more than 50% of children were living in poverty in ten large UK districts. This represents a huge market failure. So the free market equilibrium for fresh fruit and new trainers may be far from the 'proper' (optimal) equilibrium.

Grade A* The critical perspective

Equilibrium might be harder to establish in the real world than in the classroom. My local Morrisons is repeatedly out of stock of masses of fruit and vegetable items by early evening. Matching supply and demand is harder than it looks.

Equilibrium: transmission mechanism (to get the top response level)

Chain 1. If a fiery TV documentary scares people off bananas (1) … demand will shift leftwards (2) ... and piles of bananas will be unsold (3). Price will fall sharply, pushing supply down and demand up (perhaps only slightly) (4) … until a new banana equilibrium is established (5).

Chain 2. If an over-enthusiastic entrepreneur builds a Thai restaurant that's too big for the local demand for Thai food (1) … the excess supply will force him/her to cut prices to stimulate more demand (2). That might draw demand from people who usually eat Fish & Chips (3) … and help build a new equilibrium (4) … but at prices too low to make a reasonable profit from the Thai restaurant (5).

Use of supply and demand diagrams

Grade C. What is it?

A supply and demand diagram is the bread-and-butter of micro-economics. It shows the equilibrium point between supply and demand, but perhaps in the context of a disruptive factor such as a government-set maximum price level. This is not difficult economics – but you must get close to perfection on this topic.

Grade B (i) Where's the beef?

The beef comes from understanding the arithmetic of a diagram such as the one below – and understanding the mechanism that inclines supply and demand to revert to the equilibrium position.

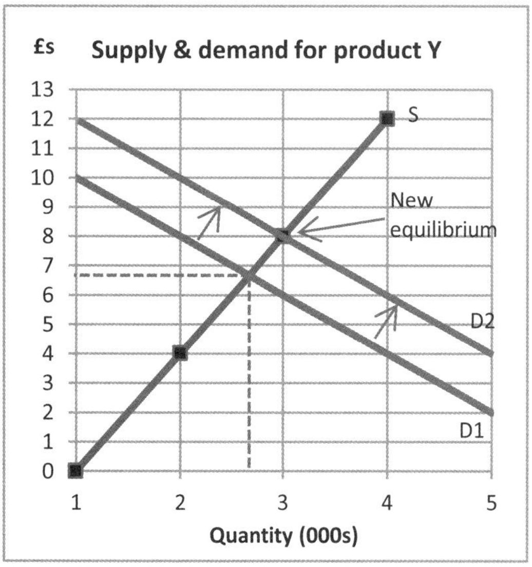

Worked example:

At a price of £6.75, product Y's sales have settled down at 2,600 a week. Then sales start to rise quite sharply, providing an opportunity to increase product Y's price.

Q1. Calculate the change in revenue caused by the rightwards shift in product Y's demand curve.

Q2. Outline 2 reasons to explain the upwards shift in demand for product Y.

Q3. Use the D1 curve to calculate Y's price elasticity of demand when the price increases from £4 to £6.

Grade B (ii) Why it matters

It matters because governments can get lured into acting when all that's needed is to allow the market mechanism to take its course. In 2015 and 2016 there were regular news items about dairy farmers and the low price of milk. From 35p per litre in November 2013 the price had fallen below 25p. The farmers were furious – and so was the Daily Mail. Government must act. Well, in effect the government did nothing and by 2018/19 the price of milk was back above 30p a litre. Some supply disappeared as farmers switched to more profitable animals or crops; and demand slipped as people switched to soya and almond milks.

Grade A The counter argument

Relying on equilibrium is alright in theory, but may be vicious in practice. Farmers may be driven out of dairy farming through bankruptcy – with huge impacts on the families. The bitterness shown by Brexiteers towards London politicians probably has its origins in the callousness of allowing 'the market' to destroy communities.

Grade A* The critical perspective

As presented in the graph above, the business world looks very static, with equilibrium at a (sort of) fixed point. For firms such as Ryanair and Center Parcs, computer models use dynamic pricing that constantly update demand pressures to establish prices that reflect an ever-changing real-world equilibrium point.

Do remember that markets should settle into equilibrium because in any other event supply and demand will be out of balance. That means either empty shelves if supply is below the level of demand (and possibly queueing or even rationing if the situation is unresolved) or a build-up of unsold stock if supply is too high.

Don't be skimpy on your labelling of graphs. Yes, time is a real pressure, but it's hugely helpful to label graphs clearly. In this case the labelling of the new equilibrium is helpful.

Answers:

Q1. Revenue = QxP It was 2,600 x £6.75 = £17,550
Now it's 3,000 x £8 = £24,000
So it's risen by £6,450.

2. One may be that it's become fashionable; a second is that it might be a luxury good enjoying the effect of a rise in real GDP.

3. As price rose 50% from £4 to £6, sales fell by 25% from 4,000 to 3,000. So the PED is 25%/50% = -0.5.

Economic calculations: test yourself; answers in back of book

Grade B question:

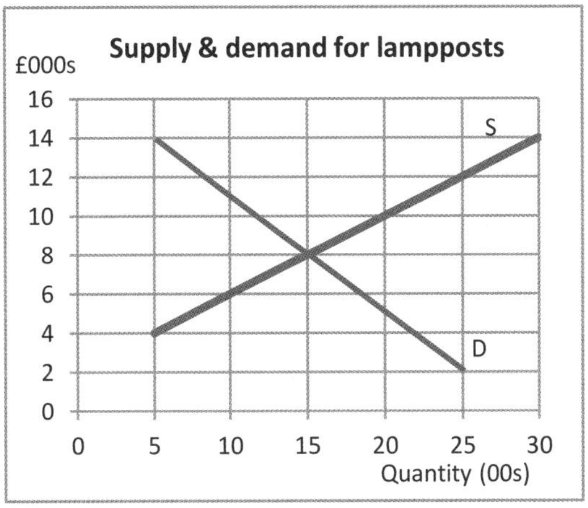

Answer these questions based on this graph:

1. What is the value of the lamppost market when it's at equilibrium?

2. What's the shortfall between demand and supply if lampposts are priced at £14,000 each. Express your answer in units and in £s.

3. Briefly explain what would happen to supply and demand if the price of lampposts was £14,000.

Grade B/A question

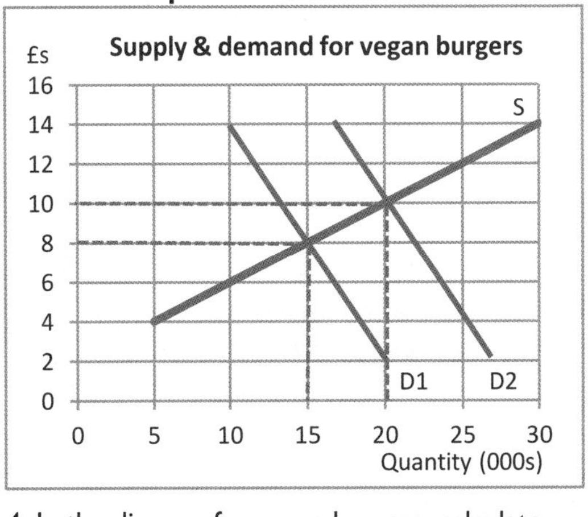

4. In the diagram for vegan burgers, calculate the change in revenue when the demand curve shifts from D1 to D2.

5a) If a firm chose to keep its price at £8 even though the market price had moved to £10, approximately what sales volume might it achieve, according to the graph?

5b) Use your estimate of the new sales level to calculate the % growth in sales volume.

Economic calculations: cont.

Grade A/A* question

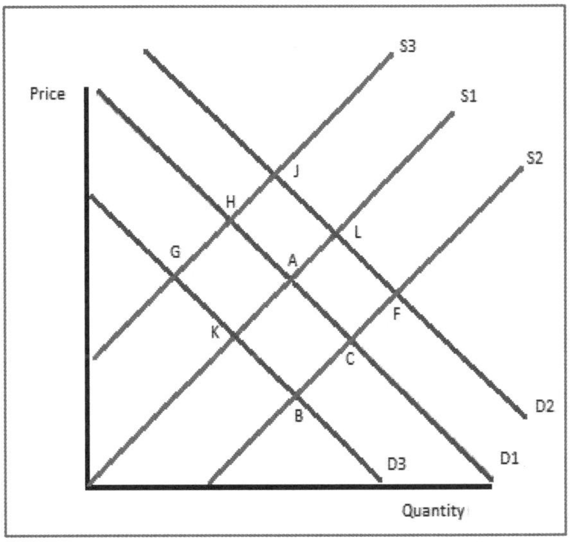

On the above diagram, A is the existing market equilibrium for Quality Street chocolates. But what if things change? Identify the letter that represents the new equilibrium, given each of the following circumstances.

1. A hard Brexit pushes the price of cocoa up by 15%.

2. Mars doubles its advertising budget for Celebrations chocolates.

3. A social media superstar has been attacking chocolate for weeks, causing a slump in sales and in the global commodity price of cocoa.

4. The government introduces a 20% tax on full-sugar chocolates such as Quality Street.

5. Nestle decides to relocate production of Quality Street from the UK to a cheaper European location in Poland.

6. A Quality Street promotion goes viral, leading to a new wave of buyers among the 16-24 age group.

7. A rise in commodity prices (cocoa and sugar) causes Mars to increase the price of Celebrations.

8. Labour shortages after Brexit force Nestle to increase salaries at the Quality Street factory.

9. A rise in the value of the £ cuts the cost of buying cocoa and sugar.

10. Quality Street is featured on a Chinese TV programme, causing a huge increase in export sales.

For answers, see Appendix A, near the back pages.

Price mechanism

Grade C. What is it?

The price mechanism is the means by which producers' decisions on supply and consumers' demand choices come together at the equilibrium point. This is achieved through three forces: rationing, incentives and signalling. The price level rations (potentially infinite) demand to those who can afford – and wish – to buy. Incentives are what spark interest from producers: the higher the price, the greater the incentive to supply. And signalling takes place when prices move: a price rise tells entrepreneurs that this is a market worth entering; but also signals to customers that perhaps they should be looking for acceptable substitutes.

Do think about the difference between markets. Just because the price mechanism is great for many consumer goods, it's not necessarily right for all. Medical supplies and education may be examples of the limits of the price mechanism.

Grade B (i) Where's the beef?

The beef, in this case, comes from the student's ability to distinguish between the three 'functions of the price mechanism' identified above. Most will memorise the three terms without being able to separate them out.

Grade B (ii) Why it matters

Quite possibly the price mechanism is the single most important concept in micro economics. It is what makes Adam Smith's 'invisible hand' work. In other words in a free market, what ensures that there are enough strawberries in the shops to meet consumer demand is the price mechanism. The attempt in command economies for government to decide on the level of strawberry production has proved very much less successful.

Don't muddle the three 'functions': rationing, incentives and signalling. For top grades it's vital to disentangle things that can easily get a bit muddled.

Grade A The counter-argument

However, the free market approach has limitations. The price mechanism makes sense for triggering allocation decisions for Mars Bars or strawberries. If strawberries in February are too expensive, I'll buy apples instead. But what if the product is Herceptin, a drug that helps millions of cancer patients worldwide? Do we want demand to be rationed by price, as happens with strawberries? Many people would feel that the price mechanism is inappropriate in some markets.

Exam tip: think carefully about the market context on the exam paper. Is it a truly free market, as for strawberries? Or is it dominated by a few big firms – who may have the power to resist market signals?

Grade A* The critical perspective

In addition to economic factors there are psychological ones. In the market for Ed Sheeran concert tickets, the price mechanism can successfully ensure that those with the deepest pockets – and the greatest love for Ed – are sitting in the front row. But people hate to see tickets changing hands for £1,000, so they demand intervention to limit or stop the price mechanism.

Price mechanism: transmission mechanism (to get the top response level)

Chain 1. If an egg producer sees that falling prices are making production unprofitable, s/he may buy in fewer day-old chicks (1) … meaning that in 6 months there will be a fall in egg production (2) … limiting the individual farmer's losses (3) … and cutting egg supply to the market (4). Thanks to this signalling process, market prices will start to rise again. (5)

Chain 2. If a government sets a minimum price that's above the market price (1) … the market mechanism ceases to work (2) … with suppliers facing the wrong incentives and therefore overproducing (3). Resources will be mis-allocated because more will be supplied than customers want to buy (4) … and because the price won't fall back, there's no signal to suppliers to slow down. (5)

Consumer surplus

Grade C. What is it?

Consumer surplus is the benefit customers get when the equilibrium (actual) price is below the price they are willing to pay. See the graph below. The actual price paid by 3,000 customers is £6. Yet according to the demand curve, 1,500 customers are willing to pay £9; they're getting a £3 surplus. And 2,000 are willing to pay £8, so they're also enjoying a bonus. In fact every one of the 3,000 customers is willing to pay more than £6, apart from the last marginal consumer – the one at point c.

Do remember this phrase about consumer surplus: that 'every consumer gains a surplus bar the last marginal customer'. This gives a fair account of the thrilling 'selling point' of consumer surplus: we're all winners.

Grade B Where's the beef?

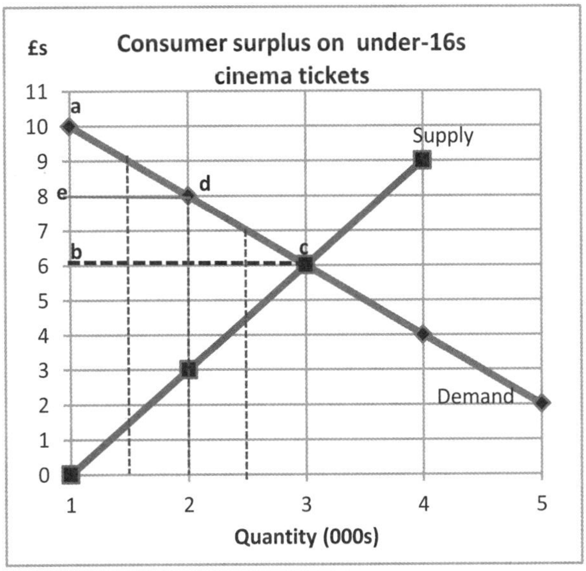

The diagram shows a supply and demand diagram for cinema tickets. The consumer surplus is often shaded in (within the area abc) and shows the extra benefit to consumers of free market prices. They are buying at a fair price of £6, when all but one is prepared to pay anything up to £10.

And if the price rose to £8 the consumer surplus would shrink to the triangle: aed.

Don't hesitate to question the real-world reality behind the theory. Many families buy their annual holiday having been convinced that it's 'worth' £6,000 even though the selling price was £3,999. So when it proves more like £4,500's worth, they're disappointed.

Grade B (ii) Why it matters

It matters because this concept helps explain the passion shown by some towards free market economics – every consumer benefits by more than they realise.

Exam tip: seize the opportunity to use this theory frequently. There are masses of questions on supply and demand, but very few answers that voluntarily include consumer surplus in the analysis of a firm's demand conditions. There should be more.

Grade A The counter-argument

Consumer surplus would be a wonderful thing if all market participants had perfect information. In fact, years' ago people rushed to buy 'timeshare' houses; to take out 'personal pensions' and endowment mortgages – and were robbed.

Grade A* The critical perspective

The theory of consumer surplus envisages a world where everyone pays the same equilibrium price. But iPhones come in a range of types and prices so that those willing to pay £1,000 can buy one. So Apple absorbs the surplus into its own profit

Consumer surplus: transmission mechanism (to get to the top response level)

Chain 1. The free market equilibrium is established as a result of market forces (1) … in other words the interaction of demand conditions (2) … and supply conditions (3). Sloping downward towards this equilibrium is the demand curve (4) leaving every consumer in surplus bar the last marginal one. (5)

Chain 2. If a cinema-lover decides a particular film isn't worth the price (1) i.e. its utility is too low (2) ... they simply won't pay, and therefore do not waste their money (3). Those that buy gain a consumer surplus (4) ... whereas those that don't are acting rationally as they don't think it's worth it. (5)

Producer surplus

Grade C. What is it?

Producer surplus is the benefit producers get when the equilibrium (actual) price is above the cost level at which firms are willing to supply. See the graph below. The actual price paid by 3,000 customers is £6. Yet according to the supply curve, firms are willing to supply 1,500 tickets at £1.50 each and 2,000 tickets at £3. So the producers are doing wonderfully well out of the market price of £6. In fact firms are willing to supply every one of the 3,000 tickets at less than £6, apart from the last marginal ticket – the one at point c.

Grade B Where's the beef?

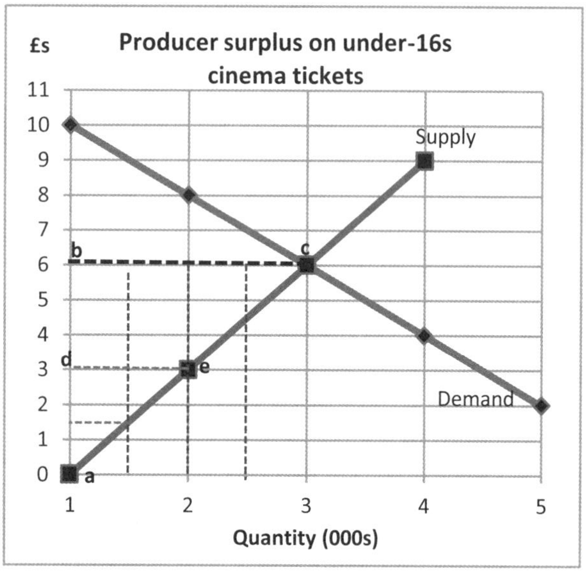

The diagram shows a supply and demand diagram for cinema tickets. The producer surplus is often shaded in (within the area abc) and shows the extra benefit to producers of free market prices. They are selling at the market price of £6, but all but one is prepared to sell for as low as £1 or £1.50.

If the price fell to £3 the producer surplus would shrink to the triangle: ade.

Grade B (ii) Why it matters

It matters because producer surplus is an important Year 12 concept, but an even more important one for Year 13 economics such as understanding the impact of trade tariffs.

Grade A The counter-argument

Producer surplus is an awkward idea because it seems to be about profit, when it really isn't. It takes into account marginal costs only, so it ignores fixed costs.

Grade A* The critical perspective

In its assumption that all goods share the same equilibrium price the theory of producer surplus assumes homogenous products. This is vanishingly rare in a world of product differentiation and ever-changing consumer tastes.

Do tackle these questions:
1. From the graph, state the area that shows the fall in producer surplus if the market price falls from £6 to £3.
2. Calculate the producer surplus available for the supply of 2,000 tickets.

Don't be fooled by the win-win appearance of this theory. All consumers and producers seem to be in the money (bar the last marginal ones). But in reality many firms go under, bogged down by a failure to generate enough revenue to cover all their costs. Business life is harder than is implied by producer surplus.

Exam tip: be willing to criticise the excessive simplifications of this theory. It appears to show profits for all – but that's not anyone's experience in the real world.

Producer surplus: transmission mechanism (to get to the top response level)

Chain 1. If a demand curve shifts leftwards the equilibrium sales level will fall (1) … and effectively squashes the producer surplus triangle (2). The leftward shift also pulls down the equilibrium price level (3) … squashing the surplus down vertically (4). So the producer surplus falls sharply. (5)

Chain 2. A threat to producer surplus arises if a new, efficient firm enters a competitive market (1). Its low costs allow it to charge lower prices (2) ... pulling down the equilibrium price (3) ... by forcing the supply curve to the right (4) This boosts consumer surplus, but leaves rival firms struggling. (5)

Impact of indirect taxes

Grade C. What is it?

Indirect taxes are levied on goods, not on income. They have been used for centuries, often levied as a way to generate government income and therefore put on essentials such as salt or windows. These days such taxes are given a more social rationale, such as the 2018 sugar tax – on added sugar soft drinks such as Pepsi. The tax is justifiable as it fulfils the social objective of reducing sugar consumption/obesity. There are two types of indirect tax: a 'specific' tax is levied by weight or volume (such as the 2018 sugar tax); an 'ad valorem' tax is levied by value, e.g. VAT which is taxed at 20% of the value of an item.

Do remember to tell the examiner whether you are treating the tax as specific or ad valorem. It will usually be spelled out, but if not, choose whichever graph is easier to draw – probably the specific tax as it's quite easy to draw parallel lines.

Grade B Where's the beef? 1. Ad valorem tax

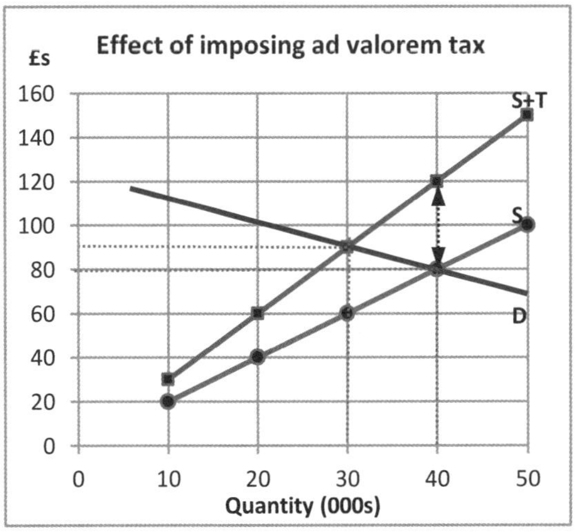

The diagram shows an ad valorem tax rate of 50%. This can be seen at 40,000 units of output, where an arrow shows the imposition of a tax that pushes the cost of supply from £80 a unit to £120. Because the tax is by value, the higher the price the higher the tax. Therefore the Supply + Tax (S+T) curve rises at a steeper angle than the original supply curve (S). The tax pushes the price up to £90 and demand down by 25% to 30,000 units.

Don't forget that Edexcel treats taxation as something that's levied on suppliers rather than consumers. So it affects supply curves rather than demand curves. This may seem illogical at times, but it does make exam answers a little easier.

Grade B Where's the beef? 2. Specific tax

Because it is levied by weight, the tax is not related to the supply price. So, as below, the Supply + Tax curve should be drawn parallel to the supply curve.

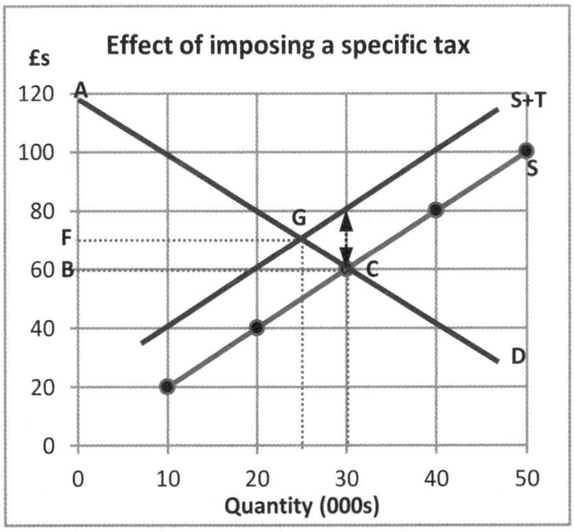

The diagram shows a specific tax rate of £20 per unit. The arrow shows this £20 at 30,000 units of output, but because they are parallel lines the same is true at every output level. The tax pushes the equilibrium price up from £60 to £70 and demand down from 30,000 to 25,000 units. This cuts the consumer surplus on this item from ABC to AFG.

Therefore the loss of consumer surplus is FGBC.

Exam tip: examiners try to ask questions that touch on every part of the specification over a 3-4 year period. Indirect tax comes up in section 1.2.9 and then again under externalities section 1.4.1. Featuring in two micro sections makes it likely that exam questions will feature more frequently than some other topics.

Grade A The counter-argument

Indirect taxes are often levied on 'bad' products such as cigarettes and alcohol that are consumed disproportionately by those on relatively low incomes. So the taxes are regressive, taxing the poor at a higher rate than the rich.

Incidence of indirect tax on producers & consumers

Grade C. What is it?

The graph below shows the effect of imposing an ad valorem tax on a particular good. In an exam you need to disentangle the effects of this on producers, consumers and government. The letters shown on the diagram are the best way to answer the questions.

Grade B Where's the beef? 1. Ad valorem tax

Examiners like to ask questions on the effect of the tax on producer and consumer surplus, and on the winners and losers from the tax. Beneath the graph come important questions and their answers, but before that let's establish a few things:

1. That in this case the consumer price rises from £70 to £100. This reduces the consumer surplus from LGE to LFC
2. At the new equilibrium sales quantity of A, the government is charging C-J in tax (£50) and therefore collecting FCJH in tax revenue.

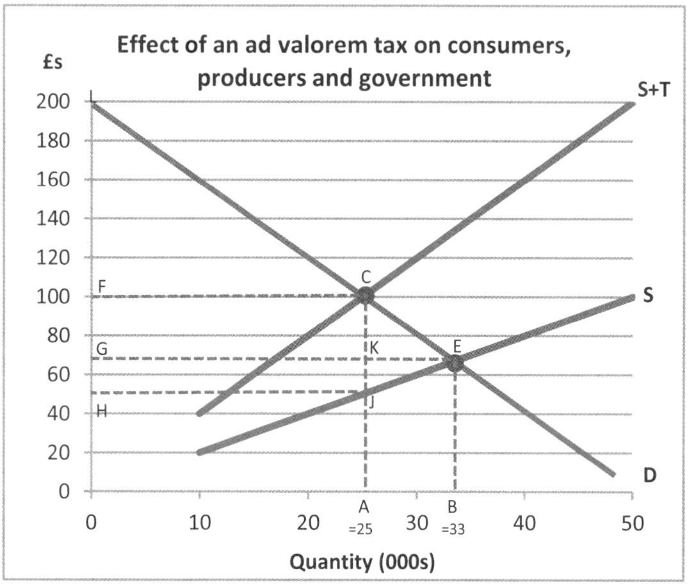

When an ad valorem tax pushes the supply curve to S+T:

1. Consumers pay FG in tax per unit
2. Producers pay GH in tax per unit
3. Consumers' total tax bill is FGCK (or FG x 0A)
4. Producers' total tax bill is GHKJ
5. Total tax revenue for the government is FCJH
6. The change in producers' revenue is GEB0 – HJA0
7. The change in consumer expenditure is GEB0 – FCA0

Grade A The counter-argument

Firms won't passively do just what theory suggests. When the sugar tax came in 2018, Coca-Cola boldly increased the prices of its taxed (sugary) and non-taxed (zero-cal) brands equally. Economic theory couldn't predict that.

Do remember the purpose behind many indirect taxes. They aren't trying to penalise consumers or firms. The plan is to cut demand and therefore cut back on smoking, or sugary drinks. Indirect tax doesn't have to be wrong.

Don't dodge these questions about the graph (answers below):
1. Calculate the loss in producers' revenue as a result of the ad valorem tax.
2. Calculate the extra government income as a result of the new tax.
3. Calculate the tax paid by consumers after the tax imposition.

Answers:

Q1 The loss in producer revenue is GEB0 – HJA0
GEB0 = 33,000 x £70 = £2.31m
HJA0 = 25,000 x £50 = £1.25m. So loss is £1.06m

Q2 Extra taxation: 25,000 x £50 = £1.25m

Q3. Consumer tax bill: 25,000 x £30 = £750.000.

Incidence of indirect tax: transmission mechanism (to top response level)

Chain 1. No firm wants an indirect tax levied on its own products because of the obvious effect on demand (1). Prices will rise so sales will fall (2) … to an extent determined by the products' PED (3). But at least there's a level-playing field (4)… as every UK or overseas firm pays the same UK taxes. (5)

Chain 2. The limit to indirect tax comes with smuggling (1) … especially for countries with contiguous borders (2). Even the UK has a smuggling problem with cigarettes (3) ... because the indirect tax is so high (4)… that the financial rewards for smuggling are enormous. (5)

Impact of subsidy on consumers and producers

Grade C. What is it?

A subsidy is a hand-out by government to encourage supply of an item that is thought to be at risk of under-supply. Usually the term 'grant' means a one-off hand-out, so subsidy tends to mean an ongoing payment, perhaps monthly or per unit produced. Often, subsidies are provided because the private sector struggles to cope with a timescale that is too distant, e.g. investing in a nuclear power station that will take a minimum of 12 years to start generating some revenue.

Grade B Where's the beef?

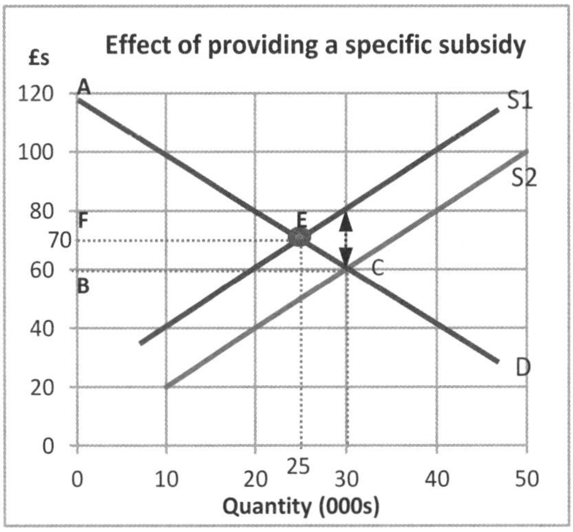

The diagram shows a supply and demand diagram for a 'smartmeter'. The government wants more households to use the meter to reduce energy consumption and help meet CO2 emissions targets. The monthly take-up rate for the meters has been 25,000 a month. The government wants to push this figure up to 30,000 by offering suppliers a subsidy of £20 per installed meter. This is an example of a 'specific' subsidy.

Grade B (ii) Why it matters

Subsidies matter because they are easy to introduce, but politically difficult to remove. Many developing economies have addressed inequality by subsidising staple products such as rice, but struggled to remove them when excessive demand caused big import levels and damaged the country's trade balance.

Grade A The counter-argument

The key counter-argument is opportunity cost. In 2019 an EU report said that the UK gives higher subsidies to fossil fuels than any other EU country (£10.5 billion). That's crazy enough environmentally, but even worse in terms of opportunity cost. It's more than enough to reverse all the 'austerity' cuts to disability benefits.

Grade A* The critical perspective

Even though governments dress them up with a 'positive', evidence-based rationale, subsidies tend to be rooted in normative decision-making – often influenced by media pressure. That makes economists very wary.

Do answer a couple of questions about this subsidy graph.
1. Calculate the monthly cost to the government (taxpayer) of this subsidy plan.
2. State the area that indicates the rise in consumer surplus as a result of the subsidy.

Don't hesitate to question the motives behind a subsidy. In some cases there may be questionable financial motives, but more often the questions will be about the political motive. Britain subsidises nuclear energy despite the problems of radioactive nuclear waste. Very odd.

Answers:
1. They will be paying a £20 subsidy on 30,000 meters a month. That's £600,000 a month.
2. The old consumer surplus was AEF; the new is ACB. The difference is FECB.

Subsidy: transmission mechanism (to get to the top response level)

Chain 1. Electric cars are expensive to buy and awkward to run until there are more charging points (1) … so there's a clear logic in subsidising their purchase (2) … as has been done massively in Norway and China (3). Promoting electric car purchasing (4) ... also promotes local production (5).

Chain 2. Subsidies increase both consumer and producer surplus (1) ,,, so they're never short of supporters (2). The cost of the subsidies can then get spread across millions of taxpayers (3) … so nobody really notices the cost (4). This is why governments should think about opportunity cost. (5)

Incidence of subsidy on producers & consumers

Grade C. What is it?

The graph below shows the effect of a government providing an ad valorem subsidy on a particular good, or service such as residential care for the elderly. In an exam you need to disentangle the effects of this on producers, consumers and government. The letters shown on the diagram are the best way to answer the questions.

Do remember that producers benefit from subsidies (often by a similar amount to the consumers) and will therefore lobby for them. Farmers have always been effective at this, as have the steel and motor industries.

Grade B Where's the beef? 1. Ad valorem subsidy

Examiners like to ask questions on the effect of the subsidy on producer and consumer surplus, and on who gains what from the subsidy. Beneath the graph come important questions and their answers, but before that let's establish a few things:

1. That in this case the consumer price falls from £100 to £68. This extends the consumer surplus from LFC to LGE

2. At the new equilibrium sales quantity of B, the government is providing a subsidy of M-E (£138-£66 = £72) and therefore spending NMEG.

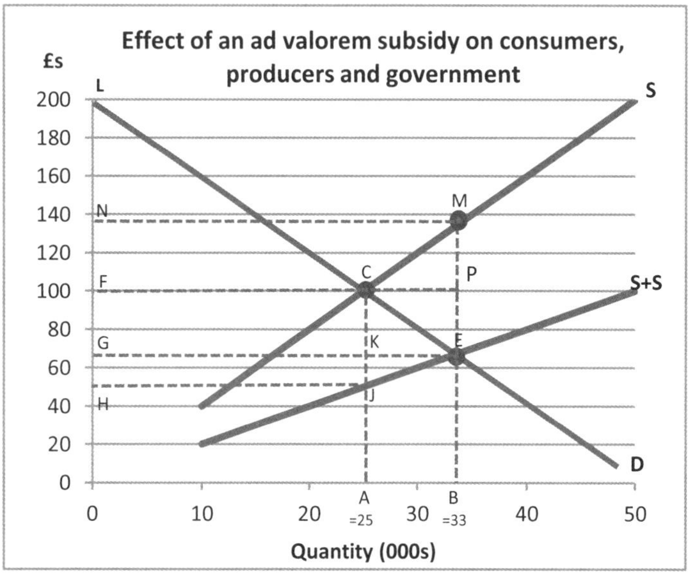

When an ad valorem subsidy pushes the supply curve to S+S:

1. Consumers benefit by FG per unit
2. Producers benefit by GH in subsidy per unit
3. Not all the subsidy is passed on to consumers. Producers keep part of it.

4. The change in consumer expenditure is FCA0 – GEB0

Don't dodge these questions about the graph (answers below):
1. Calculate the total benefit to consumers from the subsidy.
2. Calculate the total cost of the subsidy to the government.
3. Calculate the increase in production volume as a result of the subsidy.

Answers:

Q1 The consumer buys 33,000 units at £100 - £68 = £32 less than before. So gains 33,000 x £32 = £1,056,000

Q2 The subsidy costs £72 x 33,000 = £2,376,000

Q3. Production increases from 25,000 to 33,000, i.e. 8,000 units

Grade A The counter-argument

Economists are instinctively suspicious of subsidies, but sometimes they make sense. The world market in large passenger planes is dominated by a near-100% duopoly (Airbus & Boeing). Japanese and Chinese companies are trying to develop competitors, but will inevitably need subsidies to overcome huge barriers to entry. Started up in 2008 China's 'Comac' hopes to deliver its first C919 plane in 2021!

Incidence of subsidies: transmission mechanism (to get the top response level)

Chain 1. A government could decide to put a 20% ad valorem subsidy on fresh fruit (1). This would cut the price of fruit (2) … boosting demand to an extent determined by the price elasticity of each fruit (3) … but also giving extra profit to importers (4)… straight from taxpayers' pockets (5).

Chain 2. When subsidies are removed, prices rise (1) … and the fall in demand may put suppliers in trouble (2) ... if they increased their production capacity too much in response to the subsidy (3). A temporary subsidy would damage firms (4)… that mistook the short-term for the long-term. (5)

Alternative views of consumer behaviour

Grade C. What is it?

Micro-economic theory is heavily based on the assumption of rationality on the part of consumers. They act in their own best interest to maximise utility. But the specification suggests three exceptions: the influence of other people's behaviour; habitual behaviour; and consumer weakness at computation. Each is covered in more detail in the boxes on the right.

Grade B (i) Where's the beef?

The most significant issue here is weakness at computation. People may invest their whole life savings in something that's 'too good to be true' – and is. Or may get saddled with debts they cannot escape from, due to the destructive power of compound interest. If ever there was a case for effective regulation, it's in financial services.

Grade B (ii) Why it matters

These three issues matter in economics because they call into question the free-marketeer's assumption that the correct default position for government should be 'let it be'/'laissez-faire'. People don't need protection from over-sweetened chocolate – buy once, but never again; in this case the market mechanism works. But if one bad decision by someone with poor maths can damage the rest of their life (and their family's) the case for regulation is much stronger.

Grade A The counter-argument

Consumers may become overly brand loyal, or be prone to adopting the views of social media influencers – but that's up to them. Whereas there may be a case for consumer protection of young children, the decisions of adults should surely not be controlled by a 'nanny state'. Adults should learn the key phrase 'caveat emptor', i.e. let the buyer beware. Let people make their own mistakes – and learn from them.

Grade A* The critical perspective

This topic is at the heart of the argument between free-marketeers and those who want the free market tempered by regulation to protect the vulnerable. Research shows that most consumers believe that others are influenced by advertising or social media – but not themselves. We assume that our purchasing decisions are rational, but the evidence contradicts that. So alternative views of consumer behaviour should be taken seriously.

Consideration of others takes into account the importance of social media where lifestyle 'blogs' may have a powerful effect on consumer behaviour. More powerful, perhaps, than advertising. This may stop people from acting in their own best interests.

Habitual behaviour weakens the effect of the price mechanism, as consumers may not even see the signals, let alone act on them. Some iPhone fans only have eyes for Apple – so even if Samsung brought out a better phone, they wouldn't notice.

Computation: if consumers are weak at maths, they are vulnerable to mis-selling, especially with financial services, where information asymmetries are already a problem.

Alternative views: transmission mechanism (to top response level)

Chain 1. An individual follower of a fashion b/vlogger might buy products he or she believes to have utility (1) … even though they are over-priced and possibly poor quality (2). Most economists would say 'caveat emptor' and assume the individual would learn to be more sceptical (3) … but possibly social pressures make it hard to stay rational (4) … meaning social media may need more regulation.

Chain 2. Weak computational skills make some consumers vulnerable to buying goods on credit terms such as a 129% interest rate (1). This traps them into a cycle of debt that is near-impossible to escape from (2). Better regulation might prevent such extreme interest charges (3) ... or require easier get-out clauses for customers (4) … rather than allowing the innumerate to rot. (5)

Types of market failure

Grade C. What is it?

Market failure occurs when the free market mechanism leads to an inefficient allocation of resources. There may be partial market failure as the decisions of private firms and consumers lead to an under or over-allocation of resources. Or complete market failure, when the absence of incentives means no production at all, a so-called 'missing market'. The specification lists three types of market failure:

- Externalities
- Under-provision of public goods
- Information gaps

Each is dealt with in the boxes on the right.

Grade B (i) Where's the beef?

The beef lies in the graphical analysis of externalities, as set out in the following pages. It is also hugely important to get a clear understanding of the terminology, such as public goods and quasi-public goods. And although Edexcel makes no reference to 'merit' and 'demerit' goods, these are terms that are helpful when writing about externalities. (See 'transmission mechanisms' below.)

Grade B (ii) Why it matters

Market failure matters because it's the mechanism economists use to tackle various social issues in an objective, rational way. You may hate the idea of eating meat – but that opinion is normative and therefore looked down on in economic debate. Far better to research the effects of animal-rearing on the emission of greenhouse gasses – and make an informed estimate of the cost of the negative externalities associated with meat. Examiners use the term 'thinking like an economist'; the analysis of market failure is a classic way to show that skill.

Grade A The counter-argument

The main counter-argument is that 'market failure' is still an attempt to frame all human activity in terms of 'the market' – even those that don't easily fit into that framework. Is global warming best understood as an example of market failure? Or as an existential threat to future generations – requiring exceptional government engagement and cash? And what of a modern UK in which more than 25% of children grow up in poverty? Market failure? Or political failure?

Grade A* The critical perspective

The best leaders listen to the best-available evidence – and then make decisions in line with their philosophy. In football, it may be Jurgen Klopp's attacking instinct; in business it may be to stay at the forefront of technology. Restricting decisions to calculations based on market optimisation is often plain wrong.

Externalities are costs or benefits created by economic activity that impact on 'third parties', i.e. outsiders to the activity. For example, a boom in usage of an online fashion company warehouse might make life a misery for people living nearby.

Under-provision of public goods means the private sector has no incentive to supply certain goods for which no revenue can be gained, such as public roads or parks.

Information gaps cause market failure because an efficient free market depends on perfect information. It's not enough that a new competitor has entered a market – consumers must know this. For the consumer to be Sovereign, the consumer must have perfect knowledge.

Types of market failure: transmission mechanism (to the top response level)

Chain 1. Goods that are under-consumed by people who don't understand their benefits are known as merit goods. (1) If only people knew more, they'd buy more (think fruit and veg) (2) ... boosting the selling price and the sales volume (3). This boosts social welfare (4) while profits can still be made. (5)

Chain 2. Demerit goods are those that we would be better off if we consumed less, such as chocolate (1) We buy too much and consume too much (2) … which helps explain why the sugar tax arrived (3). Internalising the external costs (4) … provides incentives to tackle the market failure. (5)

External costs

Grade C. What is it?

Private costs are those borne directly by the business, such as wages, raw materials and rent. External costs are those caused by the business, but borne by third parties. For example pollution from a factory chimney may hit the value of local residents' houses. The firm creates the cost but doesn't pay for it. That's an external cost. If all the private and external costs are added together, that sum total is known as social cost. Formula: private costs + external costs = social costs.

> **Do** be clear about the term 'third party'. It means someone who is outside the transaction taking place. In the sense of external costs, the third party when you fly into Heathrow Airport are those living in Hounslow or under the flight path.

Grade B (i) Where's the beef?

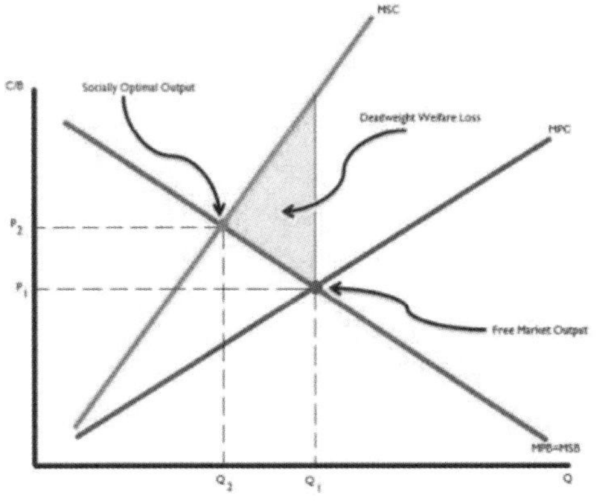

The big issue here is graphical analysis of the situation. The graph shows that unless the pollution issue is tackled the firm will over-produce with an output level of Q1. If the firm had to bear its external as well as private costs, its supply curve would shift leftwards and it would cut production to Q2.

The deadweight welfare loss shows the cost to society of ignoring the external costs.

> **Don't** muddle external costs with social costs. Remember that social costs are external costs plus private costs.

Grade B (ii) Why it matters

It matters because it shows the role of government. Private companies pursue private profit, not social profit. Their owners are shareholders, not society. So unless government intervenes, the factory will go on polluting. The government's job is to identify the best way to force the firm to bear the external costs, for example by a meter that measures the pollution and taxes the firm in proportion.

> **Exam tip:** it's best to change your labelling to MPC (marginal private costs) for Supply and MPB (marginal private benefit) for Demand. And if negative externalities are taxed, the new supply curve is MSC (marginal social cost).

Grade A The counter-argument

The firm may protest loudly, saying a pollution tax will force its costs up and make it uncompetitive with untaxed producers in other countries. This might be true of developing countries, but most developed ones have similar policies to ours.

Grade A* The critical perspective

The problem comes in identifying the exact socially optimum equilibrium. In 2018 the UK introduced a 20% tax on added-sugar drinks. That reduced the welfare loss caused by obesity – but was 20% the *right* level? Why not 25% or 30%?

External costs: transmission mechanism (to get the top response level)

Chain 1. If external costs are ignored, the producer has no incentive to limit the negative factor (1) … because the costs are borne by third parties (2). Company bosses think first about their shareholders' interests (3) … so cutting the negative factor is wrong (4) .. if it gets in the way of profit. (5)

Chain 2. If government finds a market-based solution to negative externalities (1) … by taxing the negative factor proportionately (2) … the external factor is internalised, i.e. the tax becomes a private cost to the business (3). Now that it's a private cost the firm has an incentive to minimise the externality (4) … in the same way that a business tries to minimise other costs such as wages & rent. (5)

Use of diagrams for external costs and benefits

Grade C. What is it?

Market failure lends itself exceptionally well to diagrammatic analysis. There are two basic diagrams: positive consumption externalities and negative production externalities (dealt with on the previous page), plus two other very helpful ones: the impact of regulation and the impact of pollution permits.

Grade B (i) Positive consumption externalities

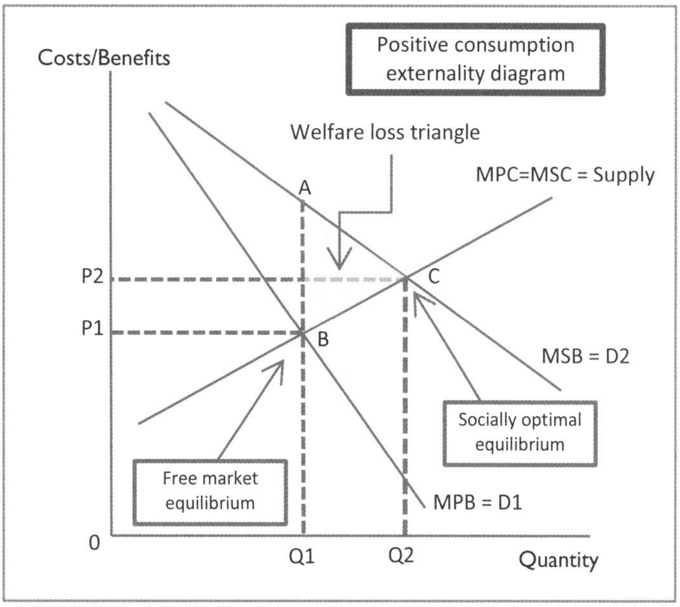

The labelling is important: demand curves now need to be labelled either MPB standing for marginal private benefit. This is the utility (the benefit) the customers perceive in the product. Or MSB meaning marginal social benefit, i.e. all the benefits to customers and third parties from the consumption, e.g. flu vaccine.

Grade B (ii) Why it matters

The above diagram matters because it shows the net welfare loss when positive externalities are ignored (such as going by bike instead of by car). Equilibrium point P1Q1 shows the free market level of demand. Once government action has pushed the demand curve to the right (by subsidy or by advertising) the new equilibrium P2Q2 involves a much higher sales level. If the government has got its sums right, this new equilibrium will be at the socially optimum point.

Grade A Understanding the welfare loss triangle

In the diagram, P2Q2 is the socially optimal level of consumption. At the market equilibrium of P1Q1, marginal social benefit is greater than marginal social cost. This yields a hypothetical social profit as measured by A-B. By moving along the sides of the triangle to point C, extra social profit is being accumulated. That profit is maximised at point C. Therefore, by leaving the market equilibrium at P1Q1, society is losing out on the whole of the triangle ABC.

Grade A* The critical perspective

It is relatively easy to identify externalities, but difficult to quantify them. London's air may be smelly and full of carbon monoxide, but people still come and house prices seem unaffected. But if the externalities cannot be quantified, how do you establish exactly where the social optimum should be – and the policy measures required to get there. There are clear problems of implementation.

Do be clear about the welfare loss triangle. It shows the economic value to society of operating at the socially optimal equilibrium rather than the free market equilibrium. On the diagram on the left, though, a more important measure may be the increase in consumption, from Q1 to Q2.

Don't forget to label the non-active curve with care. In this case it's the supply curve, which is assumed to have zero externalities (a ceteris paribus assumption to focus analysis on demand.

Exam tip: make sure to label the equilibrium points, to show that you understand the key issue: the difference between the free market and socially optimal equilibria.

Use of diagrams for external costs and benefits (ii)

Grade B (iii) The impact of regulation

The diagram below shows a standard, market-based approach to negative production externalities with an ad valorem tax pushing the supply curve leftwards to MSC. But it also shows an alternative approach a government could use: regulation that bans any supply beyond Q2. In effect this is what China is doing with car exhaust emissions – bringing in tight new maximum levels for CO2 and NOX (nitrogen oxide) from 2023.

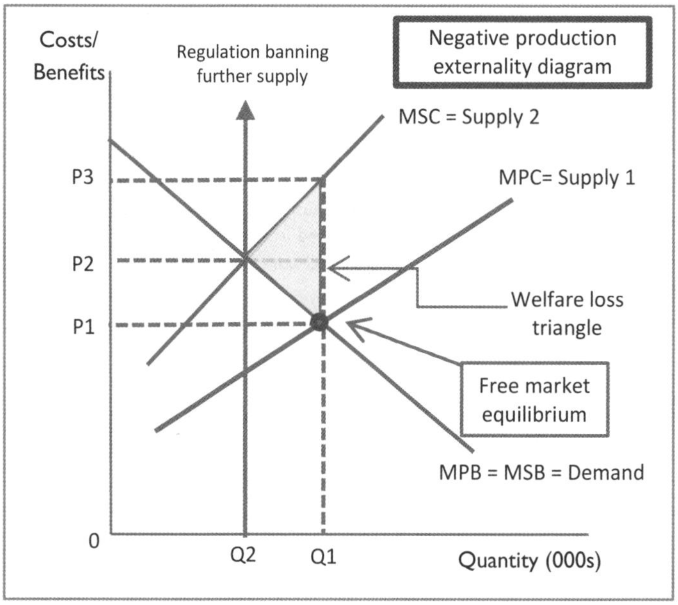

Market-based systems such as taxation allow consumers to make utility-based decisions ("I know this car's expensive but I love it so much!") whereas regulation stops everyone from breaking certain limits. Economists prefer market-based approaches, but many environmentalists prefer regulation.

Do make sure you can interpret the graph on the left. It shows two ways to achieve the same objective: to shift consumption down from Q1 to Q2. One way is to tax (pushing the equilibrium to P2Q2) and the other is to pass a law, i.e. regulation. This prevents a market drift above Q2, whereas the market-based approach allows sales to rise above Q2, if consumers are keen enough.

Grade B (iv) Extending property rights

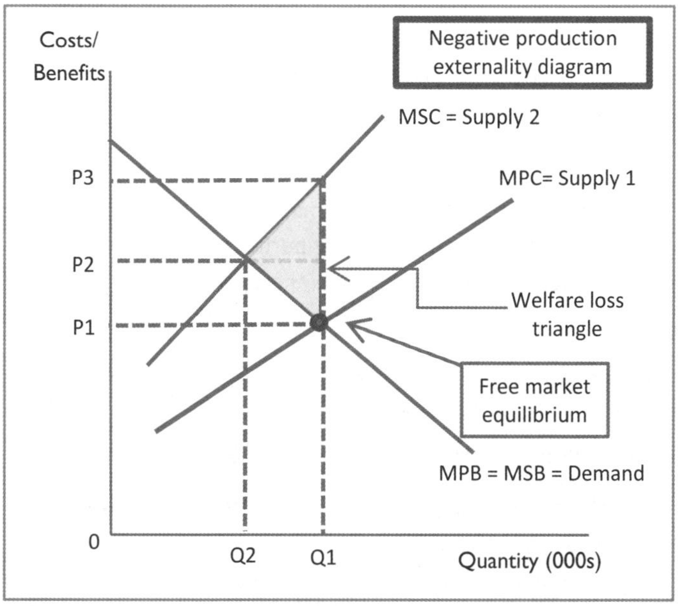

If there are no property rights assigned to a river or a piece of land, there are two negative out-comes: first, there may be over-usage such as over-fishing as no-one has an incen-tive to act respon-sibly (known as 'the tragedy of the commons'); 2nd is the incentive to dump waste on 'no-one's' open land.

To solve the problems caused by lack of property rights, either the government regulates, or the land needs to be taken into private ownership, so that the owner acts responsibly to look after the long-term interests of the land & environment.

Don't miss the logic of graph (iv). If a private owner took control of open land or river, s/he would spend money on the security methods needed to protect the property. This additional cost would push the supply curve leftwards, ideally to MSC (Supply 2).

Exam tip: make sure to evaluate all these pieces of graphical analysis by questioning a) whether extern-alities can be quantified accurately and b) whether optimum outcomes can ever be known.

Economic agents, externalities and government

Grade C. What is it?

Economic agents include producers, consumers and third parties such as local residents. Externalities have a particular effect on third parties; the attempt to correct the externalities affects consumers and producers. Government intervention has been successful in the markets for cigarettes and added-sugar soft drinks, but proved mistaken in relation to diesel fuel for cars.

Grade B (i) Where's the beef?

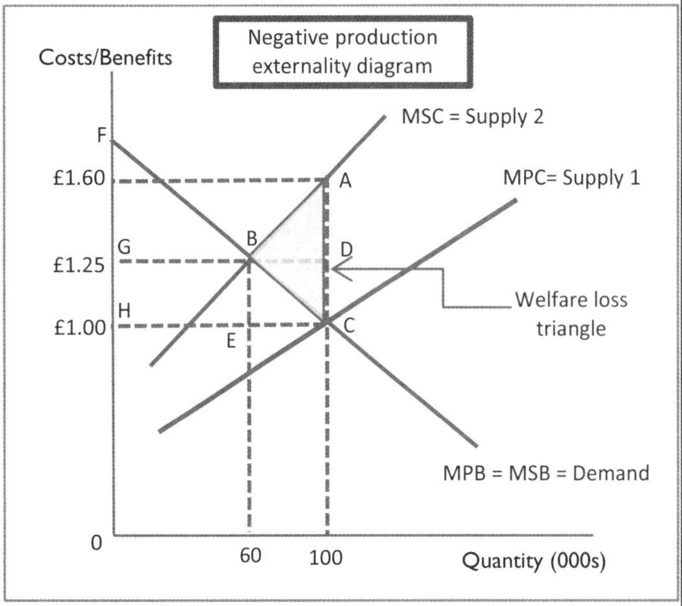

In this diagram there are three economic agents:

the consumer, whose behaviour is reflected in the demand curve;

the producer, whose private (marginal) costs are shown in curve Supply 1;

and the government, whose imposition of indirect tax has pushed the supply curve to Supply 2.

Grade B (ii) Why it matters

The impact on economic agents matters because if governments decide to get involved in market transactions, they must make sure not to make things worse. The innocent bystander (the third party) tends to get the media/public's sympathy.

Grade A The counter-argument

Some might argue for longer-term, strategic prioritisation. Third parties may dislike land-based wind-power turbines and argue against further planning permission. But those thinking of global warming may demand *more* renewable energy.

Grade A* The critical perspective

With market failure it's often the government that's stuck in the middle, trying to get the right balance between competing interests. Often businesses have the loudest (and best-funded) voice, but sometimes popular opinion is overwhelming.

Questions relating to the graph

1. Which letter gives the socially optimum equilibrium point?
2. Assume the shift to the MSC curve was caused by indirect taxation. State the area that shows the fall in consumer surplus.
3. Calculate the amount consumers will pay as a result of this indirect tax.

Don't under-estimate economists' concern for third parties. The maximisation of consumers' utility counts for little if it is at the expense of third parties such as local residents. And the local residents really suffering may be young children, as with air pollution and asthma.

Answers: 1. B
2. GBCH
3. Consumers will pay 25p a unit x 60,000 units = £15,000

Economic agents: transmission mechanism (to get to the top response level)

Chain 1. If medical research showed that whisky caused cancer (1) … producers would fund strong counter-arguments (2) … and whisky-loving consumers would shout hands-off! (3). But socially-based arguments may prevail (4) … leading to higher indirect taxes and upset producers and consumers. (5)

Chain 2. If government raises the indirect tax on a good (1) … a new equilibrium is established at a lower-volume social optimum (2) … eliminating the welfare loss triangle (3) but with consumers paying higher prices (4) … while producers suffer a fall in their income. (5).

Public goods – and free riders

Grade C. What is it?

Public goods are unusual because they cannot be bought and sold within the normal market mechanism. Examples include public parks, street drainage and street lighting. There are no profit incentives to supply these items, therefore they are only provided by the public sector (local councils or national government). Public goods have two important characteristics:

- **Non-rivalrous**, meaning one person's consumption doesn't prevent another's (whereas with a private good such a Mars Bar, my consumption prevents yours)
- **Non-excludable**: there is no way to stop people from benefitting from the good/service. In a rainstorm, we all benefit from street drainage. So if a private company tried to charge local householders for new, better drains, they would come up against the free-rider problem: non-payers would still be able to benefit (so no-one would pay).

Do practise using the terminology of public goods: 'free-rider', 'non-rivalrous', and 'non-excludable'. These are testing terms; getting their usage right is a significant advantage in an economics exam.

Grade B (i) Where's the beef?

The beef lies with the difficulty of categorising goods. Some are clearly private, such as grocery items; some are clearly public such as street lighting. But in the middle come puzzling ones, such as Google. My usage doesn't prevent yours, and whereas private goods are 'excludable', Google really isn't (within the west, anyway). So is Google's search service a private or public good? And if it's public, how come Google's making fabulous profits out of it?

Don't confuse public goods with goods provided by the public sector. An NHS hospital bed is provided by the public sector, but is technically a private good, not a public one. This is proven by the existence of private hospitals providing private sector healthcare. The private sector has no incentive to provide public goods.

Grade B (ii) Why it matters

The existence of public goods can be taken as a proof of the need for a public sector, even within a free market economy. Almost no-one would deny the need for public goods such as street lighting, public roads and public parks. Therefore there's a need for a public sector that raises revenue by general taxation, then uses that tax income to spend on public goods.

Grade A The counter-argument

Free market economists want to disprove the notion of public goods. The Institute of Economic Affairs publicises the work of economist Ronald Coase who investigated the assertion that lighthouses are a public good. He showed that many were privately financed in the UK in the 17th and 18th centuries – therefore questioning whether state intervention was necessary.

Exam tip: remember that public goods tend to be social necessities, such as sewage systems or public parks. The private sector might provide these services to some people – but not to all.

Grade A* The critical perspective

Public goods is a technical term at the heart of the fundamental economic debate between free market and interventionist views. This is why free marketeers attack the idea of public goods – as a way to attack state involvement in economics.

Public goods: transmission mechanism (to get to the top response level)

Chain 1. If a private sector business built a beautiful park it would need to charge an entrance fee (1) … to provide revenue to cover its costs (2) … and a big enough profit to satisfy the shareholders (3). This would exclude those with low income levels (4) … and turn a public good into a private one. (5)

Chain 2. As I write, Manchester City's players parade in triumph in Manchester (1) … with fans having free access in streets and squares (2) … making this a public good/service (3) with no direct ability for anyone to make a profit (4) … a rare example of a privately-provided public good (5).

Information gaps and asymmetries

Grade C. What is it?

Almost all of micro-economic theory is underpinned by a rarely-mentioned assumption: perfect information. In other words every consumer knows everything about every supplier (and vice versa). This is critical because without perfect knowledge, markets become much 'stickier', with consumers unable to turn away from a disappointing product because they don't know enough about rivals to trust them. Information gaps therefore undermine real competition

Grade B (i) Where's the beef?

The beef lies with the relationship between information gaps and resource allocation. This is clearest to see in the case of so-called 'merit' goods – those with positive consumption externalities. In many cases, the reason why these goods are under-supplied is because demand is lower than it 'should' be. Yes, we know fruit and fibre are good for us, but do we know enough to affect our behaviour? If we were clear about the health benefits we would demand more of these items – and perhaps fewer packs of crisps or Haribo. So resource allocation would be closer to the social optimum if only we had fewer information gaps.

Grade B (ii) Why it matters

What matters is the scope for incumbent suppliers to benefit from consumer inaction, as they stay with the same bank or broadband/gas/electricity supplier because they lack the confidence to switch. So these (often large) incumbents enjoy more price inelastic demand and therefore more pricing power than they deserve. Great for them; bad for the consumer and bad for new market entrants.

Grade A The counter-argument

The term 'information gaps' is passive – and sounds like the consumer's own fault. But financial scams are often backed by pages of (literally) small print, perhaps written in deliberately obscure language. So the information gap may be contrived by suppliers. Similarly there must have been many a second-hand car bought from a seller who didn't say all they knew about its faults. Economists make much of the saying 'caveat emptor', or let the buyer beware. Plugging information gaps reduces the need to beware, but suppliers may be making it hard to find out the facts.

Grade A* The critical perspective

Some transactions have information symmetry between buyer and seller – notably in regular deals between supermarkets and their suppliers. Both sides would want to build a long-term relationship based on honesty and openness. The problems arise with major one-off purchases, such as buying a house or arranging a pension. Here, there may be major information asymmetries, with the supplier happy to have 'the upper hand' in the transaction. Buyers certainly have to beware.

Do get comfortable with the term 'asymmetric' information. It means one side knows more than the other. Potentially, that makes a negotiation unfair, especially if one party doesn't even realise their weakness.

Don't over-state the importance of deliberately contrived information gaps. Plenty are unplanned. Consumers can be lazy about getting the facts they need, relying on brand names, perhaps, instead of doing some proper research.

Exam tip: when answering exam questions about information gaps it would be sensible to emphasise the importance to the market mechanism of the often-unstated assumption of perfect information.

Information gaps: transmission mechanism (to get to the top response level)

Chain 1. A well-informed consumer knows the strengths of different suppliers (1) … so when let down by one, s/he can switch to the best of the rest (2). This sends a message to all suppliers to try harder to be more efficient (3) ... and keep prices competitive (4). The customer is King/Queen (5).

Chain 2. A clothes retailer might keep quiet about very-low-cost production in a country such as Myanmar (1) … in order to keep costs low enough to charge low prices (2) … to keep competitive with Primark (3). Even a wave of bad publicity (4) … might fall away as consumers focus on value (5).

Purpose of government intervention

Grade C. What is it?

In 1947 the UK suffered 1,725 deaths at work from accidents in just four sectors: mines, quarries, factories and railways. No data was collected from other sectors, including today's two most dangerous: construction and farming. In 2017/18 there were just 144 in the whole of the UK. In the USA there were more than 5,000 and in China around 50,000. The UK's exceptionally safe working world is, in part, due to legislation, notably the 1974 Health and Safety at Work Act. The purpose of government intervention is to fill in where the free market creates the wrong incentives.

Grade B (i) Where's the beef?

The beef comes from the ability to see how broadly one can apply the concept of market failure. The 19th century free market failed children in coal mines and sweeping chimneys because the financial imperative to work forced employees to ignore risks and dangers. In 1850 the life expectancy of a male baby was 39.9 years; today it's 79 years. The free market works brilliantly in many ways – but those blind to its shortcomings manage to keep the eyes and ears very tightly shut.

Grade B (ii) Why it matters

Government intervention (and the lack of it) matters when you see people asleep in shop doorways or hear of kids supported by foodbanks. Our governments, voted in by us, make decisions that make these things more or less likely. Fortunately for us, governments from long ago made remarkable decisions about intervention in the markets for health and education – as well as legislating on health and safety plus the national minimum wage. With every change there were warnings of disaster due to government 'interference'; the country survived.

Grade A The counter-argument

The main counter-argument is Hayek's view that government intervention is the start of a slippery slope on the 'Road to Serfdom'. This book (published 1944) is hugely influential among extreme free marketeers in America. Hayek believed that a move away from free market economics would go hand in glove with the removal of freedoms of expression and thought. Written at the time of Stalin's greatest power and influence, this was an understandable viewpoint.

Grade A* The critical perspective

In exams, a good starting point is to view every piece of information and data with scepticism. If the extract is strongly pro-free market, be questioning and critical. If it's strongly in favour of re-nationalisation or new, more prescriptive company laws, also be questioning and critical. Nature hates a vacuum. So do examiners.

Pro: the purpose of intervention is to tackle the effects of free market activity that firms lack the incentives to solve. The most probable is the failure of market incentives to protect the weak and the poor. It is only the paying customer who is King.

Con: the strongest argument against government intervention is that no-one can make a better purchasing decision than the consumer her/himself. The 'nanny' state deciding on someone's behalf can – and perhaps should – feel oh-so-wrong.

Exam tips: don't be afraid of showing passionate support for your argument as long as you root it in theory and evidence. Examiners get bored by bland answers – just as you'd probably feel when writing one.

Government intervention: transmission mechanism (to the top response level)

Chain 1. Goods that are under-consumed by people who don't understand their benefits are known as merit goods. (1) If only people knew more, they'd buy more (think fruit and veg) (2) ... boosting the selling price and the sales volume (3). This boosts social welfare (4) while profits can still be made. (5)

Chain 2. Demerit goods are those that we would be better off if we consumed less, such as chocolate (1) We buy too much and consume too much (2) … which helps explain why the sugar tax arrived (3). Internalising the external costs (4) … provides incentives to tackle the market failure. (5)

Diagrams for government intervention

Grade C. What is it?

There are 4 diagrams needed, but one has already been covered fully in relation to externalities, and that's the diagram showing indirect taxation (negative production externalities). So we won't repeat it. That leaves three: maximum prices, minimum prices and subsidies.

Maximum prices: questions on the diagram (answers below)
1. Identify two likely short-term consequences of this imbalance between supply and demand.
2. What benefits are there from the imposition of a maximum price for chickens?
3. If this maximum price continues, what is the likely long-term result?

Grade B (i) Maximum prices

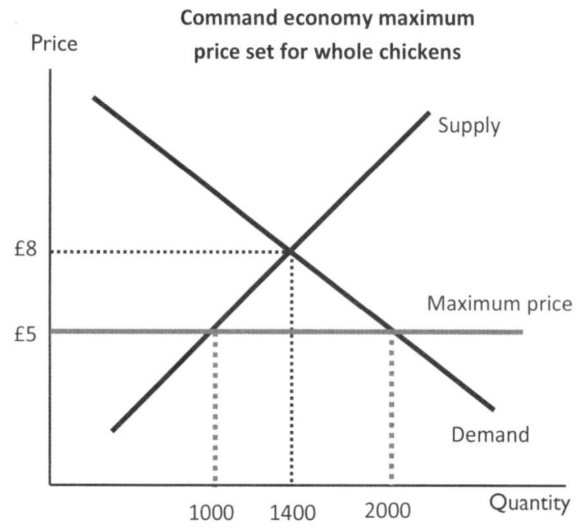

The diagram on the left looks back to Britain in wartime or a command economy today. The government believes the market price of £8 per chicken is too expensive. At that price 1,400 are bought per day. So it sets a maximum price of £5. Now shoppers want 2,000 chickens a day, but farmers only want to supply 1,000.

Don't forget the price interventions that don't matter: minimum prices set <u>below</u> the free market equilibrium and maximum prices set above the equilibrium.

Grade B (ii) Minimum prices

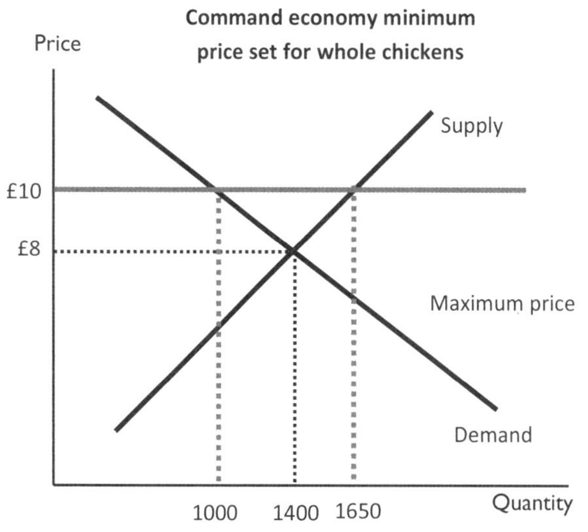

The diagram on the left shows a government persuaded by farmers that they have no economic future without government help. They may also have convinced the media and politicians that high animal welfare standards require high minimum prices. So a minimum price of £10 is set – above the free market equilibrium of £8.

In this situation customers only want (or can afford) to buy 1,000 chickens, but farmers want to sell 1,650. This glut of chickens would pull the price down and demand up until the equilibrium of 1400 was reached – unless government acts. What it would have to do is buy up the unsold chickens, i.e. pay farmers £10 each for the 650 unsellable birds. That's OK in the short-term (especially if the chickens can be frozen) but over the weeks, months and years there would be constant additions to the chicken stockpile – leading perhaps to a chicken mountain. This could end up being very expensive.

Answers:
1. Empty shelves, then queuing
2. Equitable frustration; everyone will moan, but lower income families will have as much chance of chicken as the wealthy.
3. A 'black market', ie unofficial trading in high-priced chicken.

Diagrams for government intervention (ii)

Grade B (iii) Subsidy (i)

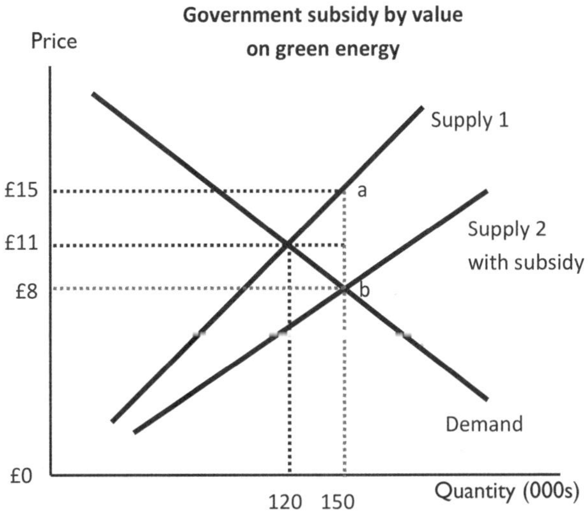

The diagram on the left looks at the effect of subsidy on a market. In this case a government subsidy of a-b brings production costs down, shifting the supply curve to the right. This encourages 30,000 extra people to buy the green energy – though this 'extra' is simply a result of moving along the downward-sloping demand curve.

Subsidy: Qs on the diagram on the left

1. Calculate the cost to the government of this subsidy.
2. Quantify the gain to customers from this subsidy.
3. Explain whether this subsidy leaves producers better off or worse off.

Grade B (iv) Subsidy (ii)

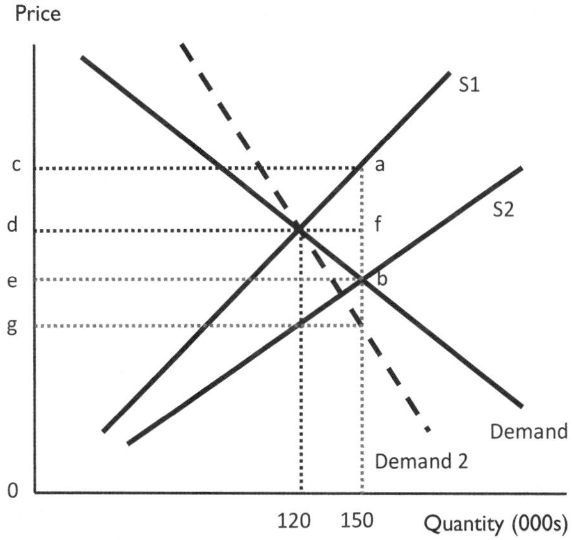

The diagram on the left is an expanded version of the one above, but with an extra demand line (D2) added. Ignoring D2, the government's subsidy of ab costs it ab x 150,000. The consumer receives a price cut of d-e, and buys 150,000 units. So the consumers' benefit is debf. The remainder of the subsidy ends up in the producer's pocket.

Further Qs (from graph ii)

4. The Demand 2 curve shows a product with relatively price inelastic demand. Does subsidy help consumers more or less when demand is price inelastic?
5. If subsidies are removed, what will be the equilibrium sales volume?

Answers:

1. £7 x 150,000 = £1,050,000
2. £3 x 150,000 = £450,000
3. Producers are hugely better off – by £4 x 150,000 = £600,000
4. Consumers are much better off. They gain (e – g) x 150,000
5. 120,000 units

Grade A* The critical perspective

All these diagrams depend on a degree of precision that is fanciful. Governments have often been surprised by poor demand for subsidised services, from loft insulation to green energy. If people don't notice it, they can't buy it, however cheap.

Government intervention: transmission mechanism (to top response level)

Chain 1. Faced with an obesity crisis a government might set a maximum price below the market equilibrium (1) … so that more people can afford the good (2). But higher demand would be met by falling supply (3) ... creating shortages, empty shelves (4) … and serious consumer dissatisfaction (5).

Chain 2. A minimum price set above the equilibrium (1) … sets a floor, just like the national minimum wage (2). This makes things fairer for poorer producers (3) ... especially if they can sell their product at guaranteed prices to the government (4)… who will need to build a buffer stock (5).

Other methods of government intervention

Grade C. What is it?

Edexcel lists 4 further methods of government intervention: trade pollution permits, state provision of public goods, provision of information and regulation. The most interesting (with scope for 10-mark-ish questions) is trade pollution permits. They at least appear to offer an ideal combination of setting a fixed ceiling on the total amount of allowable pollution, while still offering market-based incentives to producers. Polluters such as steel producers are each allocated a number of permits that, together, add up to the maximum allowable pollution level. The companies can then trade the permits, so that a firm that has succeeded in reducing its actual pollution can sell their permits to a heavy polluter. See the boxes for more detail.

Grade B (i) Where's the beef?

The beef is in being able to identify the market-based intervention methods compared with the non-market methods. Economists will be inclined to prefer market-based methods that provide incentives to better behaviour, rather than compulsion. State provision of public goods is clearly not market-based.

Grade B (ii) Why it matters

Governments need a wide range of options to achieve their policy objectives. With goods that are undervalued by the public, the provision of information can be the most effective way to move consumer habits and therefore the demand curve. People under-consume fresh vegetables, vaccinations such as MMR and flu jabs. Financial incentives may be hugely expensive and relatively disappointing – but government advertising and promotion might be successful.

Grade A The counter-argument

To absolute free-marketeers, government action and government failure are inseparable. In Britain, many self-styled 'think-tanks' find media outlets to express their condemnation of all four types of intervention. For example, they see any form of regulation on business as a burden that jeopardises international competitiveness. And government advertising is simply propaganda.

Grade A* The critical perspective

Where free market critics have a point is in the idea that 'do-gooders' often have their own agenda. There's money in poverty and money in green policies, both for those making a career in the United Nations or in charities, and for firms that fill their shop windows with messages of support for green or social initiatives. Good evaluation recognises the difficulty in knowing people's *real* motives.

Pro pollution permits: polluters have market incentives to minimise pollution and therefore can be trusted to do so; the state has a guarantee on the maximum pollution coming from the industry. This could help in meeting global warming targets.

Con pollution permits: in practice governments have used this method timidly, with maximum pollution levels set so high that companies are not that constrained, and the permits trade at relatively low figures. So it risks being a bureaucratic way to achieve relatively little.

Exam tips: remember that state provision of public goods doesn't mean the state has to be the direct provider. It might pay private sector operators to build a new park or playground

Government intervention: transmission mechanism (to the top response level)

Chain 1. The state has huge power to inform, whether by advertising or in schools (1) ... but can be called 'a nanny state' by free-marketeers (2). But information can be crucial, such as having an MMR vaccine – a clear merit good (3) ... which promotes health for all (4) ... creating a net welfare gain.

Chain 2. In the UK the quality and size of kids' playgrounds vary hugely. (1) These are quasi-public goods paid for by local councils, not central government (2) ...and therefore the quality varies in line with local resources (3). Often the playgrounds are worst in poor areas (4) ... as insufficient funding is raised and available (5).

Understanding government failure

Grade C. What is it?

A valuable Year 13 concept is 'x-inefficiency'. This is inefficiency that creeps up on organisations that operate with no pressure coming from predatory rivals. This might be part-explanation for government failure: it's simply too inefficient at what it does. Other possible causes include: inadequate information, with civil servants struggling to keep up those who truly understand the market; conflicting objectives or market distortions.

Grade B (i) Where's the beef?

The beef in this case lies with empirical evidence, i.e. what happens in the real world. A clear failure came from the encouragement of successive governments between 1995 and 2015 towards the adoption of diesel fuel cars. It was only when Volkswagen was found to have been cheating on the emissions results for its diesel cars did it become clear that the government advice must change. Diesel fuel had been regarded as a merit good compared with petrol; suddenly both diesel and petrol were treated as 'demerit' goods with merit only coming from investment in electric cars. UK and other governments had been tricked by an information asymmetry between government and the big business interests of the carmakers.

Grade B (ii) Why it matters

Government failure matters in theory, but even more in practice. At a time of great concern about global warming it's vital that government should have accurate data to help make the right environmental decisions. The idea that government action might make things worse is a huge concern. Governments need to employ enough scientific expertise to avoid being caught out in this way.

Grade A The counter-argument

The term 'government failure' has been hijacked. In economics it means failure caused by government action. But what about failure due to government inaction? What about the failure by recent governments to encourage home insulation and thereby save energy and get the country closer to its carbon warming targets? This could have been achieved by regulation, subsidy or stronger information signals. Or what about the failure of the Indian government to act against discrimination against women? The term government failure could apply to both

Grade A* The critical perspective

Arguments are often won or loss depending on how they are framed. The 2016 Brexit referendum was not framed as staying in versus a specific, defined means of exit (such as 'Hard Brexit'). It was remain versus leave. In a comparable way, an economic argument about government is framed by the definition economists have chosen to apply to 'government failure'. In an exam it's valid to question this.

Do question why some economists are so hostile to state intervention. It works quite well to have everyone drive on the left side of the road and to know that red means stop at traffic lights. Governments can be inefficient and infuriating, but so can large firms.

Don't under-estimate the difficulties governments can have when tackling market failure. No civil servants will understand the market as well as the managers and entrepreneurs who work in it daily. And hiring consultants to give advice often works out badly. So it's tough.

Exam tip: focus your argument on the (deadweight) welfare loss triangle. If government efforts add greater cost than the value of the welfare loss triangle, society is inevitably worse off.

Understanding government failure: transmission (to top response level)

Chain 1. Under-consumption of vegan food might lead to government action (1) .. by a big advertising campaign focused on the impact of meat production on global warming (2). But the message of the adverts might get lost (3) ... having little effect on customer habits (4). That would be govt. failure (5).

Chain 2. Merger between Asda and Sainsbury was stopped by the Competition & Markets Authority (CMA) (1) ... to prevent market failure due to weakened competition (2) ... that might lead to high food prices (3). This might prove wrong (4) ... if Tesco's position strengthens in years to come (5).

Causes of government failure

Grade C. What is it?

Year 13 economics includes a useful concept: 'x-inefficiency'. It's caused by the complacency of managers who work in organisations that have no competitive threat to their survival. Like government departments or the middle management of multinationals such as Nestle or Toyota. So the government efforts at correcting market failures may be ineffectual and have **excessive administration costs**. Other possible causes of government failure include: inadequate information/information asymmetry; conflicting objectives and market distortions.

Grade B (i) Where's the beef?

'X-inefficiency' is a powerful concept which could add muscle to analysis of government failure. But the main focus must be on the need to quantify the cost of the government remedy – and then compare that with the value of the deadweight welfare loss caused by the market failure. In the real world that would be extremely hard to do, as many of the elements of the equation are largely qualitative, not quantitative. And within that calculation free market economist Milton Friedman urged people to allow for the fixed, long-term cost of keeping government departments in operation for just this occasion.

Grade B (ii) Why it matters

The causes of government failure matter most when considering whether the failure is an inevitable by-product of x-inefficiency and therefore a permanent problem or caused by something more temporary, such as **information gaps**. If it's the latter, then it might be possible to devise a plan for building up the expertise of the government department – perhaps putting staff on secondment to work in a relevant private sector firm to gather real expertise.

Grade A The counter-argument

Causes of government failure are – understandably – placed on the shoulders of government. But that may be unfair. The UK government mistakenly promoted diesel over petrol cars because the industry misled it. This was worse than information asymmetry – it was effectively a conspiracy against the government and the general public. So government was the victim – and it's generally unfair to blame the victim for the crime.

Grade A* The critical perspective

Correcting market failures can never be easy. This is partly because of the different interests of all the participants: suppliers, employees and society generally. It is also because of the complex combination of quantifiable, unquantifiable and semi-quantifiable data that together form an estimation of the socially optimal position for any market. Government failure will occur, because this is tricky.

Do be clear that government involvement in market activity may fail because it means well, but actually causes **distortion of price signals**. A subsidy, for example, might confuse suppliers about where the true market equilibrium lies.

Don't miss the importance of conflicting objectives when considering government failure. Firms have the advantage of a simple focus on one thing – profit. Governments rightly need to think of the interests of many groups in society. That makes decision-making a lot tougher.

Exam tip: don't hesitate to use Yr 13 material even if you're taking an AS exam. As long as you're comfortable with a concept such as x-inefficiency the examiner will be happy to give it marks.

Government failure causes: transmission mechanism (to top response level)

Chain 1. Market distortions can occur when the attempt to correct a market failure causes another (1) ... through the 'law' of **unintended consequences** (2). Cutting disability benefits to force people to get a job (3) ... can result in a food bank boom (4) … that points to misallocation of resources (5).

Chain 2. Conflicting objectives within government (1) … can lead to confused, sub-optimal decisions (2) … that are a mess of political, social and economic policy (3). This might lead to proposed solutions to market failure (4) … that are costly but ineffective: the textbook government failure (5).

Government failure in various markets

Grade C. What is it?

There is a natural tendency to focus government failure on externality questions such as pollution. The Specification wants to shine a spotlight on other examples of government failure, i.e. where the cost of state involvement exceeds the economic benefit, or where the outcomes are overwhelmed by unintended consequences. A perfect example of the latter is the 'Help to Buy' (new homes) scheme, started by then-Chancellor George Osborne in 2013 (see right). This policy was a clear example of political convenience overwhelming economic logic.

Grade B (i) Where's the beef?

The beef may lie in examining failures of implementation rather than motive. Politicians come up with new schemes – fine. But surely the new idea should be tested in controlled real-world conditions – the political equivalent of a test market for a new product. Then, if the idea flops it can be quietly – and inexpensively – buried. And if it's a success there may still be improvements that can be identified and added as a result of the controlled trial. In fact remarkably few government policies are trialled and tested. They tend to be implemented by politicians desperate to make their mark quickly, for reasons of career progression rather than getting the best value for money for taxpayers. When reading the examiners' text, think carefully and critically about the issue of testing.

Grade B (ii) Why it matters

It matters because taxpayers' patience and cooperation cannot be taken for granted. Many forms of public spending are critical to our way of life, from roads to police to pensions to education and the NHS. The majority of the UK population has generally been accepting of the trade-off between this type of spending and the hit from taxation to our disposable income. But clear-cut government failure damages this politico-economic balance.

Grade A The counter-argument

Picking on government failure can be seen as a lazily easy task. Each year the UK government spends over £800 billion – all under the control of Ministers who may have their job switched tomorrow because the Prime Minister wants a new face in place. This crazy system is called democracy (which Winston Churchill called the worst form of government, except for all the rest). No wonder there are failures.

Grade A* The critical perspective

Even a project that performs poorly on economic criteria may be worthwhile in terms of social welfare. Financial assistance given to poorer regions of the country has never been hugely successful – but it's surely better than communities feeling abandoned. Oscar Wilde said a cynic 'knows the price of everything and the value of nothing'. There's a risk that economists could be viewed in the same way.

Do remember the Help to Buy scheme as a classic in government failure. Faced with a serious shortage of housing supply, the government brought in a subsidy for buying newly-built houses. By stimulating demand instead of supply, the result was higher house prices – and a bill to taxpayers of more than £10 bn.

Don't be surprised to see HS2 in exams for decades to come. At the time of writing this high-speed rail project had cost more than £5bn before any track had been laid. With a budget of £56bn, it is expected to end up costing over £100bn – unless a brave government decides to cancel.

Exam tip: don't lose sight of government successes such as the Sure Start early-years' education system. It was a proven success, but still scrapped by a new government.

Government failure (iii): transmission mechanism (to top response level)

Chain 1. When politicians tackle a market failure such as air pollution (1) ... they are trying to balance public health against economic cost (2) … taking into account the opportunity cost of any remedy (3). This can lead to a messy compromise (4) … focused on short-term gains rather than solutions (5).

Chain 2. Governments may unfairly get blamed for the failure of firms (1) … to accept that their wealth and power should mean accepting responsibility (2) … beyond that of maximising profits (3). If firms took market failure more seriously (4) … there would be less scope for government failure (5).

Why some firms stay small

Grade C. What is it?

At the heart of the theory of the firm is that long-run average costs have a tendency to fall due to economies of scale such as bulk buying. This provides the justification for objectives based on growth (think Amazon; think Tesla) and for mergers and takeovers. Yet some firms stay small as a matter of policy (Morgan cars, for example) and others continue to succeed despite their small size. How?

Grade B (i) Where's the beef?

The beef lies in two economic theories. The first is the balance between economies and diseconomies of scale and therefore the location of the minimum efficient scale. In certain industries this point of productive efficiency may be at quite low levels of output. In creative industries such as advertising, there are few technical or managerial economies, so the minimum efficient scale is quite low. The other key theory is that of x-inefficiency. Although associated with monopoly businesses, x-inefficiency is a feature of all large businesses with strong market positions. So small, nimbler, more enthusiastic businesses have a part to play.

Grade B (ii) Why it matters

Economists care about the survival – and the success – of small firms because they are regarded as essential to provide the consumer with variety, with innovation and with price moderation due to real competition. Without the small firms, the large ones may indulge in legal cartel practices such as covert price fixing.

Grade A The counter-argument

The counter argument is that firms don't stay small because they want to, but because big firms operate in predatory ways that force them to stay small. Facebook has bought up 79 smaller businesses over the years, including clear potential rivals: Instagram and WhatsApp. Staying small may be the only way to avoid being snapped up.

Grade A* The critical perspective

The survival – or success – of small firms is an important part of the politics of economics. Karl Marx thought firms would become ever-bigger, squeezing out the small ones – and becoming ever-more exploitative. Free market economists are confident that every market has room for new, ingenious small firms that can thrive in the face of industrial giants. Although monopolisation seems a feature of some digital markets, in general the free market view has proved more accurate.

Do think about the firms you know: perhaps an independent pizza place competing with Domino's. How does the independent survive? Possibly not by offering cheaper prices, but by offering more flexible and better service.

Don't under-estimate the entrepreneurial drive that keeps new businesses challenging the existing ones. The food industry constantly sees new firms leading the way (with free-from and vegan foods, for e.g.) with the big firms struggling to keep up.

Exam tip: always remember 'the beef', i.e. the hard theory. In this case productive efficiency and x-inefficiency are two terrific theories to use in your answers.

Why some firms stay small: transmission mechanism (to top response level)

Chain 1. Some firms stay small because they want to keep the business within the family (1) ... and therefore avoid the risk that flotation on the stock market (2) ... might lead to loss of control if the family holding falls below 50% (3). A well-run family business has drive, teamwork and motivation (4) ... making it a tough competitor for bigger, corporate businesses. (5)

Chain 2. In some business sectors (especially in services) small firms dominate (1) ... because there are no significant economies of scale to be gained (2) ... and whereas big firms would suffer from x-inefficiencies (3) ... smaller firms know they have to stay efficient to survive (4) ...making them useful sources of good products, service and prices – and therefore invaluable to consumers. (5)

Ownership, control and principal-agent problem

Grade C. What is it?

Most theory in micro-economics assumes that firms profit maximise. This in turn assumes that firms are owned and run by a single person: the entrepreneur. Therefore the firm's decision making is rational in its pursuit of a single objective: profit maximisation. This may be true of private family businesses, but is much less so in the case of big public companies. These have thousands of small shareholders who – together – own the business, but may have little or no influence over the decisions made by the firm's senior management. The owners are the 'principals'; the managers are the 'agents'.

Do learn to spot when the principal-agent problem may become crucial. For example in a take-over bid, senior managers may fight for what's in their own best interests. This may explain why so many takeovers turn out badly.

Grade B (i) Where's the beef?

In the real world the key problem is that the agents have the day-to-day power to spend the company's money – and may do it in ways that maximise their own comfort and convenience. The people who have to pay for this indulgence are consumers who end up paying higher prices and the shareholders who end up with lower-than-expected profits and dividends. In economic theory the main issue is that the 'agents' may make decisions that are not in the best interests of the firm – and therefore get in the way of assumptions about rational behaviour.

Don't forget that the principal is the one with theoretical power but the agent has actual power. The same relationship occurs between the electorate and MPs. The people are the principals, but the agents (the MPs) have the real power. Brexit turned from problem into crisis due to this.

Grade B (ii) Why it matters

Economics is built on a series of models, so if large firms act in unexpected (irrational) ways, the models are undermined. This, of course, calls into question their validity.

Grade A The counter-argument

Few would argue that plc owners and senior managers have diverging interests. Senior managers may spend a lot of time on the reward packages that can pay them £multi-millions. But free market economists play down the significance of this, arguing that the principal-agent problem rarely gets in the way of major business decisions. Most of the time, managers act in the firm's best interests.

Exam tip: with every question about oligopolies or monopolies, consider whether the principal-agent problem may be an underlying issue.

Grade A* The critical perspective

The principal-agent problem can be seen as a market failure like any other. At the heart of it is asymmetric information: the managers know everything about the business, but the shareholder/owners only know what they are told. Calling it a market failure places into context: the principal-agent problem is an important fact that needs to be allowed for – but no more important than other market failures.

Ownership and control: transmission mechanism (to top response level)

Chain 1. Shareholders may be hoping for rising profits and higher dividends (1) … but the company's directors may decide to diversify by launching into Germany (2) … as Domino's Pizza UK did (very unsuccessfully) (3). The German market proved too difficult for the UK managers to succeed in (4) ... but the Directors and managers did fine, while the owner/shareholders lost out (5).

Chain 2. Some firms try to align together the interests of shareholders and senior managers (1) … by offering huge share option incentives linked to the firm's medium-term share price (2). This should overcome the principal-agent problem (3) … but instead it creates another problem (4) …as decisions start to be focused on the medium-term share price, not the firm's best long-term interests (5).

Distinction between organisations

Grade C. What is it?

Edexcel is looking for clear distinctions to be drawn within two types of organisation. First, between public and private sector organisations (this is a hugely important distinction in economics exams). Second, between profit and not-for-profit organisations. The overall point to be made here is that it's hugely risky to generalise about organisations. Every firm is different, and although many – or even most – are pursuing profit maximisation, that's not true of all. Even some private sector companies have a social purpose that overrides the pursuit of profit.

Public and private sector organisations differ due to ownership and objectives. Public sector organisations are owned by the state and have to meet goals set by the state, e.g. running bus services from 6.00 AM to 11.00PM. Private sector firms are owned by shareholders who want high dividend pay-outs generated by high profits.

Grade B (i) Where's the beef?

Exam candidates often seem confused about where the public sector ends and the private sector begins. Most of the UK economy is 100% in the private sector, including just about all limited liability businesses (Ltd and plc) plus many other cooperative or charitable organisations. At the other end of the spectrum come state-provided services such as the NHS and state education, plus some bus and train services. In the middle it gets messy, as there are many services paid-for by the state, but supplied by private sector contractors, including a lot of 'care', such as old people's homes. In effect, all public goods are provided by the state, but also a perhaps-surprising number of private goods as well, such as a hospital bed.

Grade B (ii) Why it matters

It matters because it seems like a flaw in otherwise-excellent students if they don't really understand the boundary between the private and public sectors. This would be a valuable topic to ask teachers and parents; in the latter case they may know nothing about economics, but still know where the public sector kicks in.

Profit and Not-for-profit organisations differ in their ownership, their objectives and their treatment of any surplus made when revenues are greater than costs. Above all else, profit-makers are judged by the dividends they pay their owners, whereas not-for-profit organisations look to invest any surpluses back into the business to make it grow in size and reach.

Grade A The counter-argument

Some might argue that in a mixed economy such as the UK it shouldn't matter about the boundary between private and state sectors. Managers in either should be striving to provide the best service possible – whether for the profit that comes from repeat custom or the satisfaction that comes from a job well done. In reality, though, some love private sector education while others criticise it bitterly.

Grade A* The critical perspective

Beware of making assumptions about any of the four sectors mentioned here. Some charities are a disgrace to the not-for-profit sector, with too much money focused on management and fund-raising – and too little spent on the charity's target group. And while much of the private sector is efficient, by no means all.

Distinction between organisations: transmission mechanism (to top response level)

Chain 1. Not-for-profit organisations should have objectives based on social, not financial targets (1) … such as Surfers Against Sewage (2). Their clear focus could stimulate staff to work harder (3) … making it easier to be efficient and successful (4) ... perhaps outperforming profit-focused firms (5).

Chain 2. The public sector offers franchises for private sector firms to bid for contracts such as running train or bus services (1). This is hoped to provide private sector competition (2) … alongside public provision of public goods (3) … such as trains/ buses late at night or on Sundays (4) when there are too few passengers to cover business costs – so it's an attempt to overcome market failure. (5).

How businesses grow

Grade C. What is it?

Businesses can grow in one of two ways: organically (from within) or inorganically, known as external growth. Organic growth is achieved by using the firm's marketing and human resources to increase sales of existing or new products/ services. Examples include Boohoo.com persuading more shoppers to buy clothes online and Jaguar Land Rover persuading Chinese and Indian drivers to buy a British car. Inorganic growth is achieved by takeover or merger. It is growth not by the firm's own skills but by buying up another firm and adding their sales total to your own.

Do take on board the idea that takeovers sound great but often turn out badly. Especially mistrust the boss that talks about 'synergies' (cost efficiencies that come from being together/ bigger). A famous U.S. business leader wrote a business book called 'Synergy and other lies'.

Grade B (i) Where's the beef?

The tough part is understanding how takeovers happen. They start with an announcement to the stock market, which might be a 'paper' bid or a cash bid. If the bid uses paper, it means one company is buying another by offering to swop share certificates, e.g. 'we're offering 2 of our £4 shares for every 3 of your £2 shares'. By offering shares valued at £8 to the holders of shares worth £6, the bid can proceed without any cash changing hands. The alternative method (paying cash) almost always means having to borrow that cash from the bank. As a generalisation, most takeovers mean higher debt levels for the company that makes the bid – making the firm vulnerable to recession or a rise in interest rates.

Don't forget diseconomies of scale. They can't be quantified, but imagine a U.S. business boss deciding that merging Arsenal and Spurs would boost profits. She or he will learn plenty about diseconomies of scale.

Grade B (ii) Why it matters

It matters because periods of economic growth and booming stock markets see lots of takeover and merger deals. Then, when recession hits, over-extended firms with high debt levels struggle to survive – doing so simply by making staff redundant – even though the high debt levels are no fault of those staff.

Grade A The counter-argument

Those who see climate change as an emergency will see economic growth as a negative – and therefore question why firms should want to grow. Getting bigger means using more resources, more energy and perhaps generating more pollution. So the counter-argument is to question the validity of the growth objective.

Exam tip: remember the terms organic and inorganic. Examiners love to see that you've made the effort to learn the language of economics.

Grade A* The critical perspective

Economic and business journalists are inclined to believe that takeovers make sense. No doubt because they believe in the power of economies of scale and they tell themselves that highly paid business bosses know what they're doing when they make a takeover bid. They don't. Research shows two thirds of takeovers are failures, in that they fail to show economic value in the 3 years following the bid.

How businesses grow: transmission mechanism (to the top response level)

Chain 1. A great business grows by finding more and more keen customers (1). A good example is Apple, which has made few moves to spend its huge cash reserves on takeovers (2). It grows organically, by bringing out new, brilliantly-designed phones (3) ... and stretching the business to watches and streaming (4) ... i.e. using modest diversifications to find new markets and customers (5).

Chain 2. When Sainsbury tried to grow inorganically by buying Asda (1) … it showed that its management had given up on making Sainsbury grow by making it better (2). Fortunately competition authorities turned the bid down (3) … to protect consumers from a horizontal merger that would reduce competition (4) ... and almost certainly result in higher prices in the shops (5).

Organic versus inorganic growth: pros and cons

Grade C. What is it?

There are three types of takeover/merger: vertical (either forwards, buying a customer or backwards, buying a supplier), horizontal (buying a competitor) or conglomerate (buying an unrelated business, perhaps opportunistically or because of a plan to spread risk by diversifying. All three have advantages and disadvantages, especially when compared with the alternative of growing from within, i.e. growing organically.

Grade B (i) Where's the beef?

The beef lies in understanding the problems of inorganic growth. Firms aren't simply assets in the way an A.I.-robot is an asset. When firm A buys firm B it can't know how staff will react. If firm B's best staff look for other jobs rather than accept the takeover, there may be much less residual value than firm A's bosses expected. Takeovers in the service sector are very vulnerable to this problem.

Grade B (ii) Why it matters

It matters because, for many years, free market economists persuaded governments to stop their competition regulator from intervening much in takeover bids. In the UK lots of bids were accepted without much consideration about the impact on competition. Bafflingly, in 2017, Tesco was allowed to buy the Booker grocery wholesaling business. Since then the Competition & Markets Authority (CMA) has been sharper, for instance stopping the merger between Sainsbury and Asda. These days, takeovers are more likely to be seen as an attempt by a firm to seize control of competitors and other businesses – to no-one's benefit apart from the shareholders.

Grade A The counter-argument

Free market economists persist in seeing takeovers as a force for good – as a way to get new management into older, lazier businesses that deserve to disappear. Sometimes this is absolutely true. There may be firms where the managers are padding their own pockets rather than acting on behalf of the business – and it's great that there's a mechanism for putting a stop to this – the takeover.

Grade A* The critical perspective

The fundamental problem with takeovers is that vested interests can overwhelm economic logic. City advisors can earn hundreds of millions on a single takeover – so they are understandably keen to push for this approach rather than recommending slower but safer organic growth. There's just too much cash involved.

Pros: vertical takeovers enable a firm to build stronger, better relationships with suppliers and/or customers; this can help with new innovations. **Horizontal** takeovers eliminate duplication, e.g. two sets of delivery drivers; this should be better environmentally. **Conglomerate** takeovers spread risk by diversifying.

Cons: there's less pressure to be efficient if you've bought up your suppliers and customers; this hurts customers and shareholders. The least successful takeovers are **conglomerate** ones. Managers at the bidding company don't know enough to succeed.

Exam tip: make sure to identify whether a takeover is vertical, horizontal or conglomerate – and make sure to tell the examiner.

Organic v Inorganic: transmission mechanism (to the top response level)

Chain 1. A successful horizontal merger gives greater market share and control (1) … which is likely to give more pricing power, especially if the market has an oligopoly structure (2) … giving scope for more effective covert collusion (3) ... taking pressure off all the big companies in the marketplace (4) ... and giving scope for a significant increase in supernormal profits (5).

Chain 2. A backward vertical takeover gives full control over supplies (1) … which might boost profits as the supply company's margins are absorbed into the main company (2). On the other hand those working at the supplier now feel their sales are guaranteed (3) … and that relaxation from market pressures can lead to x-inefficiencies (4) ... making costs jump and profits fall (5).

Constraints on business growth

Grade C. What is it?

Constraints are the factors that limit a firm's ability to achieve all it might want to. The constraints on the growth of a firm include the size of the market; access to extra finance; the objectives of the owners/shareholders; and government regulation. Taken collectively across UK businesses, the constraints on individual firms become the limits to macro-economic growth. This is why access to a Europe-wide market was one of the original arguments for joining the E.U. – to increase the size of the 'home market' accessible to UK firms and thereby remove that constraint on business growth.

Grade B (i) Where's the beef?

Although 4 constraints are listed by the exam board, argument among economists would tend to take three together – and pitch them against the other one. Market size, access to finance and the objectives of owners are relatively neutral issues – largely outside the direct influence of economists. The outlier is regulation, which is a way of saying that the actions of government can be a constraint on business growth. This is why many free marketeers in America are sceptical of climate change; they see it as a trick to give the state more power over firms.

Grade B (ii) Why it matters

This topic matters because it's a huge focus of government policy. Every Chancellor tries to boost the long-term growth rate of the UK economy. They try to do this by supply-side-orientated macro policies often supplemented by interventions in micro markets: housing, perhaps, or steel, or air travel. Recently, the track record of such interventions has been between unimpressive and awful.

Grade A The counter-argument

The main counter-argument should concern the proper response by government to these apparent constraints. Governments are often influenced strongly by the views of business, as put forward by lobby groups such as the Confederation of British Industry. They have trimmed legislation or cut corporation tax to address apparent constraints such as access to finance. Often, these lobby groups use economic arguments to gain advantages that benefit directors (no pay constraints) and shareholders (lower corporation tax), without changing business behaviour.

Grade A* The critical perspective

Business leaders, just like farmers, do love a moan. There are always constraints to blame – proving that poor performance isn't their fault. Governments need to be braver, rejecting calls to action (or inaction) by people with big vested interests.

Objectives of owners means some, perhaps family, businesses don't want to get big; the business is a way to allow an entrepreneur to create perhaps a great restaurant – with no wish to copy Jamie Oliver. So the owner's rational response to new circumstances is different from a firm seeking growth.

Access to finance may be a big constraint on ambitious young firms operating in high-risk, perhaps high-tech markets such as artificial intelligence (A.I.)

Exam hint: this topic is perfect for Paper 3, because there's a strong overlap between micro thoughts on firms' growth and macro thoughts of the country's GDP growth rate. The best way to improve your understanding is to read more, day-by-day, in the business pages of newspapers and websites.

Constraints on growth: transmission mechanism (to get to top response level)

Chain 1. To tackle the growth constraint of obtaining extra finance (1) ... recent Conservative Chancellors have slashed corporation tax (2) ... so that firms keep more of their profits (3) to be used to increase business investment (4). Unfortunately the tax cuts have been used for higher dividend payments to shareholders – there has been no boost to business investment (5).

Chain 2. Planning permission regulations have been cut to boost housebuilding (1) ... boosting supply to try to tackle the housing shortage (2) ... and therefore hold down house prices (3). If houses are more affordable for younger people (4)... this helps labour mobility and therefore GDP growth (5).

Demergers

Grade C. What is it?

The clearest proof of the failure of a merger or takeover is when a demerger happens a few years' later. A demerger is the reversal of an earlier decision to merge. Recently the giant Prudential insurance business demerged its UK M&G Prudential business from the rest of the company. It declared that it would increase efficiency to separate the businesses – but that's exactly what bosses say when they make a takeover move – that it'll increase efficiency. So which is it? Does merging make you more efficient or is it demerging? Surely it can't be both.

Reasons for demergers include the existence of sharp diseconomies of scale, which push up average costs and damage profit margins. Others include a new boss's choice to focus on fewer management divisions or a desire to empower bosses to run a smaller unit the way they want.

Grade B (i) Where's the beef?

The beef comes from your analysis of the situation. If a company is demerging today what it bought three years' ago, that sounds like a mistake. Either the business failed to achieve the cost reductions it was looking for, or the world must have changed dramatically. And what if it's simply down to a new boss turning up – and wanting to show off his/her power? That surely is a dreadful reason for a takeover – implying normative rather than rational decision making.

Grade B (ii) Why it matters

It matters because shareholders may be happy to see ownership of organisations chop and change, but others will not. Staff want to feel they are part of something – in effect part of a family that will be theirs, perhaps not for life, but for as long as they want. Some employees at John Lewis are proud to be part of this employee cooperative, with its generally ethical approach to business. They don't want it suddenly taken over by Tesco, then sold to WH Smith, then to a Russian firm.

Don't assume that managements always act rationally. Sometimes demergers are fashionable – so a demerger announcement makes the share price rise. That's a big temptation to a boss of a struggling business.

Grade A The counter-argument

Some economists argue for a freely functioning market in which firms can merge one year and demerge the next; typically they would see the firm's share price as the proper test of this approach. Others feel uncomfortable that it means the staff are being treated as 'assets', whose 'ownership' can be transferred from Firm A to Firm B overnight. That may be acceptable when there's full employment, but may feel wrong if a weak economy means people are trapped in their current job.

Exam tip: beware of proposing a demerger in an economic downturn. When times are tough it's more important to cut costs throughout the business. A demerger would be a distraction.

Grade A* The critical perspective

City advisors seem as confident recommending a demerger as when they pushed for a merger a few years' beforehand. It's as if any deal/change must be a good thing. With the fees and commissions involved, this is no surprise. But in economic terms, there should be an optimum size and scale for a business: either inside a merger or outside it. Logic – and the interests of staff – deserve more stability.

Demergers: transmission mechanism (to the top response level)

Chain 1. If a firm is struggling with management overload and indecision (1) … it is threatened by x-inefficiencies (2) …that will boost average costs and cut into profit margins (3). This may make a demerger highly attractive (4) … especially if shareholders are pushing for higher profits (5).

Chain 2. When Whitbread demerged Costa Coffee by selling it to Coca-Cola (1) … it left a business focused heavily on its Premier Inn hotel division (2). This is good because it focuses minds on the desperate need to make Premier Inn a success (3) … but may put the company at risk if a new U.S. hotel chain enters Premier Inn's market sector. (4) Firms can come to regret demerger decisions (5).

Different business objectives

Grade C. What is it?

A business objective is a goal, usually set by the owners of the firm (the shareholders if it's a limited company). The goal determines the decisions made by managers throughout the firm. Some years ago Tesco was pursuing the objective of growth. It was the world's Number 3 grocery business – and seemed determined to challenge for the top spot. So the Tesco boss invested £2 billion into Tesco USA – which after 6 years of struggle was given away to an American company. Tesco was trying to achieve revenue maximisation instead of the more common profit maximisation. The third objective is sales maximisation.

Grade B (i) Where's the beef?

The beef comes from the graphs on the following two pages. These set out the actual point at which each objective is maximised. You need to be able to show that point on a graph, understand the graph in general, then also know the formula for working out the maximising point for each objective. It may take some time to get to grips with these three graphs. Please find the time.

Grade B (ii) Why it matters

It matters because objectives affect decisions. A firm pursuing short-term profit maximisation risks ending up on *Watchdog* because it promises customers a lot but delivers very little. If the business aimed for long-term revenue maximisation it would look after its customers – to try to turn them into loyal regulars.

Grade A The other side

Economic theory is often based on extreme assumptions such as 'perfect' competition. Many economists question whether many firms are really pursuing the maximisation of a specific goal. They argue that in the real world owners and senior managers of firms look for a balanced approach, rather than maximisation. They think that firms look for optimisation, not maximisation. That requires a balance between short-term profit and longer term revenue maximisation.

Grade A* The critical perspective

No-one who runs a large public company would recognise the objectives set out by Edexcel. Profit maximisation, in particular, would be avoided. This is because if you get the best possible profit this year, you have the challenge of beating that figure next year. Instead of a 40% profit increase this year then a dip next year, bosses know their jobs are safer if they achieve 15% profit increases in both years. So they generally look to optimise profit, not maximise it.

Do take your time over the graphs on the next two pages. Start with Figure 1 (profit maximisation) and make sure you understand it. The other two graphs build on Figure 1, so if you grasp the first one the next two should be approachable.

Don't forget that there are four things to learn here: profit, revenue and sales maximisation; and then the idea of optimisation, i.e. finding a satisfactory compromise between them.

Exam tip: Level 4 analysis requires depth, which can be shown by clarifying the assumptions that underpin your arguments (such as that firms are profit maximisers) and by breaking down a heading such as objectives into the three types graphed on the next 2 pages.

Different objectives: transmission mechanism (to the top response level)

Chain 1. If a firm seeks revenue maximisation it produces where MR = 0 (1) … which can yield a substantial supernormal profit (2) ... even if profit is not maximised (3). A business may choose this objective to make its market share less of an attraction to potential rivals (4) ... which may help it generate higher profits in the long term than a short-termist approach would do (5).

Chain 2. A firm pursuing sales maximisation produces where AC = AR (1). This means there will be no supernormal profit (2) … but that may be acceptable to a holiday company in the winter months (3) … or a producer of inferior goods during an economic upturn (4). No firm is likely to choose sales maximisation as a long-term objective, but in the short-medium term it may be necessary (5).

Diagrams to illustrate different objectives of firms

Objective 1: Profit maximisation

This is the default business objective that is the underlying assumption throughout micro-economics. Profit maximisation means that if firms had perfect knowledge of the cost and revenue conditions under which they operate, they would seek to produce the output level at which marginal revenue = marginal cost (MR=MC). The graph below is for a business in monopolistic competition. Therefore it has temporary monopoly power that it can use to gain from supernormal profits. Those profits will be maximised where MR = MC.

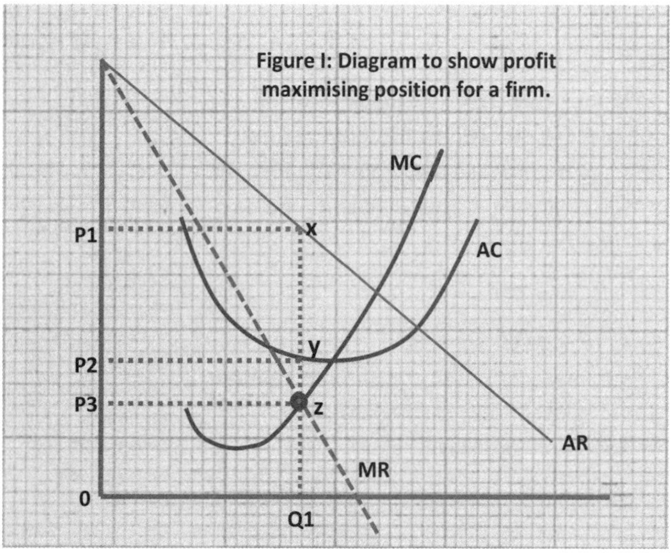

In this graph profit maximisation takes place when MC = MR, which is at quantity level Q1 (point Z). And the super-normal profit generated is within the rectangle P1,X,Y,P2. This is the area where average revenue exceeds average costs.

Questions on Figure 1:

1. What price is the consumer paying?
2. Which of the following shows the firm's total costs?

a) 0,P3,z,Q1

b) P3,P2,y,z

c) 0,P2,y,Q1

3. What would happen if this firm's fixed costs rose?

a) The MC and AC lines would shift up

b) Only the MC line would shift up

c) Only the AC line would shift up.

Don't panic when faced with a graph as complex as Figure 1. Take your time to really figure out what's going on. And explain the graph with care.

Profit maximisation: formula

The rule is simple: whatever the market structure (perfectly competitive, monopolistic competition, oligopoly or monopoly), the same formula will identify the quantity and price at which profit is maximised:

Profit maximisation formula: MC = MR, i.e. where marginal cost = marginal revenue.

This formula applies to short-run conditions. If a firm chooses to maximise its long-run profit, it might use limit pricing to discourage new entrants to the market. This would mean charging a price below the point where MC = MR, to act as a barrier to entry to potential competitors.

Objective 2: Revenue maximisation

Although profit maximisation explains a great deal of business behaviour, it fails to explain everything. Sometimes takeover bids seem based more on a desire to get bigger than to become more profitable. Economists have suggested that the divorce of ownership and control leads to a situation in which owners want profit maximisation, but managers seek revenue maximisation. This is because the bigger (and more complex) the business, the easier it is for senior managers to get higher salaries and greater promotion prospects.

So revenue maximisation is a plausible business objective. This is shown in Figure 2 on the facing page. Note that the revenue-maximising point is at a lower price but higher volume level than the profit maximising position shown on Figure 1.

Answers on Figure 1:

Q1. Consumers pay P1

Q2. Answer: C. (You start by identifying where the profit-maximising quantity Q1 cuts the AC curve (point Y), then identify the rectangle below the AC curve)

Q3. Answer: C. Whereas an increase in variable costs would shift the MC *and* AC upwards, a rise in fixed costs only affects AC.

Diagrams to illustrate different objectives of firms

Objective 2: Revenue maximisation

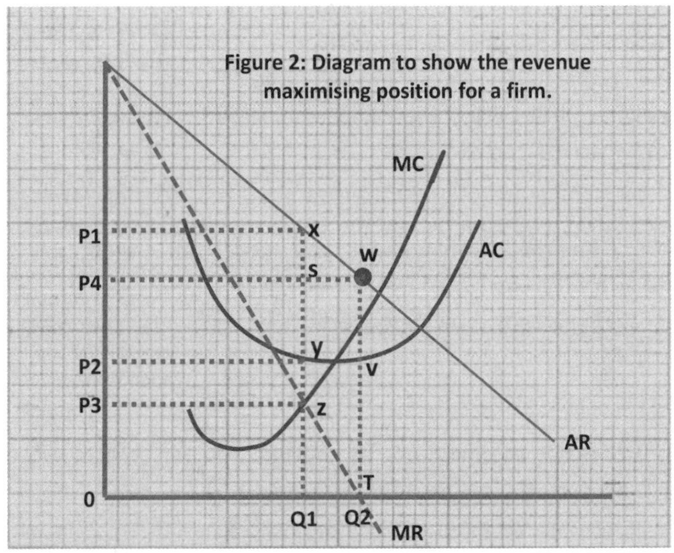

Revenue is maximised at the point on the horizontal axis where MR = 0 (point T). While MR is falling, but still above zero, every extra unit of output adds to total revenue. So revenue is maximised when MR = 0. Beyond Q2, total revenue will fall.

Questions on Figure 2:

1. What is the price change if the firm switches from profit to revenue maximisation?

2. Which of the following shows the revenue maximiser's total revenue?

a) 0,P4,W,T

b) P4,W,V,P2

c) P4,S,y,P2

3. What is the benefit to this firm of charging P4 rather than P1?

a) Higher revenue means higher profits

b) Lower price and higher sales act as a barrier to entry

c) Boosting production cuts unit costs

Don't panic when faced with a graph as complex as Figure 1. Take your time to really

Answers on Figure 2:

Q1. A price cut from P1 to P4

Q2. Answer: A. The consumer is now paying P4 and the sales volume is Q2. So total revenue is 0,P4,W,T

Q3. Answer: B. (A is plain wrong; higher revenue only boosts profits if costs stay low; C is wrong according to the graph: Figure 2).

Revenue maximisation: formula

Revenue maximisation formula: MR = 0, i.e. where the marginal revenue line cuts the horizontal axis.

Objective 3: Sales maximisation

Sales maximisation is a theoretical business objective that may be valid towards the end of a product's profitable lifespan. The idea is to sell as many units as possible without making a loss. That means operating at the sales volume level where AC = AR.

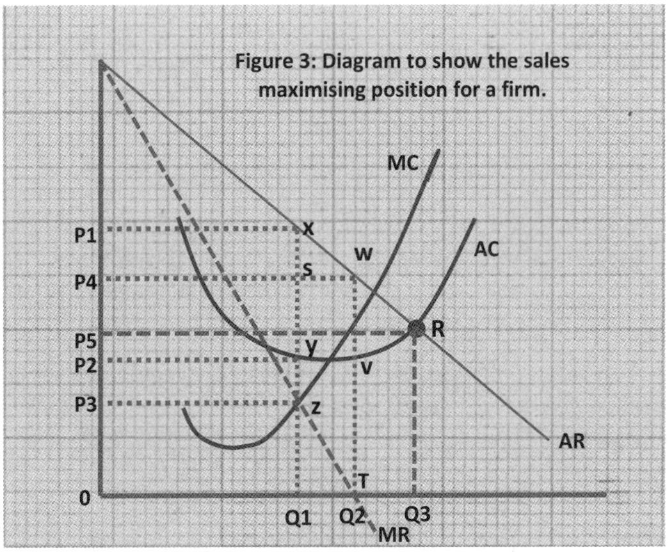

At the sales maximising point R (where the AC line cuts the AR line) the price is cut to P5 while the quantity of output is Q3. This shrinks the supernormal profit to zero as there is no profit margin between AC and AR. A firm might do this on occasions such as the January sales.

Possibility 4: Optimised objectives

It is also possible that a firm might choose against a maximised objective, instead opting for a compromise between two or more objectives. A price set between P1 and P4, for example, might be the management's view of the optimum price level – compromising between profit and revenue maximisation.

Revenue

Grade C. What is it?

(Total) revenue is the value of all sales made in a trading period, such as a year. It is needed to cover all the costs of the business, ideally with some surplus to generate a profit. Average revenue is total revenue / the number of goods sold, which means that average revenue is simply the selling price. Most important of all is marginal revenue: the revenue gained from selling one extra unit.

Do remember the 3 formulae:
Total revenue = Quantity sold x Selling price

Average revenue = $\frac{\text{Total revenue}}{\text{Quantity sold}}$

Marginal revenue = New total revenue *minus* Previous total revenue

Grade B (i) Where's the beef?

The beef comes from the graph below, as is often the way. In addition, you need to have confidence in the concept itself: that profit is maximised where marginal revenue = marginal costs. That helps in analysing graphs showing perfect competition but also monopoly and oligopoly.

Grade B (ii) Why it matters

Micro-economics revolves around the idea of profit maximisation. This occurs when marginal revenue (MR) equals marginal costs (MC). If MC<MR (see graph) more profit can be made by selling more items until the point where MC and MR are equal. After that point, MC is greater than MR so the profit is shrunk as every extra unit generates higher costs than revenues.

Don't forget the importance of price elasticity in questions about revenue. A price rise on a price elastic product cuts revenue. A price rise on a price inelastic product boosts revenue, as the % price rise outweighs the % fall in sales volume.

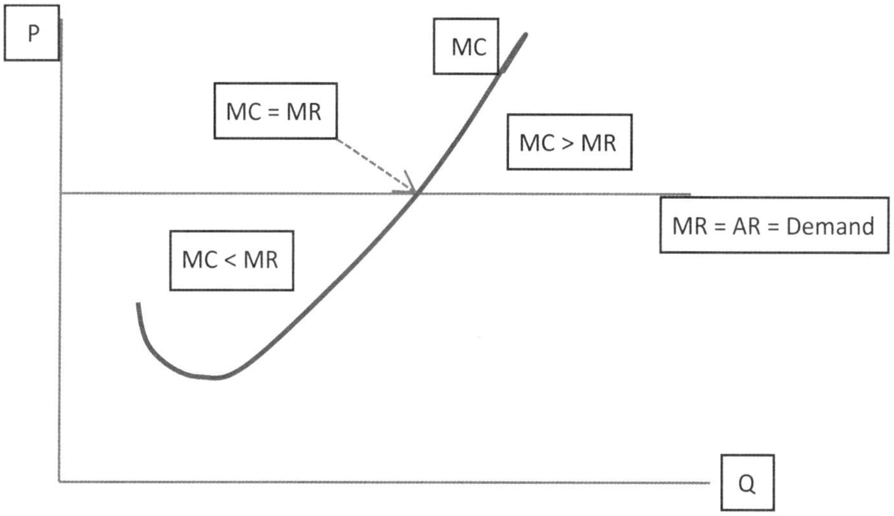

Grade A The other side

Economics focuses a lot on revenue, but for most businesses profit is a far more important measure. Profit, of course, is revenue *minus* the costs of operating. You can't get rich by generating revenue, only by generating profit.

Exam tip: 9 times out of 10 an exam graph showing average revenue (the demand curve) is down-ward sloping. If it's horizontal it's because the firm is a price-taker in a perfectly competitive market.

Grade A* The critical perspective

Some bosses seem more interested in revenue than in profit. This may be because of the pride that can come from size (we're Number 1!) or because executive pay often reflects size and scale. If company A buys company B, company A's boss often ends up with a big salary hike – to reflect the company's greater size. This is where economists talk about the **divorce of ownership and control** – what suits senior managers may be divorced from the best interests of shareholders.

Revenue (ii)

Extra graphical analysis of total revenue

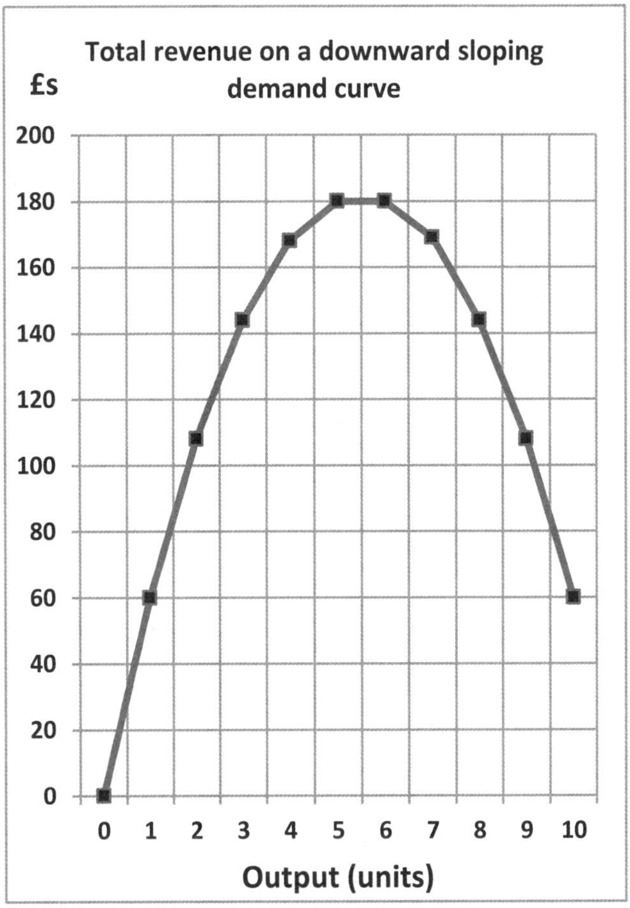

The graph on the left shows total revenue for a firm with the following downward sloping average revenue (demand) curve

Price	Output
£60	1
£54	2
£48	3
£42	4
£36	5
£30	6
£24	7
£18	8
£12	9
£6	10

This illustrates that in the top half of the curve a price cut boosts revenue, because the product is price elastic.

Do remember that if price is constant, the price-taker will enjoy steadily rising total revenue, with a constant marginal revenue

Don't be shocked if marginal revenue is negative. It may seem all wrong, but a firm may be happy to cut prices to beat off a competitor, even if it causes a fall in revenue.

Test yourself (answers in tiny print at the foot of the page)

1. Calculate the PED when the price is cut from £54 to £48.
2. Calculate the PED when the price is cut from £24 to £18.
3. Calculate the marginal revenue when the price is cut from £54 to £48.
4. Calculate the marginal revenue when the price is cut from £24 to £18.

Revenue: transmission mechanism (to get the top response level)

Chain 1. If a firm cuts its price the average revenue also falls (1) … but total revenue may rise as long as sales volume rises by a higher % than the % price cut (2) … meaning that the product is price elastic (3). If total revenue rises marginal revenue will also rise (4) and can be measured by taking the previous total revenue figure from the latest one (5).

Chain 2. When the average revenue (demand) curve is downward sloping (1) … the top half will be price elastic (2) … so a change in price changes demand by a higher percentage (3). The bottom half is price inelastic and in the centre price elasticity is unitary (4) … meaning that the marginal revenue will be zero as any % price change is cancelled out by an equal but opposite % change in demand (5)

Answers: 1. = *minus* 4.5 (highly price elastic) 2. = *minus* 0.57 (price inelastic) 3. £144 - £108 = +£36 4. £144 - £168 = *minus* £24

Price elasticity of demand and revenue

Grade C. What is it?

If the Morrisons price of Pot Noodles is cut from £1 to 50p, sales volumes can rise from 800 to 3,200 packs per week (in just one store). This dramatic rise in sales not only shows how price elastic the product can be, but also points towards the huge effect of price on revenue. Instead of 800 x £1 = £800, the sales of Pot Noodles rise to 3,200 x 50p = £1,600. So halving the price doubles the sales revenue. For other products consumer behaviour is quite different. The graph below shows what happened when the price of the Financial Times newspaper was increased overnight from £1 to £1.80.

Grade B (i) Where's the beef?

The beef is to become expert at the calculations involved. Some recent exam papers have included easy calculations of % change. Examiners surely should be testing fully the calculations on the specification; one of those is the effect on revenue of a price change, given a specific measure of price elasticity. See right.

Grade B (ii) How it's shown

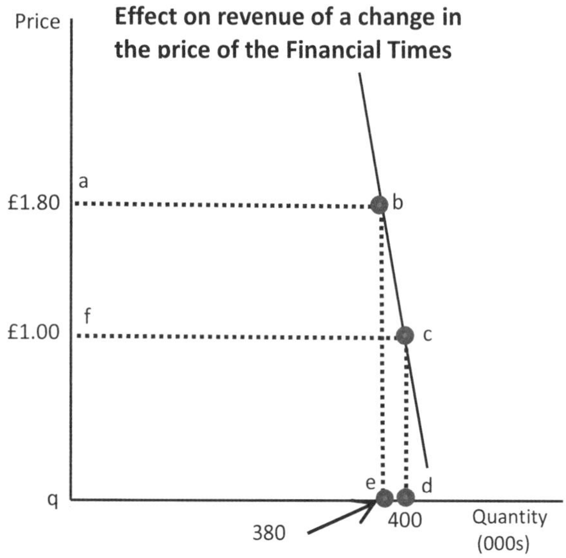

Grade A The graph

When the Financial Times increased its price from £1 to £1.80, sales slipped by 5% to 380,000 a day. The steeply sloped demand curve reflects the newspaper's low price elasticity of demand.

Answer these questions:

A. Calculate the price elasticity of the Financial Times at the time of its price rise to £1.80.

B. Use the letters on the graph to indicate the change in revenue when the price was increased to £1.80.*

(Answers at foot of the page)

Grade A* The critical perspective

Calculating the effect of a price change on revenue needs to be backed up by 'ceteris paribus', i.e. other things being equal, which means holding all other variables to be constant. The most obvious intervening factors are the response of competitors and the degree of consumer knowledge. A further consideration is timescale, i.e. the impact on revenue may change over time in line with PED.

Do these calculations (answers below)

1. A firm sells 200 units a day at £5 each. The PED is *minus* 2.0. Calculate the effect on revenue of a 20% price cut.

2. A firm sells 1000 units a day at £4 each. The PED is *minus* 0.2. Calculate the effect on revenue of a 25% price rise.

Don't ruin your calculations by muddling up your answer. This calculation is about the effect of a price change on revenue, not profit. Oddly, students often use the words inter-changeably.

Answers:

1. Old revenue was 200 x £5 = £1,000
New sales up by -20% x -2.0 = +40%
New revenue is £4 x 280 = £1,120
So ANS = +£120

2. Old revenue was 1000 x £4 = £4,000
New sales down by +25% x -0.2 = *minus* 5%
New revenue is £5 x 950 = £4,750
So ANS = +£750

PED and revenue: transmission mechanism (to get to the top response level)

Chain 1. When price is cut on a price inelastic product (1) … sales rise, but by a lower percentage than the price cut (2). Therefore the revenue gain from extra sales volume is outweighed by the reduction in revenue per unit, ie. price (3) So a price cut on a price inelastic product leads to a fall in revenue (4) ... though this may work in the long term if new customers stay loyal to the product. (5)

*A. Sales -5%/Price +80% = -0.0625 B. NEW = abeq *minus* OLD = fcdq

Costs: formulae and calculations

Grade C. What is it?

There are three categories of cost that you need to understand: total costs, average costs and marginal costs. Read the box on the right for definitions of fixed and variable costs. In the table below you can see the rise in total costs as output increases. It's only when you calculate the average total costs that you can see how costs per unit are falling from £610 at 100 units to £264 when 500 are produced.

Do note that fixed costs are unaffected by the amount of business a firm is doing. These costs include rent on premises and interest payments on debts. Landlords and banks demand to be paid every week. Variable costs vary as output varies, such as raw materials.

Grade B Where's the beef?

Output	Total fixed costs £000s	Total variable costs £000s	Total costs (£000s)	Average fixed costs (£s)	Average variable costs (£s)	Average total costs (£s)	Marginal costs £s
0	40	0	40	-	0	-	
100	40	21	61	400	210	610	+21
200	40	40	80	200	200	400	+19
300	40	57	97	133.3	190	323.3	+17
400	40	74	114	100	185	285	+17
500	40	92	132	80	184	264	+18
Formula:			TFC+TVC	FC/Output	VC/Output	TC/Output	The difference in total costs

The formula for calculating each cost is in the final row above. Now answer these questions based on the table above.

Q1. Calculate the average fixed costs if 250 units are produced.

Q2. Calculate the total variable costs at 250 units, if total costs are £90,000.

Q3. Calculate average total costs at 350 units if total variable costs are £66,000.

Don't shut your eyes to the apparent contradiction that as output rises, total costs rise while average total costs fall. Try to make sure it makes sense to you.

Answers: 1. With 250 units produced, AFC will be £40,000/250 units = £160.
2. If total costs are £90,000 and fixed costs are £40,000, total variable costs are £50,.000.
3. If TVC = £66,000 and fixed costs are £40,000. then TC = £106,000 and ATC is £106,000/350 = £302.86p

Grade A The counter-argument

There can't be any serious counter-arguments on a factual matter such as total and average costs. Nevertheless it's important to remember it depends on the business context. When producing tins of baked beans, Heinz will know the fixed and variable costs to a high degree of accuracy. But when starting on a huge project such as HS2 no-one truly knows what the costs will end up being.

Grade A* The critical perspective

Within a build-up of economic analysis it's easy to forget that 'costs' in business often means people. So cutting costs could mean redundancies – or forcing people to switch from permanent to zero-hours contracts. This is important in evaluation.

Costs: formulae & calculations: transmission mechanism (to top response level)

Chain 1. If a firm's average costs are higher than their selling price (1) … the business will be making actual losses (2) ... threatening to strip the firm of its cash and therefore its ability to survive (3). But when thinking how to cut costs (4) … it is only right to consider the impact on the staff involved (5).

Chain 2. Fixed costs are usually 'sunk' (1) … meaning that the money has been spent and cannot be recovered (2) ... such as spending on advertising at the time of a new product launch (3). Because sunk costs cannot be recovered (4) they are not taken into account when making business decisions (5).

Derivation of short-run cost curves

Grade C. What is it?

When a start-up firm enjoys rising sales it is easy for staff to find more efficient ways to do things, so productivity increases. Rising marginal productivity is shown in Figure 1 below. But as the firm increases its output by adding more of a variable factor such as labour, marginal productivity declines. As explained in the **Do** box, the rise and then fall in marginal productivity forms a mirror image (Figure 2) in relation to costs. Diminishing marginal productivity leads to rising marginal costs.

Do recognise that productivity changes have an inverse effect on costs. If labour productivity rises from 10 units per hour to 20, the cost per unit for an employee earning £10 an hour falls from £1 per unit to 50p. Similarly, diminishing marginal productivity will push costs up.

Grade B Where's the beef?

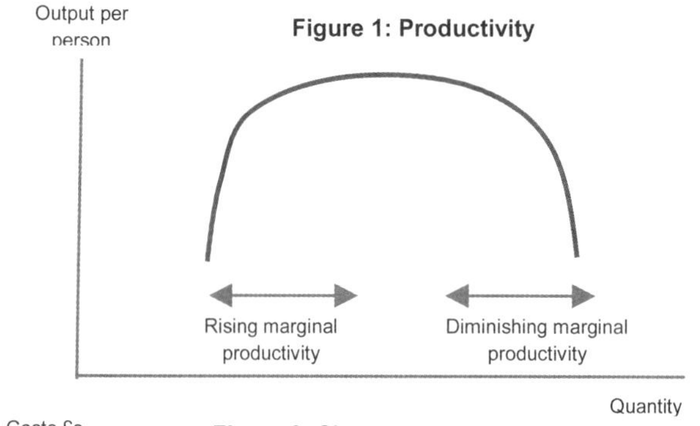

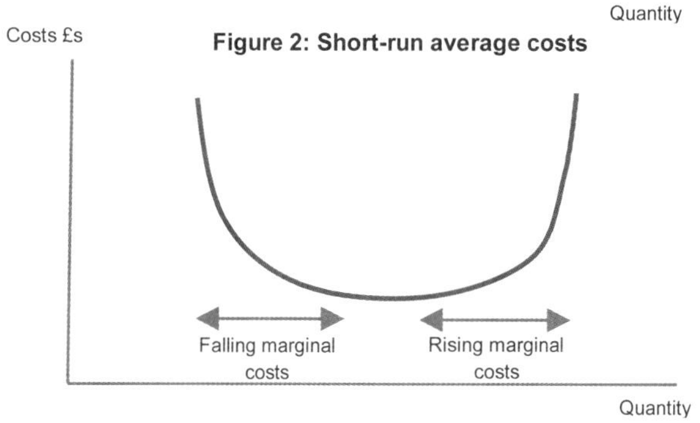

The beef lies in the importance of the underlying assumption: of diminishing marginal productivity. Businesses would find it hard to understand why productivity doesn't keep rising as the business produces more. The key is that economists are assuming extra output achieved by adding variable factors only, which would unbalance the production method.

Don't forget that short and long-run cost curves are the same (U) shape, but for different reasons. Here, the short-run cost curve is due to rising then diminishing marginal productivity.

Grade A The counter-argument

Although businesspeople may find it hard to recognise this picture of a short-run cost curve, it is an important part of micro-economic theory. It is plausible within its own assumptions. The important thing when answering exam questions is to make it clear that you recognise its logic (within those assumptions).

Exam tip: one of the most important definitions in micro-economics is 'the short-run'. Remember that it's: 'a period of time in which the quantity of at least one input is fixed, forcing supply increases to stem from increasing other, variable, inputs'.

Grade A* The critical perspective

Micro-economic theory was largely developed in a world dominated by goods, not services. A theory such as the U-shaped short-run average cost curve fits into a world of manufacturing cars or candles. It's harder to visualise in these days of service businesses such as solicitors or designers.

Deriving short-run cost curves: transmission mechanism (to top response level)

Chain 1. When a new firm enjoys an increase in output it finds it easy to improve efficiency leading to higher productivity (1) ... and falling unit costs (2). Even when efficiency is limited by a fixed, long-term factor (3) .. it boosts output by adding variable production factors (4) .. at the cost of falling efficiency (5).

Chain 2. If short-run productivity is diminishing (1) … it may be wise to boost the scale of output (2) ... by increasing a fixed factor such as the size of the factory (3). With the new factory, rising output should mean rising productivity (4) until marginal productivity diminishes, so short-run costs rise again (5).

Short and long-run average cost curves

Grade C. What is it?

Imagine a growing family living in a flat. As the years go by it becomes increasingly overcrowded and inefficient to live in. So the family moves to a 3-bed house. Life improves (two bathrooms now; no queueing) but a new baby plus growing kids make it seem overcrowded and impractical again in a couple of years. Time to move again into a 4-bed house.... And so on. This is like the relationship between cost curves shown in the first half of the graph below. Short-run inefficiencies are relieved by moving to bigger premises – but only for a short time before the situation repeats itself.

Do note the potential power in an answer of the combination: diminishing marginal productivity … leads to rising labour costs per unit … causing average costs to rise … until production bottlenecks can be relieved by increasing the scale of output.

Grade B (i) Where's the beef?

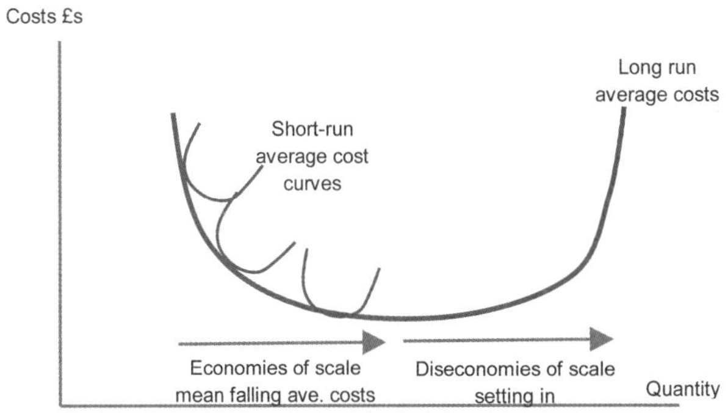

The diagram on the left shows the long run average cost curve – falling due to economies of scale then rising as diseconomies set in. The short-run cost curves touch the long run curve at their point of lowest cost.

Don't forget that economists classify costs into fixed and variable. Fixed costs include rent, the depreciation on machinery or vehicles, interest payments on loans and the cost of advertising and promotion. Variable costs include piece-rate labour, raw materials and packaging materials

Grade B (ii) Tackling the numbers. Fill in gaps 1-8.

Output	Total fixed costs £s	Total variable costs £s	Total costs (£s)	Average fixed costs (£s)	Average variable costs (£s)	Average total costs (£s)	Marginal costs £s
0	5000	0	5000	-	0	-	-
10	5000	2500	7500	500	250	1.	+2500
20	5000	2.	9600	250	3.	480	+2100
30	5000	6900	4.	166.7	230	396.7	5.
40	6.	9400	14400	7.	235	8.	+2500
50	5000	12000	17000	100	240	340	+2600

Answers:
1. £750
2. £4600
3. £230
4. £11900
5. £2,300
6. £5000
7. £125
8. £360

Grade A* The critical perspective

Cutting costs as Primark has done can lead to over-consumption, with people buying clothes, wearing just a few times, then scrapping them and buying again. This works well in a traditional free market economy, but may come to be seen as anti-social and anti-environmental in times of concern over finite resources and global warming.

Costs: short & long-run curves: transmission mechanism (to top response level)

Chain 1. Production costs can rise in the short term when commodity market prices move upwards (1) … and there's little the firm can do about this (2). But this type of cost increase is irrelevant (3) ... to the issue of short v long-term costs (4) … which is focused on costs relating to time and sales volume (5).

Chain 2. The long-run average cost curve (1) … is drawn from all the minimum points on the short-run cost curves (2). So although they have different causal factors (3) … they are more closely related than appears to be the case (4) … and are therefore the same managers at firms deal with them both (5).

Economies and diseconomies of scale

Grade C. What is it?

This concerns the long-run relationship between the firm's size (scale) and its average costs, also known as its unit costs. Economies of scale are the factors leading to lower average costs as the firm increases its scale. So although total costs rise as the firm expands, costs per unit may fall, perhaps because of bulk-buying. Diseconomies of scale lead to rising costs per unit as the firm expands, perhaps because of faltering motivation or greater difficulties in coordination.

Do remember the causal factors involved. For economies, the main causes are purchasing economies (bulk buying), plus technical and managerial economies. Causes of diseconomies include problems with communication, coordination and staff motivation.

Grade B (i) Where's the beef?

There are two big issues with this topic: first is the need to be comfortable distinguishing between costs (implying total costs) and unit costs (total costs divided by the number of units). The second is that minimum efficient scale (see graph) is important in economics because it shows the point of maximum productive efficiency. And productive efficiency, together with allocative efficiency, represent the free market ideal within an efficient market economy.

Grade B (ii) How it's shown

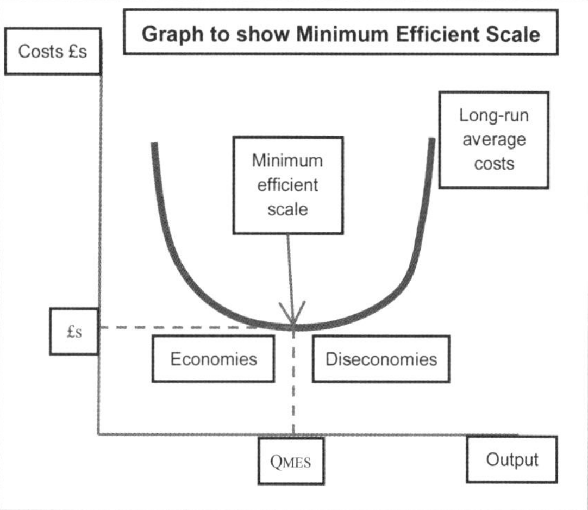

Grade A The other side

The argument against this graph is that it paints the wrong picture. It looks like economies of scale bring the costs down, but then diseconomies kick in, bringing unit costs back up. In fact, diseconomies of scale kick in as soon as a firm begins to grow. They start to outweigh the economies after the point of minimum efficient scale.

Don't confuse economies of scale with improved capacity utilisation. The latter is an important short-run cause of falling average costs. Economies of scale are about falling long-run average costs.

Exam tip: remember that both economies and diseconomies occur when scale is increasing. There are no equivalent terms to discuss what happens when a business shrinks.

Grade A* The critical perspective

Economies of scale are often accepted quite uncritically, because they seem obvious. Yes, buying more bulk means lower costs per unit and yes, technical economies (such as robots) make sense. But when two companies are brought together in a merger or takeover, the diseconomies of scale often outweigh the economies and many so-called synergies evaporate away.

Economies and diseconomies: transmission mechanism (to top response level)

Chain 1. An example of increasing scale in when a firm buy new, faster, automated machinery (1) … that can produce more per hour or per person (2). This increase should allow the new, higher fixed costs to be spread over far more units (3)… allowing the unit costs to fall (4) ... unless there are unexpected diseconomies caused as a result of the automation, e.g. worsening staff motivation. (5)

Chain 2. A firm is productively efficient when it's operating at the lowest point on its long-run average cost curve (1) … but there's no point in this unless people want to buy that number of units (2) … shown on the graph as QMES (3) … in other words the point of allocative efficiency (4). So the ideal point for efficiency is the point where allocative and productive efficiencies are maximised. (5)

Condition for profit maximisation

Grade C. What is it?

Profit maximisation occurs when MC = MR. On the graph below a firm operates in a perfectly competitive market. It is a price-taker, as shown by the horizontal demand curve. Profit maximisation is at Q_1, i.e. where MC = MR at the point where MC is rising past MR. At Q_2 MC also equals MR, but between Q_2 and Q_1 is an area where marginal revenue is always higher than marginal cost – so there is profit to be made. Therefore Q_1 is the relevant point to choose.

Do remember the definitions involved. **Marginal cost** (MC) is the cost of adding one more unit of output. **Marginal revenue** (MR) is the extra income gained by selling one more unit. **Profit maximisation** is when MC = MR.

Grade B (i) Where's the beef?

The beef lies in being unshakeable in your conviction that profit maximisation occurs when MC = MR. The examiner's skill is in writing questions where that economic truth is hidden within other data, perhaps average revenue and average costs. And on a monopoly graph it is easy to miss MC = MR in a raft of other lines

Grade B (ii) How it's shown

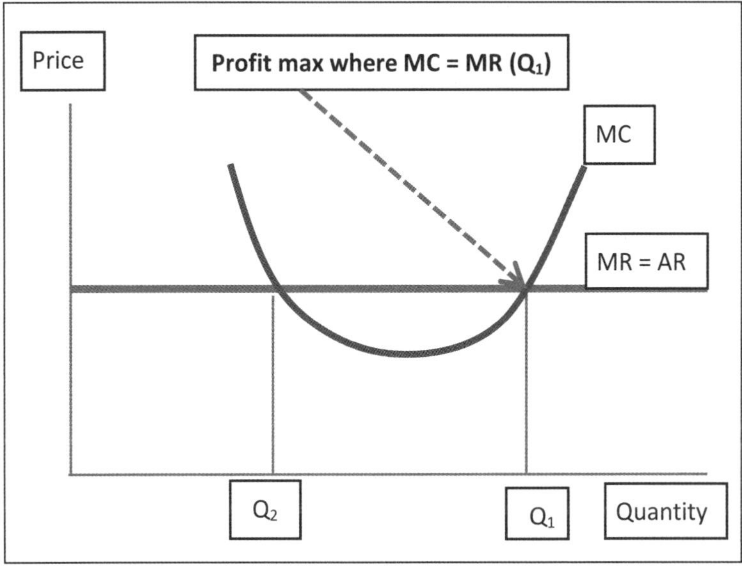

The other side

The main counter-argument is that firms' cost data lacks the accuracy to know exactly where their MC = MR. So this can't happen in the real world.

Don't forget that in a graph such as the one on the left, MC = MR is profit maximising because at every point up to Q_1 there's more to be made by selling more, as MC<MR. Beyond Q_1, as MC rises above MR, the profit is being eaten away.

Grade A* The critical perspective

Only in the world of perfectly competitive markets is survival dependent on maximising profits and therefore on identifying where a firm's MC equals its MR. Most firms operate in a state of oligopoly or monopolistic competition, where profits are optimised rather than maximised. It would be hard to find an example of a firm working hard to identify the point where its MC equals its MR.

Exam tip: Profit maximisation is the underlying assumption behind all micro analysis of the actions of firms. So it's helpful to be able to show the examiner where it occurs – and why.

Condition for profit max.: transmission mechanism (to top response level)

Chain 1. To maximise profit firms need to operate at the point where marginal costs equal marginal revenue (1). This is also the point at which losses are minimised (2). By implication, if demand is greater than the profit-maximising quantity (3)… a firm should turn down the offer of extra orders (4). In the real world this would be hard to do without upsetting customers. (5)

Chain 2. For a business operating within an oligopoly (1) … profit maximisation is at the output level where MC=MR (2) … but the (supernormal) profit is the area between AR and AC (3) … multiplied by the profit maximising output quantity (4). In monopolistic competition the same analysis is used, though in this case it is assumed that competition erodes the supernormal profit in the long run. (5)

Normal and supernormal profits

Grade C. What is it?

For profit maximisation (given current market conditions) firms should operate where marginal costs = marginal revenue. If the market is highly competitive, MC = MR may just yield 'normal' profits, i.e. no more than enough for the firm to keep going. Normal profits give enough to pay lenders their interest charges and shareholders sufficient in dividend payments to keep them happy.

Grade B (i) Where's the beef?

The big issue is to understand normal profits – that they are high enough to keep a business going, but not big enough to create reserves of profit to get a business through a really bad time. And most firms will face a bad time once every few years, either because of a recession or due to excessive competition.

Grade B (ii) Why it matters

It matters because it explains what happens in every high street and shopping centre. There are always shops or restaurants that are struggling – yet keep going. They may stay in business for years longer than you expect. Yet suddenly the *Closing Down Sale* is on – and they've vanished within a few weeks. They were struggling on making little or no real profit, and when the landlord demanded a signature on a new, higher rent the shop closed down.

Grade A The other side

Free market theory sees normal profit as 'normal', implying a profit rate that only just covers the cost of the capital being used. In fact recent figures show that UK companies enjoy a profit rate of over 12.5% a year, which is far higher than that. By implication, many firms are constantly making profits that are higher than 'normal'. This suggests that far more firms have highly differentiated products than text books suggest – perhaps plenty of them operating in oligopolistic markets.

Grade A* The critical perspective

Almost every economist agrees that highly competitive markets are good for consumers, whereas monopolistic markets are bad. Where they disagree is on prevalence. Free marketeers think that free markets and normal profits are the norm. More critically-minded economists think that oligopolies and the power of brands make supernormal profits quite normal. They question the assumption that brands in monopolistic competition will see their supernormal profits eroded away quickly. Today independently-produced *Irn Bru* has a 4% share of UK soft drinks. It's been in a similar position for decades – and remains very profitable.

Do think about opposites when revising. If the focus is on supernormal profits, what about supernormal losses? What might they be? Perhaps temporary as a new company has started a price war to break into your market. And any firm should be able to cope with temporary trouble.

Don't treat supernormal profits as a matter of chance; company executives will have worked hard to create the differentiation that allows high prices to be set – and maintained.

Exam tip: a good economist would never treat profit as a dirty word. Usually profit pays for investments in the future, such as newer machinery or a better website. Occasionally, though, profit is excessive.

Normal and supernormal: transmission mechanism (to the top response level)

Chain 1. A firm making normal profit may try to boost its profitability (1) … by pushing its brands towards more highly differentiated segments of the market (2) … allowing price elasticities to fall and profit margins to increase (3). It will be hard to sustain this newly differentiated position, however (4) … without a strong (and expensive) marketing campaign.

Chain 2. If profit is to be maximised a firm must have precise knowledge of its costs (1) … especially marginal costs (2). When these are below marginal revenue the business boosts its profit with every extra sale made (3)… up until marginal costs = marginal revenue (4). After this point marginal costs will be higher than revenues, making the profit start to drain away (5).

Normal and supernormal profits (ii)

Figure 1: Normal profit made in perfectly competitive market

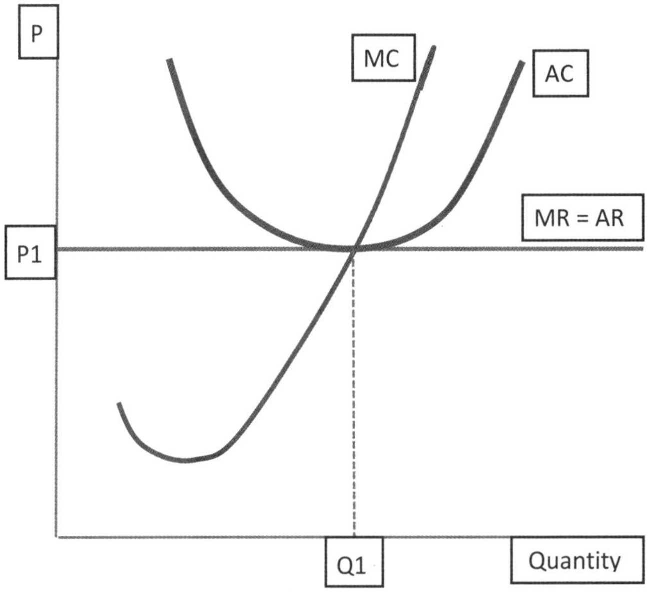

The graph on the left shows a stable equilibrium position for a firm in a perfectly competitive market. It is operating at its profit-maximising position (MC = MR), but no supernormal profits are being made because AC = AR. So there are no incentives for new entrants to join the market.

Do think about how tough it would be to operate a firm in a highly competitive market with no supernormal profit. It would mean a constant struggle to find the capital to finance expansion.

Figure 2: Supernormal profit in perfectly competitive market

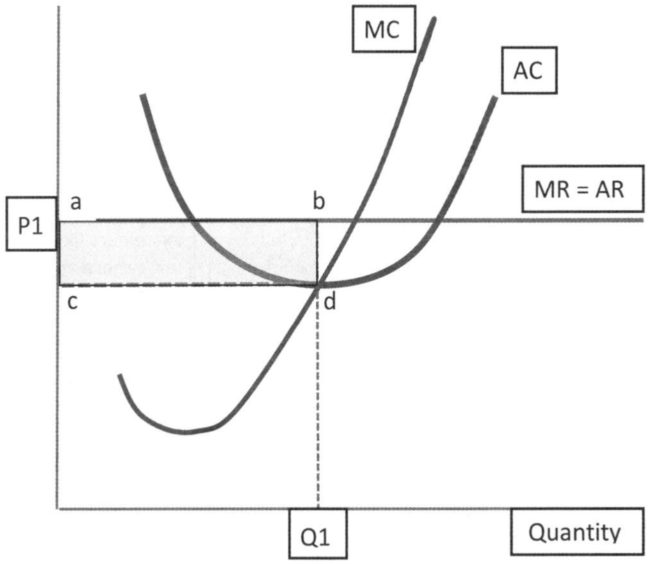

The graph on the left shows an unusual position for a firm in a perfectly competitive market. Its profit maximising position (MC=MR) generates a supernormal profit within the area abcd. This is where AR > AC. So there are incentives for new entrants to join the market; they'll probably arrive soon.

Don't forget the natural tension in an economist's mind between producers and consumers. Business owners pray for supernormal profits – as big and as often as possible. But customers want prices low enough to squeeze the super-normal profits down to zero.

Test yourself (answers in tiny print at the foot of the page)

1. If extra competition arrives, what will be the effect on Figure 2?

2. Why might one firm have average costs that are lower than its rivals?

3. Why are supernormal profits best to have when the firm is a monopoly?

1. Market prices fall, so the AR line falls, perhaps eliminating the supernormal profit. 2. It may be more efficient; or may pay administrative staff badly. 3. Because barriers to entry maintain the supernormal profits for as long as the monopoly persists.

Short and long-run shutdown points

Grade C. What is it?

In the long run it is impossible for a business to stay in business if it cannot achieve 'normal' profit. In the graph below this is achieved at point a, where average costs are £66 – exactly the same as the selling price. If market prices slip down to £42 then the business is only covering its variable costs. This is the point where any further price slippage and the business will shut down, at least in the short-run.

Grade B (i) Where's the beef?

This topic is all-beef. It's hard to remember these details in an exam, and the graph below is a tough one to remember (and to draw). But the keys are to remember:

Short-run shutdown point: when price (AR) falls below average variable costs

Long-run shutdown point: when price (AR) falls below AC for a sustained period. Once the firm believes the loss-making position is permanent, it will close.

Do remember that it's hard for firms to identify all their costs. So the short-term shutdown point will be hard to identify. Businesses tend to close down rather than (temporarily) shut down – because they've run out of the money needed to pay the bills.

Grade B (ii) How it's shown

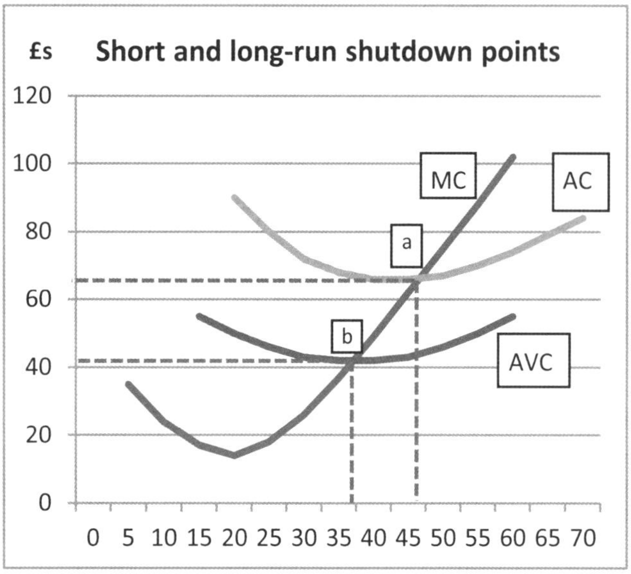

Grade A: The counterargument

The main counter-argument is that real-world shutdown points rely on two further factors: does the firm have the cash to continue in business? And do its owners/investors believe there may still be success in the very long term. Otherwise firms like Tesla and Snapchat would have shut down by now.

Don't forget that long-run shut down is mainly about cash, not costs. Firms such as Carillion and Interserve find themselves drained of the cash they need to survive. They may still believe in the firm's future, but lack the cash to keep it going.

Exam tip: examiners like to think there are plenty of small firms willing to enter and exit markets freely. In this view, a short-run shutdown is temporary – just part of the gig economy.

Grade A* The critical perspective

The short-term shutdown point forms an important part of neo-classical economic theory because 'contestable markets' require suppliers to be able to enter and exit market freely. Do firms *really* exit a market but stay waiting for an opportunity to re-enter when prices rise? Not many, surely, as it sounds highly impractical.

Shutdown points: transmission mechanism (to the top response level)

Chain 1. When business is going badly a firm may consider closing down (1). In the short run it can survive as long as it covers its variable costs (2). Fixed costs are assumed to be sunk (3) … and therefore irrelevant to the short-term decision (4) … though in the long run all costs must be covered. (5)

Chain 2. Even when market prices are below a firm's variable costs it may choose to keep going (1) … as long as it believes there are long-term profit opportunities (2) … and has the cash to keep going despite the lossmaking. (3) The digital age has been full of examples of huge lossmakers kept afloat by optimistic investors (4) … who ignore the economics in favour of what Keynes called *animal spirits* (5)

Productive and allocative efficiency

Grade C. What is it?

Productive efficiency is maximised when a firm is operating at the lowest point on its average cost curve. So it is maximised within an economy when every firm is operating at its lowest average cost. An economy has full allocative efficiency when the marginal cost of production equals price in all markets. This can only occur if there is no market failure in any market; and, in effect, there will only be allocative efficiency when all markets are perfectly competitive.

Do remember the difference between these two efficiencies: 'productive' is about production costs – operating at the lowest point on the AC curve, where AC = MC. Allocative is about the allocation of resources within the economy: if MC is below price, more resources should be allocateed to this activity.

Grade B (i) Where's the beef?

The beef comes from recognising the implications of a free market economist's desire for a fully efficient economy with maximised productive and allocative efficiency. This requires every market to be perfectly competitive. i.e. price elasticities of infinity and therefore no effective branding, advertising or product differentiation. This implies plain-pack, unbranded, unsophisticated products that hark back to the early 19th century. Is this a world you recognise?

Grade B (ii) How it's shown

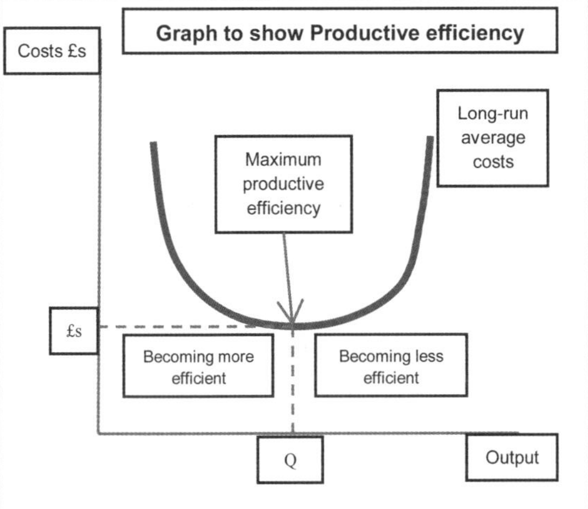

Grade A The other side

This graph looks convincing, but there's nothing great about producing at the lowest cost if customers don't want to buy Q output. This is why it's vital to look at allocative efficiency as well. If there is allocative efficiency, then every consumer's utility is maximised because what they want to buy is available in the shops – and in a perfect world, they can afford to buy it.

Don't ignore the possibility that the best outcome may be away from full productive and allocative efficiency. The Premier League is an example, with its un-market-like equality of TV payments that allows for full-blooded competition between big and small clubs. By over-riding market economics, the Premier League has created a worldwide hit.

Grade A* The critical perspective

Output will be maximised in an economy which has full productive and allocative efficiency – and makes full use of all its land, labour and capital. The problem is that no modern economy is remotely close to that ideal. Even in Singapore markets aren't infinitely perfect. People in Singapore are as enthusiastic about iPhones and luxury handbags as people elsewhere. And where there are brands there are market imperfections.

Exam tip: remember that both these efficiencies are 'static'. Dynamic efficiency is at least as important.

Productive & allocative efficiency: transmission (to top response level)

Chain 1. A firm is productively efficient when it's operating at the lowest point on its long-run average cost curve (1) … but there's no point in this unless people want to buy that number of units (2) … shown on the graph as Q (3) … the point of allocative efficiency where Price = MC (4). So the ideal point for efficiency is the point where allocative and productive efficiencies are maximised. (5)

Chain 2. Productive and allocative efficiencies take a very static view of the world (1) … ignoring, for instance, developments in digital technology (2) … that have the potential to transform firms and whole economies (3). The real world is dynamic (4) … perhaps leaving this theory behind (5).

Types of efficiency – and diagrams

Grade C. Dynamic efficiency. What is it?

Productive and allocative efficiencies take a static view of the business world. Dynamic efficiency considers how well firms manage to handle changing market and technological circumstances – and get themselves from yesterday's optimum point to tomorrow's. If there is perfect dynamic efficiency throughout an economy resources will continuously be allocated efficiently. Dynamic efficiency is helped hugely by investment in capital (e.g. the latest A.I. robots), in human capital (retraining and upskilling) and in Research & Development.

Grade B (i) Where's the beef?

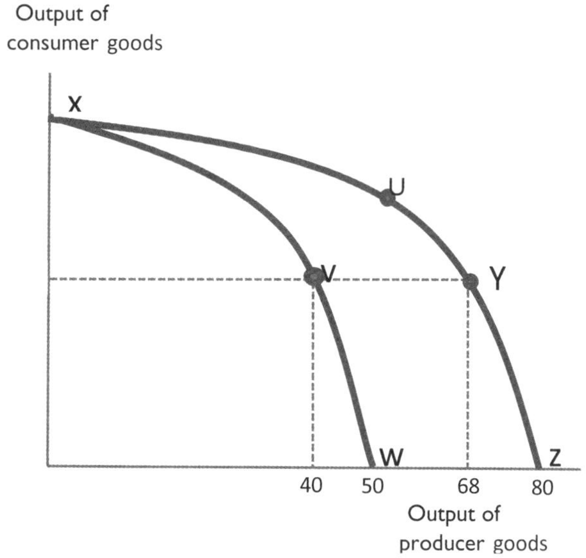

The beef:

This graph shows an economy in transition. Rising production efficiency has changed the opportunity costs between producer and capital goods. If the economy manages to transition from point V to point U or point Y, it is showing dynamic efficiency. And keeping resources fully used. And helping deliver economic growth.

Grade C. X-inefficiency. What is it?

The famous economist Schumpeter wrote a great deal about 'creative destruction' as a key positive force in free market economics. The natural clashes between firms in competition would lead to creative solutions and innovation. More recently, the former boss of Intel (Andy Grove) wrote that 'only the paranoid survive'. X-inefficiency occurs in the absence of such forces. It's the organisational slack that means that another cup of tea seems more important than planning a new initiative. Free market economists have every right to suggest that this is true in many government departments. In fact it's also true in many firms that have a market position that's assumed to be impregnable. Think Nestle with its 54% share and £400m of sales with Nescafe in the UK instant coffee market. Or Wrigley, with a 94% share of the UK market for chewing gum.

Grade B (i) Where's the beef?

The graph on the facing page shows the potential impact of X-inefficiency. It will mean that costs steadily grow above the rate of inflation, forcing the business to impose ever-higher prices on customers. An attempt at a hostile takeover of such a business might jolt it back into action. This might come from a venture capital or private equity fund. In 2017 Kraft bid for the massive multinational Unilever. Unilever fought Kraft off, but introduced a flurry of initiatives soon after.

Do remember the difference between these two terms relating to efficiency: '**dynamic**' is about the ability to change and adapt – and therefore maintain overall allocative efficiency. **X-inefficiency** relates to the effect of complacency on staff, especially managers, in organisations that are largely insulated from competition.

Don't ignore the interactions between the three efficiencies. **Productive** is about minimising costs; **allocative** is about meeting the diffuse needs of every customer and **dynamic** is providing the means to change quickly to meet changing tastes and technologies.

Exam tip: 'X-inefficiency' is a gem for exams. Instead of sounding woolly about big firms' inefficiencies, you sound like an economist. And the point made on the left about Schumpeter, competition and creative destruction would be a glorious supporting argument.

Types of efficiency – and diagrams (ii)

X-inefficiency

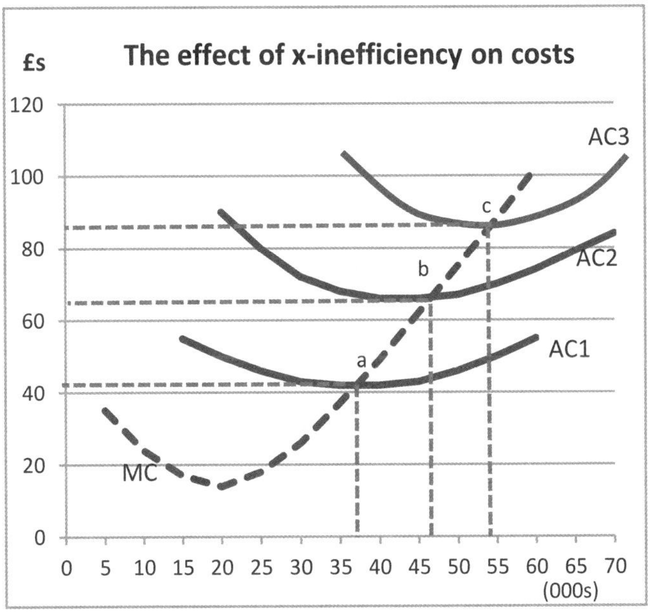

The beef:

This graph shows a firm with average costs of AC1 at the time it became powerful enough for complacency to set in. Within a few years x-inefficiency pushed average costs up to AC2 then AC3. The main cause of the rising costs was hiring more and more managerial staff.

Questions on the diagram

1. From the graph, how do we know that fixed costs are rising rather than variable ones?
2. At which point are total costs approximately £1,550,000? a, b or c?

Exam tip: if there's a Paper 3 question on micro and macro issues in boosting UK economic growth, leap at the chance to write about the 3 efficiencies – and about the threat/constraint of x-inefficiency. Could be a perfect topic.

Answers:

1. If variable costs rose the marginal cost curve would rise. Instead it's just the average cost curves. So it must be fixed costs.
2. At point a the price of £42 yields sales of 37,000 units, i.e. £1,554,000. So it's point a.

Grade A The counter-argument

The counter-argument is that x-inefficiency may be too simplistic a way to look at organisations. It is a convenient way for free marketeers to imply that big corporations and powerful monopolies inevitably self-destruct because of creeping complacency – and therefore no government intervention is needed. In fact the Coca-Cola Corporation has enjoyed No 1 status in cola for more than 125 years in the USA and the UK; any x-inefficiencies have been countered by raw market power. So although x-inefficiency is an important idea, there's a risk that it may be over-used – and used a bit simplistically.

Grade A* The critical perspective

Often in economics a thoughtful student wonders: 'but how could any firm know' the profit maximising output or the equilibrium point? The answer is that firms don't know, but the invisible hand pushes them in the right direction. It's the same here, especially with allocative and dynamic efficiencies. Firms only know when they're not at the right point, because the optimum is unknown. But market forces help point the way, via their classic signalling mechanisms such as price changes.

Efficiency & inefficiency: transmission mechanism (to the top response level)

Chain 1. Kodak was once a huge global corporation, specialising in film for cameras (1). It reacted slowly to the arrival of digital cameras (2) … so global resources were steadily re-allocated towards new giants such as Canon (3) … with Kodak forced to cut staff and close factories to try to survive (4). Kodak had productive and allocative efficiency, but failed due to weak dynamic efficiency (5).

Chain 2. Business leaders know of the risks of x-inefficiency as they look at past collapses of world No 1s such as Kodak and General Motors (1) … hence the quote 'only the paranoid survive' (2). But x-inefficiency is hard to stop because society expects more and more of large businesses (3) … forcing firms such as Facebook to act responsibly rather than entrepreneurially (4)… though the brilliance of firms like Google and Amazon makes it likely that they will prevent creeping x-inefficiency. (5)

Efficiency in different market structures

Grade C. Efficiency in different market structures. What is it?

In a perfectly competitive market, an inefficient firm will find it impossible to survive once the market has found a stable equilibrium. In the graph below, if the market price stays at P_1 this firm's excessive average costs will quickly drain it of any financial reserves, pushing it into liquidation. It needs the dynamic efficiency to re-think its current way of producing to get costs down at least to P_1.

Grade B (i) Where's the beef?

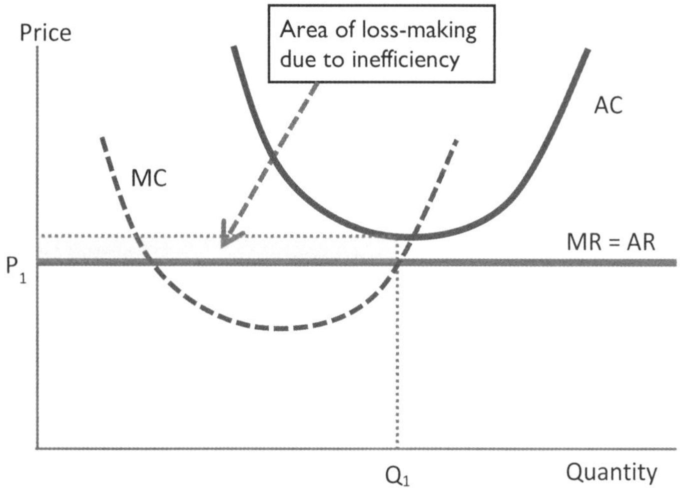

The beef: This graph shows a firm with a profit-maximising point Q1 (where MC = MR) that leaves average costs above average revenue. This means a permanent loss-making position, unless it can find a solution.

Grade B (ii) Why it matters

The market structure matters hugely when considering efficiency and inefficiency. Theory would suggest that a business in perfect competition will have to find and operate at its point of maximum productive efficiency to survive in the long-run. At the other end of the spectrum of market structures, a pure monopolist will have huge internal pressures towards x-inefficiency. Managers will always be pressing for bigger expense accounts and larger budgets.

Grade A The counter-argument

Economic and business events of the past ten or so years have proven that pure faith in market theory is doomed to disappointment. People matter, and people get in the way of theory. X-inefficiency doesn't always undermine the prospects of dominant firms; clever managers can prevent this from happening. So don't take the theory for granted; question it – and always question fatalism in economics.

Do remember the main market structures. For a firm in **perfect** or **monopolistic competition**, constant threat from competitors should keep x-inefficiency at bay. But barriers to entry for **oligopoly** and **monopoly** firms create the perfect conditions for x-inefficiencies to creep up.

Don't get caught up in the fatalism that can surround economic theory. Market forces are powerful, but that doesn't mean people should lie back and accept their fate. Entrepreneurs such as Jeff Bezos and Elon Musk move markets.

Exam tip: think hard about the competitive environment of the firm featured in the exam paper. Is competition so fierce that x-inefficiencies are unlikely or even impossible?

Efficiency in different markets: transmission mechanism (to top response level)

Chain 1. Allocative efficiency is difficult in fast-moving markets such as fashion (1). In 2018 Burberry admitted burning £28 million of unwanted stock (2) ... in a rare example of the effects of mis-allocated resources (3). If a firm understands market tastes and trends (4) ... such waste wouldn't occur. (5)

Chain 2. For the UK to maximise its output (1) … every firm should be operating at its optimum productive and allocative efficiency (2) … backed by the right responses to change in order to maximise dynamic efficiency (3). Free market economists say this can only happen if firms are small and markets are free (4). But it's still asking a huge amount of any economic system (5).

Characteristics of perfect competition

Grade C. What is it?

The characteristics of perfect competition start with a homogenous product. This means a product with no scope for differentiation such as a kilo of white flour. Other key characteristics are: many buyers and sellers, therefore no-one has the power to influence the price; freedom of entry and exit to and from the industry; and perfect knowledge on the part of all buyer and sellers (see **Do**).

Grade B (i) Where's the beef?

Perfect competition is full of beef, most importantly in the notion of 'price takers'. Unilever decides on the price of Marmite, but firms in perfectly competitive markets have to accept the market price. As I write this, the world commodity price for gold is $1,320 per ounce. If a trader tried to sell to a jeweller at $1,350 per ounce – no deal. Because one ounce of pure gold is the same as any other (homogenous) the market determines the price. Ultimately, businesses have two things to control: price and costs; to lose control of one is a scary thought.

Grade B (ii) Why it matters

These characteristics matter because they show the key assumptions that underlie every exam question about perfect competition. When the examiner says 'Firm A operates in a perfectly competitive market ...' she or he is also telling you that all these things can be assumed as a fact: homogenous goods, many buyers and sellers, free entry and exit, that every firm in the market is a price taker (and, as you can infer from the last point, price elasticities must be infinitely high). This provides huge scope for written analysis.

Grade A The counter-argument

Many students feel very unhappy about having to base a lot of analysis on such a strangely implausible market structure as perfect competition. Give me examples, they shout, but there are few that fully fit the bill. Even some that economists assumed to be perfectly competitive, such as the foreign exchange and money markets, were revealed in the 2009 financial crisis to be rigged by the banks. But economics builds models to test out theory, and perfect competition is just such a model. The lack of examples doesn't alter its value in the theory of the subject.

Grade A* The critical perspective

Although the key characteristics of perfect competition have been known for many years, the arrival of the internet has given the theory a huge lease of life. 'Perfect information' was a bizarre concept before the web, whereas now one can instantly find firms offering niche products from round the world – all with clear price information. The real world has caught up with economic theory.

Do be clear about the importance of perfect information. Signalling only works if companies can see the signals, such as a company cutting prices on the other side of town. And for consumers, they'll go on paying full price for electricity if they don't know there's a new, cheaper supplier.

Don't ignore the importance of free entry and exit. It's a very specific condition. In how many markets can there be *no* barrier to entry? Starting almost any business requires capital – and that's immediately a barrier to entry.

Exam tip: treat a perfectly competitive market as an interesting theory, but be wary of saying such-and-such a market <u>is</u> perfectly competitive. It's safer to say it shows some of the characteristics of a perfectly competitive market.

Perfect competition (i): transmission mechanism (to top response level)

Chain 1. If I hire a stall in Croydon market and start selling fruit and veg this Saturday (1) ... I'll be close to a situation of perfect competition (2). Barriers to entry are near-zero and my strawberries and cabbages will be like any others (3) ... and anyone can walk along the whole market to get perfect information (4). Unfortunately this market is declining, so there aren't many buyers and sellers (5).

Chain 2. If the market is perfectly competitive (1) ... all firms are price takers (2) ... meaning they all have the same, horizontal demand curves (3). This means that a price increase by one firm would lead to an absolute collapse in demand (4) ... proving that the price elasticity is infinitely high (5).

Diagrams of perfect competition

Grade C. Perfect competition diagrams. What are they?

Perfect competition diagrams of a firm share one important characteristic: because the firms are price-takers, the demand curve is a horizontal line. This line might be labelled AR = MR. Average revenue is the price, which is constant because the firm is a price-taker; marginal revenue is constant for the same reason. The diagram below shows an unstable position for a firm, because it's making large supernormal profits. Happiness, but short-lived given no barriers to entry.

Grade B (i) Where's the beef?

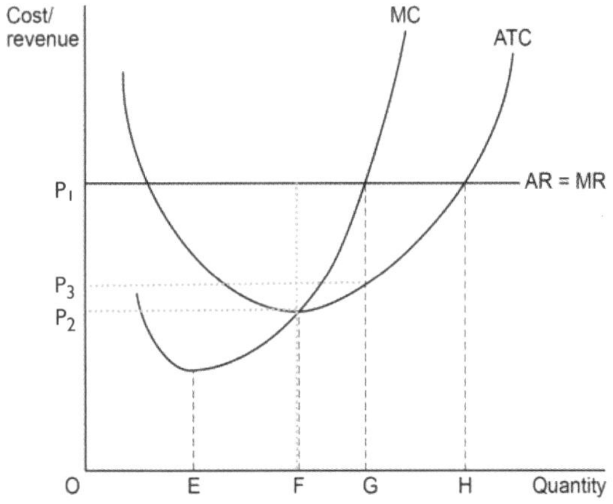

Answer these questions:

1. Which letter shows the quantity of output at which profits are maximised?
2. Does this diagram show the firm's long-run or short-run position? Briefly explain your answer.
3. How would you calculate the supernormal profits being made by this firm?
4. In the near future how are things likely to change in this market?

Grade B (ii) Relating the firm to the market

The diagram below shows the relationship between a firm in a perfectly competitive market – and the market itself. Figure A shows a firm in a short-run position of supernormal profit (AR exceeds AC). These profits attract new entrants to the market (Figure B) so supply shifts rightwards from S1 to S2 pushing the equilibrium supply quantity to Q2. As the supply rises, the equilibrium price is pulled down from P1 to P2 – eroding away the supernormal profit. Now the firm is in a stable, long-run equilibrium – making normal profit only.

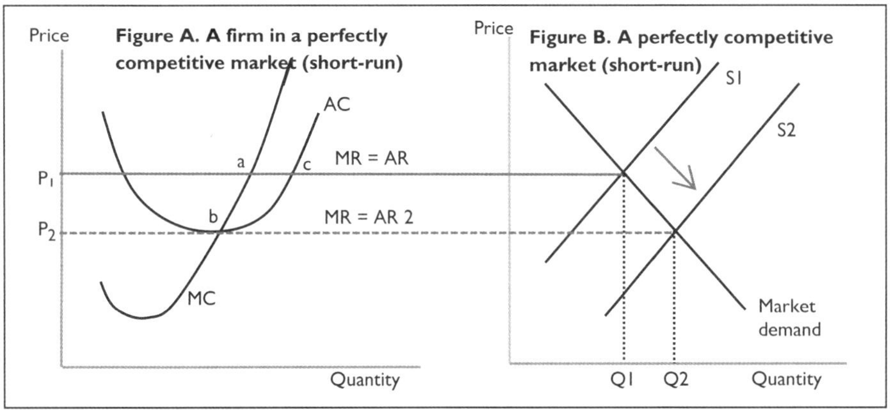

Grade B (iii) Questions on Figures A and B. (Answers on facing page)

5. Explain why commercial secrecy would be important for a firm in the position shown in Figure A.

6. With reference to Figure A, explain how you would show the firm's loss of revenue when new market entrants push the market supply curve from S1 to S2.

Do remember the standard facts about all diagrams of a firm in a competitive market:
1. The demand curve is horizontal (it's a price-taker)
2. MC cuts AC at its lowest point
3. For a stable long-run equilibrium position, the AC curve sits on the horizontal demand curve (see Figure 3 on the facing page).

Answers to Qs 1-4
1. G (where MC = MR)
2. It's short-run because it can't be sustained in the long-term (new competitors will be attracted in by the supernormal profits)
3. (P1-P3) x G OR (same thing): (P1-P3)x(G-0)
4. New entrants will be drawn in, pushing supply up and the market price down – so AR/MR will fall until supernormal profits are eroded.

Exam tip:
Practice the diagram on the left, with its connection of two graphs – the firm and its marketplace. It shows off a lot of economics – and has a naturally dynamic narrative as you explain how market changes affect the individual firm.

Diagrams of perfect competition (ii)

Grade B (iv) A firm in a stable long-run equilibrium

Figure 3 below shows a price-taker in a stable position where, as long as no changes happen in the market as a whole, it can continue in business. All it's making is normal profit, which provides an adequate reward to the providers of the firm's capital – but no more than that. So there's no reason why new entrants would bother with this market.

Figure 3: firm in stable long-run equilibrium

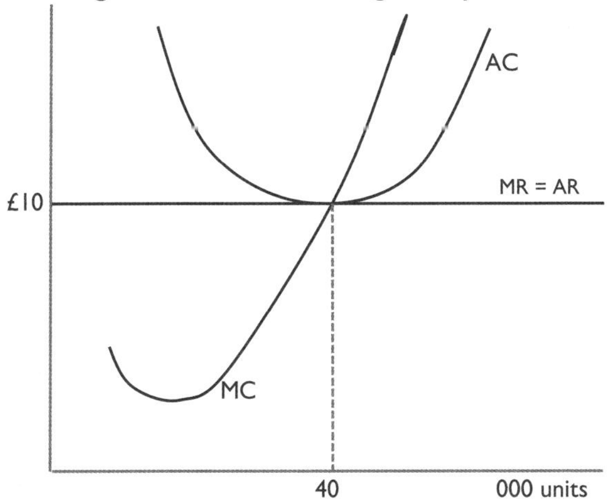

Answer these questions:

7. Calculate this firm's total revenue

8. Calculate the firm's total costs

9. Briefly explain why this firm might continue to operate in the long-run.

10. Explain what would happen to the MC and AC curves if there was a price increase on a key raw material.

Do recognise the importance of the internet in discussions of perfectly competitive markets. Price transparency has never been greater than today, forcing supermarkets to keep competitive to avoid losing market share. No-one would say the grocery market is perfectly compet-itive – but it's been pulled in that direction by online shopping and price transparency.

Grade B (v) Loss-making in a perfectly competitive market

The diagram below shows a firm in a loss-making short-run equilibrium. It won't be able to sustain this for long. Figure C shows the current position where MR = AR 1 and therefore point a is the equilibrium for the firm and the market as a whole. The losses (AC > AR) force suppliers out of the market, so Figure D shows the supply curve shifting leftwards from S1 to S2. This pushes the market equilibrium supply quantity to Q2. As the supply falls, the equilibrium price rises from P1 to P2. Now the firm is in a stable, long-run equilibrium at point b.

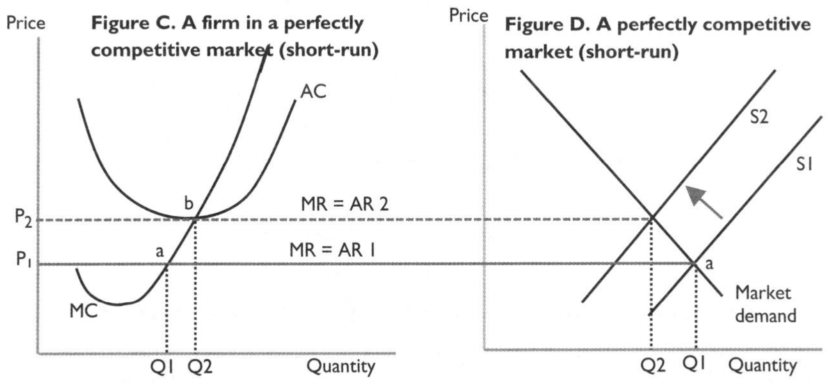

Answers

5. To prevent other firms realis-ing how much supernormal profit is made in this market.

6. Revenue was P1 x the quantity at point a; now it's P2 x the quantity at point b.

7. £40,000

8. £40,000

9. Because normal profit includes managers' pay plus dividends to shareholders. No-one's getting rich but everyone's getting paid.

10. Both the MC and AC curves would shift upwards.

Perfect competition diagrams: transmission mechanism (to top response level)

Chain. If a new firm sees an opportunity to enter a perfectly competitive market (1) … it can do so without affecting market equilibrium (2) … because its supply is insignificant among so many buyers and sellers (3). But if lots of firms are attracted in, market supply increases enough to shift the supply curve to the right (4) … pushing the equilibrium price down – discouraging more market entrants (5).

Characteristics of monopolistic competition

Grade C. What is it?

Monopolistic competition exists when a product or brand has the edge over rivals that gives it clear differentiation. This reduces its price elasticity and therefore gives some freedom to push prices up. But whereas a monopoly would have barriers to entry that would secure that differentiation in the long-run, a monopolistically competitive product has no such barriers. Therefore the product or image 'edge' gets eroded over time as new entrants come into the market.

Grade B (i) Where's the beef?

The beef lies in the implications of the definition given above. These are that a firm in monopolistic competition can enjoy supernormal profits in the short-run, but not the long-run. This argument has an unstated ceteris paribus assumption built in. In other words: 'ceteris paribus, a firm in monopolistic competition enjoys supernormal profits in the short-run only'. Needless to say, managers at these firms work hard to overcome ceteris paribus. They don't wait for competitors to catch up, they have 'new, improved' products and do clever things with advertising.

Grade B (ii) Why it matters

Polo Mints were launched in 1948 and today's sales of £25 million represent 2.5% of the UK market for sugar confectionery. And, no doubt, huge supernormal profits. With a 2.5% market share it's clearly in monopolistic competition, for can 70+ years really be considered the short run? Polo calls into question the theory that a small brand's differentiation will inevitably be eroded by competition.

Grade A The counter-argument

Economists are inclined to build micro theories as if perfect competition is the norm. Monopolistic competition is presented as a temporary phenomenon, because the ability to exploit the consumer is only short-run. Soon enough, by implication, competition will demolish producers' supernormal profits. But if you go to Tesco, you'll see a series of shelves with brands that have been around for years. Can you see a series of perfectly competitive markets or monopolistically competitive ones? There's a case for saying it's more the latter than the former.

Grade A* The critical perspective

A fair criticism of economics is that it's been too fixated on theory and too little interested in evidence. That is changing in some ways, as behavioural economics tests how consumers actually behave, rather than simply assuming rationality. But with monopolistic competition, perhaps there should be more research into the actual long-term pricing power of brands, rather than assuming the power erodes.

Do see that firms in monopolistic competition have huge, but interesting challenges. If their supernormal profits are eroded in the short run, they must use innovation, ingenuity and clever new product ideas to find new brands to replace those that have lost their supernormal edge.

Don't forget the long-lasting power of some brands in monopolistic competition. Ferrero Rocher was launched in 1982 and has just 1.75% UK market share. But that's £65 million of very profitable sales.

Exam tip: like any model, monopolistic competition can be called a simplification of a complex world. Be willing to question that simplification, as some brands will inevitably be near-oligopolies. Categorising is never simple.

Monopolistic competition: transmission mechanism (to top response level)

Chain 1. Some brands have a period of super-profitable success (1) ... but are then caught up by supermarket own-label imitations or new rival brands (2) … perhaps ending up being sold 4-for-£1 in Poundland (3). A classic of short-run supernormal profits (4) ... turning into long-run normality (5).

Chain 2. Faced with a brand success such as Lindt Lindor (1) … with more than £100 million of UK sales a year (2) … of which a substantial amount would be supernormal profit (3) ... Swiss-owned Lindt will engage highly-paid staff to keep this brand relevant and loved in the future (4) … to keep those supernormal profits coming for decades to come. Isn't that the long-run? (5).

Diagrams of monopolistic competition

Grade C. What is it?

Monopolistic competition diagrams have downward-sloping demand curves. The typical monopolistically competitive product is a brand with a limited market share within a market such as grocery or fashion retail. Even though price elasticities might be quite high, each brand may be sufficiently distinctive to set its own prices for its own products, e.g. a new, fashionable coat from ASOS. The graph below shows that coat soon after its launch, before rivals copy the product, and while it's able to generate some supernormal profit. According to economic theory, this will only occur in the short-run; in the long-run the supernormal profit will be eroded away.

Grade B (i) Where's the beef?

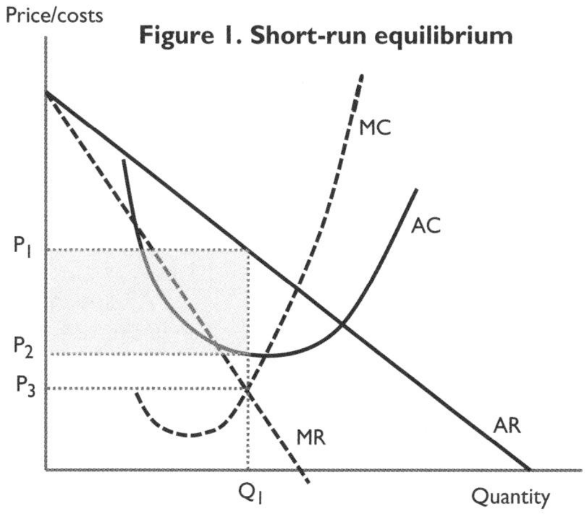

Figure 1. Short-run equilibrium

P_2

The graph shows the profit maximising output as Q1. This is where MC = MR. At this output level the firm is charging P_1 for its brand – and generating a large supernormal profit that can be calculated as (P1 – P2) x Q1. It is shown as a lightly shaded area.

A classic exam mistake would be to take P3 as the equilibrium price. In fact it signifies nothing.

Grade B (ii) Why it matters

The job of an examiner is to find out what you can do with what you know. So exams need you to understand theory rather than simply memorise it. The questions below are a fair example, as they require you to think quite widely about your economics, rather than simply testing what you know about this topic. As explained at the top of the facing page, the key to understanding monopolistic competition is to understand what an economist means by short-run and long-run.

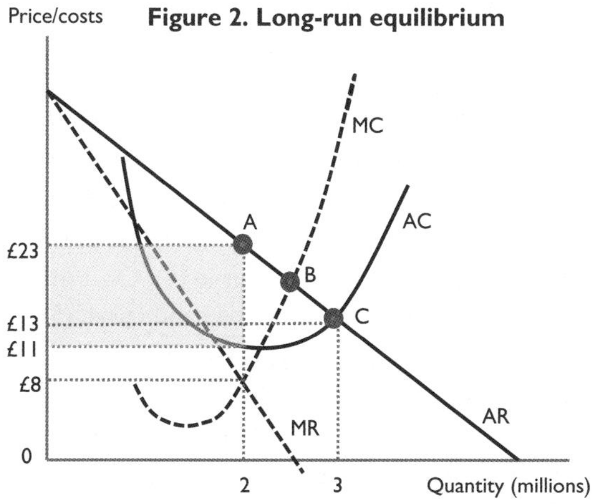

Figure 2. Long-run equilibrium

Questions

1. Calculate this firm's total costs when it's selling 2 million units.

2. What business objective is fulfilled at point C?

3. Calculate the % effect on the firm's revenue of moving from point A to point C.

4. Calculate the effect on the firm's supernormal profit of moving from point A to point C.

Do remember that in all markets other than perfect competition, the AR line is downward-sloping and the MR curve bisects the horizontal distance between zero and the revenue curve. When drawing the MR curve it's sensible to draw it going below 0 on the horizontal axis.

Don't forget that the single biggest difference between a monopolistically competitive firm and an oligopolist is that the former has no barriers to entry to protect it from competition. So whereas an oligopolist can retain its supernormal profits in the long term, the monopolistically competitive firm cannot.

Answers to Qs 1-4

1. 2 million x £11 = £22m.
2. Sales maximisation
3. At point A it's 2m x £23 = £46m At point C it's 3m x £13 = £39m. So the effect is -£7m/£46m x 100 = *minus* 15.2%
4. At point A it was 2m x £12 = £24m; now it's zero. So it's a fall of £24m.

Diagrams of monopolistic competition (ii)

Grade B (iii) Where's the beef (ii)?

P2

Figure 3. Long-run equilibrium

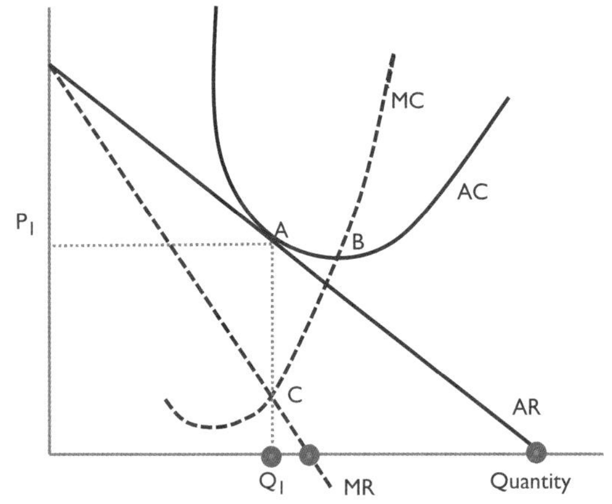

The graph shows the long-run position of a firm in monopolistic competition. It still has brands with a degree of differentiation, but they are having to compete so strongly (spending lots on advertising, perhaps) that AC has risen to be touching AR. So supernormal profits are no more. The profit maximising output is Q1, but point A shows that profits are normal-only at this point.

Questions on Figure 3

1. Briefly explain the economic significance of what's happening at point:

1.1 A

1.2 B

1.3 C

2. For marginal revenue to become negative when price (AR) is falling, does that mean the elasticity of demand is price elastic or inelastic?

Grade A The counter-argument

The counter to all this graphical theory is that the short-run, long-run distinction works very well for some, probably weaker brands. They have a degree of distinctiveness – but it's eroded over time by competition. The supernormal profits are over. But the theory falls down in the face of lots of day-to-day examples in which small brands keep hold of their niche market share for generations. Mum loves her Honda Jazz, around for decades in the UK, even though its market share is less than 1%. If a brand can hold on to super-normal profits for generations, there needs to be a more sophisticated theory than short-run/long-run.

Grade A* Critical perspective

Most of business activity in a developed economy takes place in conditions approximately like monopolistic competition. Established businesses and brands will have worked to establish some barriers to entry, but they aren't sufficient to keep out an enthusiastic new entrepreneur. Nor can they resist disruptive change such as Uber's effect on traditional taxis and cabs. So these firms have some market power, but nothing like the power of an oligopolist. Yet economics seems relatively uninterested in this market structure compared with perfect competition and oligopoly. This seems strange.

Answers to Qs 1-4

1.1 At point A AC and AR are equal so profits are normal only.

1.2 At point B MC is cutting AC at its lowest point – as it has to do

1.3 At point C MC = MR so output is at its profit-maximising point.

2. Price elasticity is high if a price cut makes revenue rise, so falling MR suggests the lower portion of the AR curve is price inelastic (cut price, falling revenue).

Monopolistic competition: transmission mechanism (to top response level)

Chain 1. Some brands are fashionable and have market power making them monopolistically competitive (1) … but over time this can be lost as the product slides into becoming a commodity (2). This may lead to the situation shown in Figure 3, where no supernormal profits are made, but there's still some element of pricing power (3) … hence the downward-sloping demand curve (4). Or it may so slip into commodity status that it ends up being a price-taker with a horizontal demand curve (5).

Chain 2. Facebook started with the motto 'Move fast and break things' … the perfect slogan for a monopolistic competitor (1) … that keeps moving to stop rivals from catching up (2). The growth of the business means it's now a monopolist (3) ... with huge barriers to entry based on the network benefits of its scale (4). It certainly never got to the point of giving up its super-normal profit. (5)

Characteristics of oligopoly

Grade C. What is it?

Oligopoly is competition between the few. For example the UK instant coffee market is dominated by two firms, while the markets for both chocolate and bread are dominated by three. In an oligopolistic market products are usually differentiated, partly by branding and advertising. And there are significant barriers to entry, as in the case of Boeing and Airbus – the two aircraft-makers that have a near-100% of the global market for large passenger planes. In an oligopoly, the few firms will be interdependent, meaning every action affects their rivals – so they rarely act without thinking how the others will react.

Grade B (i) Where's the beef?

The beef lies in the word 'interdependence'. My actions affect you and your actions. This affects the decision-making of every oligopolistic firm, from pricing through to promotions and product development – but even more importantly, it creates a huge temptation to collude. This topic is covered fully in the following page. Interdependence is a striking feature of oligopoly because it is not possible within the other market structures. In a perfectly competitive market no one firm is big enough to affect others; in a monopolistically competitive market there is differentiation, but again market shares are too small for one firm to affect others; and in monopoly, there is only one firm!

Grade B (ii) Why it matters

Oligopolies matter because their interdependence gives scope for a great deal of government activity. Many oligopolies have regulators such as the energy industry's Ofgem. And many attract the interest of the Competition and Markets Authority (CMA), which wants to check whether competition is effective within the industry and whether cartel or other collusive practices are taking place. This makes oligopolies a battle ground between free marketeers who mistrust government involvement and those who believe intervention can help competition.

Grade A The counter-argument

Perhaps oligopoly is not the problem; perhaps it's the consumer. Consumers can be lazy about finding the best deals and therefore putting pressure on firms to compete actively. Hence government support for financial literacy in schools.

Grade A* The critical perspective

Oligopolies stand out because big firms create headlines. Yes they may have a significant amount of market power, but countervailing action by government protects the consumer interests. The balance of power seems quite benign.

Do remember what is meant by n-firm calculation ratios, e.g. the top 3 UK chocolate companies have 71% of the market between them. This is a useful way to measure oligopoly power. By contrast the top 3 in UK soft drinks (led by Coca-Cola) have a much weaker 45% market share.

Don't under-estimate the term 'differentiation'. It can be the result of real consumer benefits, such as great design or exceptional quality standards. Or can be purely due to consumer perceptions, such as a trendy image or celeb backing.

Exam tip: just about every micro exam features oligopoly as a major element of the stimulus material and questions. And at the heart of oligopoly is interdependence. Get familiar with this term.

Characteristics of oligopoly: transmission mechanism (to top response level)

Chain 1. For a firm such as Mars – part of the UK's chocolate oligopoly (1) ... it would be reckless to cut prices sharply (2) ... as that will spark a price war with Cadbury and Nestle (3) ... which will keep revenues largely unchanged, but hit profits hard (4). Oligopolists hate price wars (5).

Chain 2. When the 'Big 6' energy companies pushed gas and electricity prices up faster than inflation (1) ... the government and regulator Ofgem intervened (2) ... by placing a cap on energy prices (3) ... to attempt to create a better balance between the interests of consumers and producers (4) ... but at the risk of discouraging new firms from entering a profit-capped market (5).

Collusion and cartels

Grade C. What is it?

Collusion occurs when firms act together with others, such as when setting prices or deciding on new technologies. Collusion can be overt, meaning to make a deal with a supposed rival (which is illegal) or tacit, meaning to try to achieve the same result, but by nods, winks and careful thought about how to influence a rival. A cartel is an extreme form of overt collusion, where firms get together to agree prices and production (supply) volumes. A cartel arrangement is always illegal.

Do bear in mind the term 'price leadership'. An oligopoly might be dominated by one business, as Cadbury dominates the UK chocolate market. The market leader may adopt the role of price leader, with its annual price increases triggering rivals to push their prices up in step. This could be done in an overt or tacit manner.

Grade B (i) Where's the beef?

The beef is the distinction between overt and tacit collusion. Overt is fairly obvious, based on direct communication between rivals – by word or by email doesn't matter. Overt collusion often takes place in a bar at the end of the working day – but is still illegal. Tacit is more subtle. The boss of Airbus once said publically that he was happy with the company's 50% market share. Duopoly partner Boeing could draw the conclusion that price battles between the companies could ease off if Airbus wanted no extra market share. That's an example of tacit collusion.

Grade B (ii) Why it matters

Collusion and cartels matter because they are a conspiracy against the consumer. They are an illegitimate attempt to convert consumer surplus into producer surplus. This is wrong in itself, but also may damage the living standards of certain consumers. For example, less affluent older people may spend a significant proportion of their income on heating. A cartel among energy companies might mean sufficiently higher energy bills as to cause significant distress to this group.

Don't assume that all collaboration is collusion. Jaguar Land Rover and BMW have an agreement to work together on research into electric cars. That's legal and potentially of benefit to consumers and the planet.

Grade A The counter-argument

It is easy to underestimate the ingenuity of entrepreneurs and the speed with which markets can be disrupted. Today's complacent, rich oligopolist can quite quickly be overtaken – and forced to struggle to survive. Of America's famous 'Big 3' car companies, two collapsed in 2009 with the third, Ford, lucky to survive. So market forces can make a serious dent in oligopoly positions – if governments stand back and let the free market work its magic.

Exam tip: if the exam text mentions a fine, evaluate its size and importance in relation to the finances of the company in question.

Grade A* The critical perspective

As shown above, a strong case can be made for or against government action against collusive behaviour. In reality, the arguments depend on the example being chosen. Where groups of consumers can suffer serious harm (older energy users) there's a clear case for government action. In other cases there may not be.

Collusion and cartels: transmission mechanism (to get to top response level)

Chain 1. The term oligopoly can be awkwardly broad (1). In duopolies there are two dominant firms but the term oligopoly is used for 6 energy firms (2) … and even the 10+ global car giants (3). Tacit collusion is much easier with two or may be three participants (4) … whereas overt methods may be the only way to keep ten or more companies acting together within a cartel (5).

Chain 2. Overt collusion in pharmaceuticals has involved one firm paying a rival to stop producing a drug (1) … turning a duopoly into a very profitable monopoly (2) … with price increases to the NHS of 500%+ (3). This hit to NHS budgets (4) … would have damaged the health prospects of many (5).

Oligopoly diagram

Grade C. What is it?

The oligopoly diagram shown below shows the area of supernormal profit that could be expected in the short-run by a firm in monopolistic competition, and in the long run by a monopolist (P1,X,Y,P2). If the oligopoly is based on a 3-firm concentration ratio of near 100% (such as games consoles: Sony PS4, Microsoft Xbox One and Nintendo Switch), the oligopolists would want to capture the full supernormal profit – split 3 ways, as indicated by letters A, B and C. To achieve this would probably require collusion, i.e. the three companies acting in concert with each other. As long as that collusion is tacit, it is perfectly legal.

Do remember that competition still exists among (most) oligopolists, but constrained by interdependence. The most obvious types of competition would be minor innovations such as new brands and flavours – and responses to consumer change, e.g. the trend towards plant-based foods.

Grade B (i) Where's the beef?

Figure 1.
Oligopolists share supernormal profit

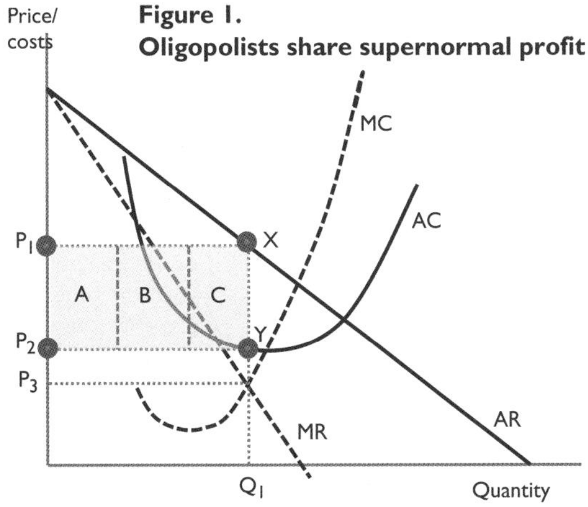

The graph shows the profit maximising output as Q1. This is where MC = MR. At this output level the firm is charging P_1 for its brand – and generating a large supernormal profit that can be calculated as (P1 – P2) x Q1. It is shown as a lightly shaded area.

The easiest way for oligopolists to maximise their own profits is to share that supernormal profit.

Don't worry about the complexity of the diagram shown. The basic diagram for monopoly, oligopoly and monopolistic competition is the same. So as long as you grasp it, it's not hard to add tweaks such as dividing up supernormal profit.

Grade B (ii) Why it matters

The diagram gives a clear idea of the potential benefits of being an oligopolist (long-run supernormal profits) and also shows the huge temptation to collude. If each of three rivals were to spend much more heavily on advertising and promotion, their AC curves would rise, squeezing the supernormal profit rectangle. Cleverer by far for one firm to tell the media their advertising budget will rise by 2% in the coming year, and for the other two to copy that approach.

Exam tip
In an exam, draw this diagram on a big scale, otherwise the labelling becomes a fiddly nightmare. Never worry about how much of the exam board's paper you're using.

Grade A The critical perspective

When there's such a temptation to collude it requires clever government action to combat this. Years' ago, the rules and the fines were too small to have much of a deterrent effect. Today, though, the UK follows the EU's approach of fines worth up to 10% of a company's global turnover. The EU's biggest fine to date is €2.93 billion for 6 price-fixing European truckmakers. Now that's a deterrent.

Oligopoly diagram: transmission mechanism (to top response level)

Chain 1. The diagram shows why oligopolists collude (1) … but not *how* they do so (2). Most will act in a covert way, because that's within the law (3). It mainly consists of making decisions that you know are unlikely to offend your rivals (4) … confident that they'll take the hint and do the same for you. (5)

Chain 2. In 2019 Boeing's best-selling new plane was grounded for months due to safety concerns after two disastrous crashes (1). Big rival Airbus did all it could *not* to exploit this position (2) … as it knew its long-term interests were served by preserving the duopoly (3) ... rather than forcing Boeing to retaliate when its planes were back in service (4). A classic of oligopoly interdependence (5).

Game theory and the prisoners' dilemma

Grade C. What is it?

One development from the idea of interdependence is game theory. This is an attempt to look in a quantified, objective way at the impact of interdependence on decision making. Game theory is a structured way of asking: 'if we do this, what will they do? And if they do that, what's the effect on us?' The process works best when there are just two players and two options, i.e. it works for a duopoly (just two dominant firms). The best-known example of game theory is the prisoner's dilemma.

Grade B (i) Where's the beef?

Edexcel has identified a single example of game theory: the prisoners' dilemma. Two robbers have been caught and are kept apart, in separate interview rooms. Both are told that if both confess they'll get 5 years each. If one pleads guilty while the other confesses, the guilty one gets 10 years, while the 'pleader' gets away free. If neither confesses they'll get 1 year each. What would *you* do? In theory the logical answer is for both to confess, in preference for either 0 or 5 years instead of either 1 or 10. The conclusion that can be drawn is that the best outcome when the robbers can't collude (5 years each) is worse than when they do collude (1 year each). This is the imperative: to collude if possible.

Grade B (ii) Why it matters

Game theory can help analyse the impact of a decision on fellow oligopolists. If we put our prices up by 5%, what will our rivals do? Will they match our price rise (yes please) or will they hold their prices down, to enjoy rising market share as our customers switch to cheaper alternatives? Game theory tends to predict that oligopolists are best off keeping prices unchanged.

Grade A The counter-argument

The main argument against 2-firm (duopoly) game theory in that it's unnecessary. You only need game theory if there's no collusion, yet game theory rightly says it's better to collude. For decades, Sony and Microsoft have had a duopoly of serious console gaming. Note the launch dates for the 5 Playstation models: 1994, 2000, 2006, 2013, 2020 (PS5 expected). Sony and Microsoft have effectively collaborated on a profitable launch schedule – every 6/7 years. Don't play games – collude!

Grade A* The critical perspective

Despite the counter-argument game theory has proved successful in modelling certain oligopoly market situations, such as the bidding process for 3G phone licences (it raised £22.5 billion for the UK government). As with many economic theories, game theory has its moments, even if it's not needed all the time.

Do remember the term 'Nash equilibrium'. Mathematician John Nash formulated the idea that individual decisions would end up with a situation in which neither side is able to improve its position. That situation is called the Nash equilibrium.

Don't forget that the prisoners' dilemma is based on ignorance of what the other player/prisoner is doing. In business a firm can see what rivals are doing – and how others are responding – so the prisoner example may not be that relevant.

Exam tip: make sure to lace your answers on game theory with references to interdependence together with ceteris paribus – because game theory assumes all variables are held constant apart from those being 'gamed'.

Game theory: transmission mechanism (to get to the top response level)

Chain 1. When an oligopolist considers a price rise (1) … it may model the likely responses by key rivals (2) … to get prepared for their response (3). A speedy response to their response could stop them from securing any advantage (4) … enabling you to enjoy higher profits from higher prices (5).

Chain 2. Game theory and the prisoners' dilemma may sound a bit childish (1) … but Directors do spend time thinking a bit like chess game (2) … if I take this, they'll take that … (3) ... so modelling markets is a reality for many (4) … even though collusion may be even more effective (5).

The kinked demand curve model

Grade C. What is it?

One theory that illustrates the interdependence of firms in oligopoly markets is the kinked demand curve. In effect, this model dismantles a standard aspect of price elasticity theory – 'ceteris paribus', or let other things be equal. This theory assumes that rival firms in an oligopoly will behave differently when faced with a price rise than when faced with a price cut.

Do remember that the kinked demand curve suggests that oligopoly is a stable market structure with stable prices. This implies a benign situation for consumers. Recent anger over the price of gas and electricity make this hard to recognise.

Grade B (i) Where's the beef?

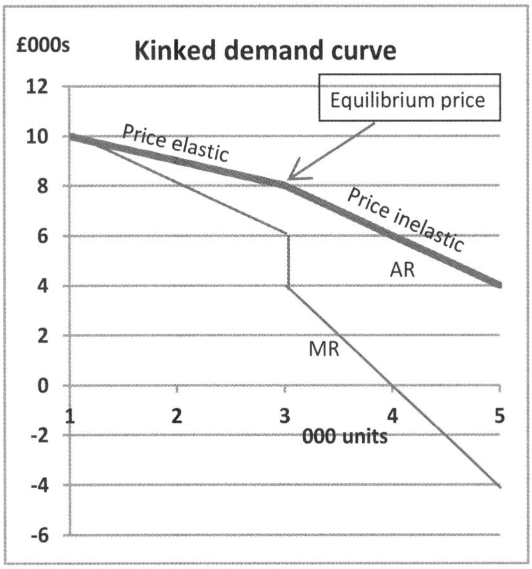

The kinked demand curve model suggests that prices hold stable in oligopoly markets because price rises meet elastic demand while price cuts face price inelastic demand. When one firm pushes its prices up, rivals hold back, enjoying rising market share – at the cost of the firm that moved first. Whereas a price cut forces an immediate response from rivals, leading to a mini or full-scale price war.

The theory says you lose out whichever price change you make – so it's better to do nothing.

Don't forget that the kinked demand curve still allows for the possibility of price wars, though implicitly it would be irrational for a business to start one. If price elasticity is high when prices are cut, the impact of a price war on profit would inevitably be bad.

Grade B (ii) Why it matters

It matters because the theory uses questionable assumptions to lead towards the conclusion that oligopolies are harmless: prices stay stable and implicitly consumers are well served. UK energy/utility customers might dispute this.

Grade A The counter-argument

The main argument against kinked-demand theory is that it is based on an odd assumption. It assumes that if one UK electricity firm pushes its prices up, rivals **won't** follow. Please show me an example! Firms usually make more profit by selling fewer units at higher prices. So a price rise by one will be followed by others.

Exam tip: make sure to lace your answers on oligopoly with references to interdependence together with ceteris paribus – because kinked demand theory is based on some unusual – and questionable - assumptions.

Grade A* The critical perspective

The kinked demand curve theory is 80 years' old, remains in text books, yet has in no sense been proven. The only conditions in which it would be plausible are in commodity oligopolies such as the OPEC cartel. In most modern oligopolies, such as the supply of electricity or chocolate, price rises by one are copied by rivals.

Kinked demand theory: transmission mechanism (to get the top response level)

Chain 1. When an oligopolist considers a price rise (1) … it will model the likely responses by key rivals (2). Kinked-demand theory assumes rivals will keep prices down (3) ... to win market share (4) … but ignores the attraction to firms of higher profit margins due to higher selling prices (5).

Chain 2. The theory is helpful in warning about the risks of price-cutting (1). If one oligopolist cuts prices others may well cut theirs (2) … which would be great for consumers (3) ... but awful for the firms and their shareholders (4) Most large firms regard price cutting as a dreadful last-resort (5).

Types of price competition

Grade C. What is it?

In micro-economics the standard assumption is that pricing decisions target the objective of profit maximisation. But there are exceptions. For oligopolies, there are three circumstances in which prices may fall below the profit maximising point. One, known as **limit pricing**, is when an oligopolist (or monopolist) chooses to price below its profit maximising point in order to limit the attractiveness of the market and therefore discourage new entrants. This might be wise if the oligopolist is worried the barriers to entry are weakening, e.g. patents are about to run out. Two other possibilities are **predatory pricing** and **price wars.**

Predatory pricing means pricing to kill: pricing low with the intention of driving a rival out of the market, and perhaps out of business. This could only be attempted by a wealthy firm attacking a smaller, weaker one.

Grade B (i) Where's the beef?

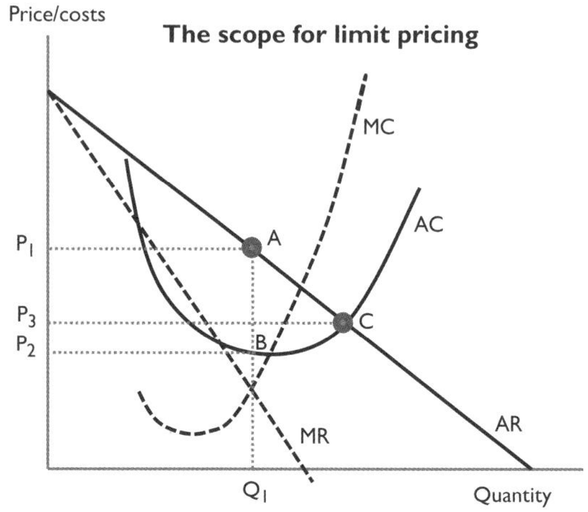

The graph shows the profit maximising output as Q1. The oligopolist is charging P_1 and generating a supernormal profit that can be calculated as (P1 – P2) x Q1.

If it is concerned about new entrants it could choose to limit its price to anywhere between P1 and P3. At P3 it would make zero super-normal profit because AC = AR. So perhaps half way between P1 and P3 would be more sensible.

Price wars can occur among oligopolists when a disruptive change is expected or is occurring. The firms may then fight to secure their own place in the new order by cutting prices deeply. This could happen if a government banned diesel and petrol cars, forcing a rapid switch to electric ones. The short-run damage to profits is to boost long-run market share.

Grade A The counter-argument

There is a lot of evidence from past prosecutions and guilty verdicts that oligop-olists are very prone to overt collusion. There is also evidence of 'buying off' rivals – especially in the pharmaceuticals industry. So limit pricing seems a relatively unlikely action; it's a bit too passive and self-sacrificial. Oligopolists are more likely to keep prices high until forced to cut them due to new competitive pressures.

Grade A* The critical perspective

Limit pricing, price wars and predatory pricing are real possibilities. The first two are legal and indeed welcomed by consumers and politicians. Who doesn't love a price cut? But predatory pricing is unlawful if the real intention is to drive a rival out of business. The problem for competition authorities is that it's very difficult to prove intent. The oligopolist can simply claim the rival's collapse was the result of other things – perhaps poorly managed finances.

Exam tips: Focus for exams on limit pricing, using the diagram shown above. This is an easy way to generate analysis marks.

Types of pricing: transmission mechanism (to get the top response level)

Chain 1. A firm with a strong national position in a service business (1) ... can cut prices locally when a new local entrant starts up (2) … making it impossible for the entrant to build a profitable market share (3) … and therefore closing (4). Any short-term losses are subsidised from national profits (5).

Chain 2. If a price war breaks out among oligopolists (1) … all may cut prices to where AC = AR (2) ... or below, to where supernormal losses will be made in the short-run (3). Each will hope the other blink first, ending the price war (4)… before all start to damage their long-term financial health (5).

Types of non-price competition

Grade C. What is it?

Non-price competition is rivalry based on anything other than price. It can either be based on real consumer benefits, such as exceptional production quality, or on psychological factors such as image. Among the real consumer benefits are great design, extra product features (ideally, unique), good service, good after-sales service and greater convenience. Among the psychological factors are branding, advertising, the effect of social media influencers and celebrity endorsement – all adding up to the brand image.

Grade B (i) Where's the beef?

Non-price competitive factors matter because they determine price elasticity of demand. Brands such as BMW or Apple are bought for themselves, not because of price. This keeps such products far away from perfectly competitive markets, providing the opportunity for long-run supernormal profit. Furthermore, in modern international markets, British exports tend to have desirable non-price attributes, such as Land Rover cars, Rolls Royce aero engines and Innocent Smoothies. Sales of these highly differentiated products are affected little by changes in the value of the £.

Grade B (ii) Why it matters

Non-price competition matters hugely because UK firms tend to have relatively high wages combined with relatively poor productivity. This makes it close to impossible for a UK firm to produce at lower cost than most international competitors. Therefore it is essential for British products to perform strongly in non-price terms, from branding through to great design. These days it's relatively easier for Burberry to sell a £1,000 coat in China than for an unknown, small UK clothing business to achieve the same with a £50 coat.

Grade A The counter-argument

Although the UK cannot compete internationally on cost/price grounds for manufactured goods, it can do so in the service sector. EasyJet and Primark are examples of globally competitive UK service businesses. So non-price competition isn't always necessary; in some service businesses we can win a price war.

Grade A* The critical perspective

Years ago price *was* the most important factor in winning market share. Today, branding and clever design are often the key factors. So keep your argument balanced between price and non-price factors, but willing to make a judgement about the product & market in question, as to whether non-price factors win out.

Do remember the importance of service as a non-price factor. It's often a matter of warmth, friendliness (a smile, may be) and a positive attitude. These strengths can be developed in a firm by good recruitment and training – but don't need to cost much at all. Managing people well is a great way to get a non-price advantage.

Don't forget the relationship between non-price factors such as differentiation – and price elasticity of demand (PED). A distinctive product will have lower price elasticity, making it easier to increase price when needed

Exam tip: when reading the exam materials, always think about the difference between products and services. Usually, services are easier to tailor to the client's needs.

Non-price competition: transmission mechanism (to top response level)

Chain 1. A firm struggling with fierce competition in its market (1) ... might invest heavily in non-price factors such as design (2) ... to differentiate the product more highly (3) ... and thereby enjoy lower price elasticity of demand (4) ... making it easier to increase price with little sales fall-off. (5)

Chain 2. If a phone shop lost experienced staff and replaced them with untrained, low-wage workers (1) ... the poor service would undermine consumer confidence (2) ... damaging sales and profits (3) ... and forcing the business to focus on price (4). Lower prices are an expensive luxury for a firm (5).

Characteristics of monopoly

Grade C. What is it?

Monopoly is the market power achieved by a single supplier within a market. This usually only happens in circumstances of natural monopoly (see right) or when the state supplies a public good. The UK government also defines monopoly as occurring when a single firm has a dominant influence over a market, which is quantified as holding a market share of 25% or more. Under that definition Tesco – with a 27.5% share of the UK grocery market – can be called a monopolist.

Grade B (i) Where's the beef?

The beef lies with the term 'the market'. 'Gordon's has a 55% share of UK sales of gin, but only a 6.5% share of sales of all 'spirits'. So does Gordon's have monopoly power? Probably not, because any price increases would be likely to get consumers to switch to other spirits such as whisky. To the examiner, the issue of 'what is a market' would always be worth exploring. If a court case arose over Gordon's gin, the producer would be sure to argue that it's part of the market for all spirits, and therefore has a 6.5% market share.

Grade B (ii) Why it matters

Today there are massive private sector monopolies in digitally-related sectors, from on-line shopping to search and social media. The monopolies in the west are rivalled by equivalents in China, such as Baidu – the Chinese 'Google' – which has a 75% share of search in China (Google's share of UK search is over 90%). This level of market dominance might be used for political motives or for commercial exploitation. Competition provides consumer choice – and keeps firms honest.

Grade A The counter-argument

Economists argue about most things, but there would be wide agreement that monopolies are against the consumers' best interest. They restrict output, push prices up and restrict consumer choice. This unanimity makes a counter-argument extra-powerful. The NHS is the UK's healthcare monopolist. It has lots of flaws but is far more cost effective than America's scattered, private sector system. So perhaps, in certain circumstances, monopoly can be an efficient market structure.

Grade A* The critical perspective

An example such as the NHS doesn't disprove the general principle that competition aids efficiency and ensures the fairest balance between consumer and producer surplus. There were once many air routes offered by a single firm – and flight prices were often ten times higher than today. If a structure gives scope for exploitation of the consumer, no-one should express surprise that firms seize the opportunity. Economics is based on rationality, and exploitation is wholly rational.

Natural monopoly: a monopoly based on physical supply. For a utility such as tap water, it would impractical and uneconomic to have two sets of reservoirs and pipelines to bring water to people's houses. So water is a natural monopoly. Either the state can supply it, or a private sector sole supplier.

Key monopoly characteristics: Substantial barriers to entry, such as patents or massive sunk costs (as in aircraft product-ion). Sunk costs make it hard for new competitors to afford the huge investment and easy for existing monopolists to price in a predatory manner.

Exam tip: even with monopolies it's important to see the upside. Huge scale might lead to low costs and higher consumer surplus.

Characteristics of monopoly: transmission mechanism (to top response level)

Chain 1. When a new drug is invented it will be patented (1) ... giving monopoly rights to the patent-holder for perhaps 20 years (2). This gives scope to charge thousands of times what the drug costs to produce (3) … excused by saying the profits will finance future drug breakthroughs (4) ... and thereby increasing social welfare (5). Somehow the shareholders also seem to do very well.

Chain 2. A state-run monopoly will suffer from x-inefficiency (1) … which might be compensated in part by a sense of staff care and commitment (2). If privatised as a monopoly (3) ... there may be some managerial efficiencies (4) … but the power to exploit pricing may leave customers worse off (5).

Monopoly diagrams (i)

Grade C. What is it?

To understand the monopoly diagram (facing page) it helps to start with a full understanding of the lines being drawn. It starts with this classic downward sloping demand curve. What this curve, plus the others on this page, can show is why the marginal revenue line behaves as it does. You'll know how to draw the MR line on the monopoly diagram, but do you know why? Carefully read the explanation to the right of Fig 1.

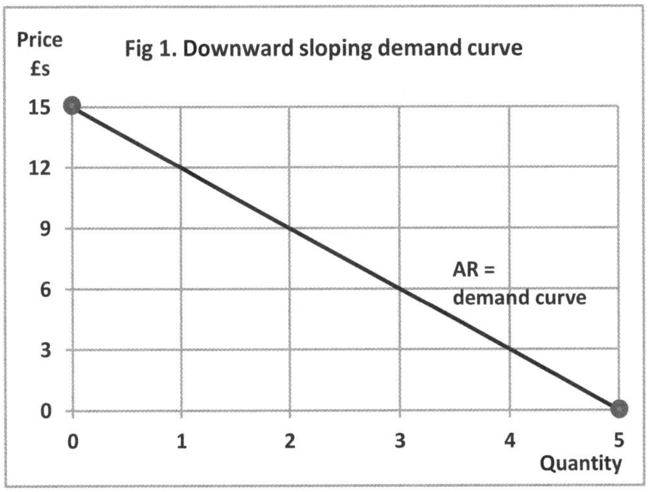

Fig 1. Downward sloping demand curve

Where's the beef? Look at Figure 1 and think about how the curve would look if it showed total revenue instead of average revenue. It would start with £0, because £15 x 0 output = £0. And it would end with zero, because 5 units x £0 = £0. Now look at Table 1.

Table 1: the numbers behind Fig 1 and Fig 2.

Quantity	Total revenue	Average revenue	Marginal revenue
0	0		
1	12	12	12
2	18	9	6
3	18	6	0
4	12	3	-6
5	0	0	-12

Grade B (i) Where's the beef (ii)?

P_2

From Table 1 you can see the AR line shown in Figure 1 and how MR responds to the changes in the total revenue column. The TR and MR lines are shown below.

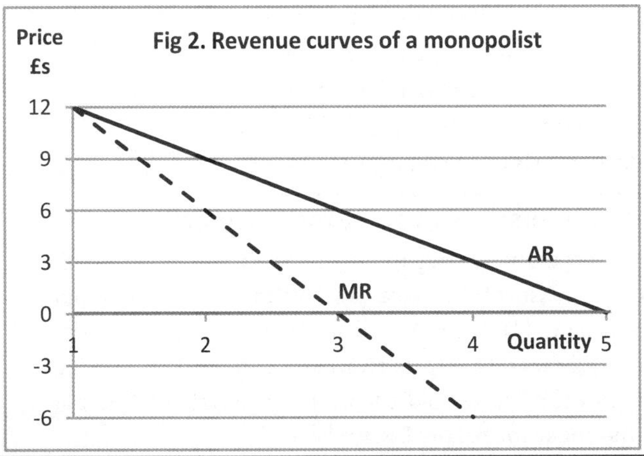

Fig 2. Revenue curves of a monopolist

From Fig 2 and the table above you can see the relationship between Marginal Revenue and Average Revenue. My hope is that this will make it easier to remember how to draw these two lines for a diagram such as Fig 3 (see right) – the full monopoly diagram.

Do remember that the logic and diagrams on these two pages apply equally to oligopoly and monopolistic competition. Getting the AR and MR lines right is a big step towards drawing a correct diagram.

Don't worry in the exam about drawing elegant diagrams. Scruffy is fine, though it helps hugely if you draw the diagrams on a reasonable large scale. (Assume your examiner is a bit old and a bit short-sighted – you won't be far wrong.) And label, label, label. Plus, show what's happening with arrows and a bit of explanation.

Exam tips.
Never forget that although every business claims to love competition, they all crave the security of the monopolist. Company directors want to forecast what's going to happen in the coming year – and see the same numbers at the year-end. Monopolists can do that; most firms face too much uncertainty to do that.

Monopoly diagrams (ii)

Grade C. What is it?

The monopoly diagram shown below shows the area of supernormal profit a monopolist enjoys as a result of charging far higher prices than would be true in a competitive marketplace. The area between the AC and AR curves (P1,X,Y,P2) represents that supernormal profit. Even that may not satisfy the monopolist, which may eye the area of consumer surplus (A, X, P1) and try to turn it from consumer surplus into producer surplus. This could be achieved if the business meets the conditions for price discrimination (see following page).

Grade B (i) Where's the beef?

Figure 3. The monopolist's supernormal profit

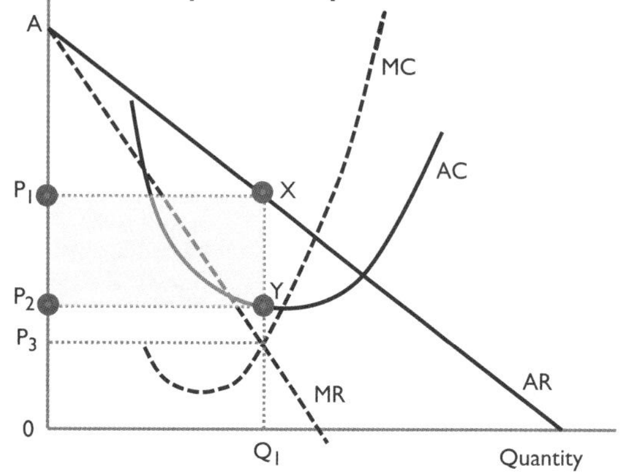

Note the key characteristics when drawing this graph:

1. MC cuts AC at its lowest point.
2. MR bisects AR and 0 along the horizontal axis …
3. … and continues below the £0 horizontal
4. Profit maximisation is where MC = MR (Q1)
5. A vertical line from Q1 shows the selling price P1 and guides the supernormal profit.

Grade A The counter-argument

In fact it's much harder than you might imagine to maintain this level of supernormal profit. Monopoly power may keep the price at P1, but that same power makes it difficult to hold average costs down. In the aviation and railway industries, monopoly power emboldens staff to join trade unions and fight for higher wages. So the staff end up with a slice of that rectangle. X-inefficiency may account for another slice. Important to remember, though, that even if the shareholders don't gain all that they might, it makes no difference to the overpaying consumer.

Grade A* The critical perspective

Monopoly is seen as damaging because it implies a degree of security and complacency that can damage the consumer's interests. Why should a monopolist spend heavily on Research & Development or on new ways to boost production quality? They simply don't need to. So governments treat monopolies with suspicion, often demanding special forms of regulation and scrutiny. Clever firms accept and participate in this; others try to fight it – risking breaking the law.

Do remember that local monopolies exist – almost everywhere. Such as the sole grocery in a local village or the only vegan restaurant in a town. These small firms are likely to behave in the same way as a giant monopoly – charging high prices for a Snickers or a vegetable curry.

Don't feel that nothing can be done about monopolies. In the past, America has been very bold in breaking up monopolies such as those affecting the U.S. oil and steel industries. UK governments have been weaker, but might find more courage in future.

Exam tip
In most exam answers only one diagram is needed – and there are only marks available for one. So take your time at the start of an answer to think of the most suitable diagram.

Monopoly diagram: transmission mechanism (to top response level)

Chain 1. The monopoly diagram is the same as the one for oligopolists and those in monopolistic competition (1) … but without the competitive pressures they face (2). This can make a monopoly hard to manage (3) .. because absence of constraints (4) … means the leader *has* to get things right. (5)

Chain 2. If a business in a competitive market managed to buy up rivals (1) ... and build barriers to entry (2) … it might be able to form a monopoly (3). This would enable it to squeeze total output down, to push prices up (4) ... to maximise the supernormal profits available (5).

Third degree price discrimination

Grade C. What is it?

Third degree price discrimination means charging different customers different prices for the same service. If a firm has the monopoly power of an Apple or a Microsoft (Windows etc) it feels the need to cash in. The diagram below shows the supernormal profits being made by a monopolist (P1,X,Y,P2), but also identifies the area under the AR curve (line) that the monopolist is failing to capture: the area of consumer surplus: A,X,P1. This, after all, shows where customers are willing/happy to pay a higher price than P1. Third degree price discrimination is the attempt by a monopolist to get their hands on some – preferably all – of that consumer surplus.

Grade B (i) Where's the beef?

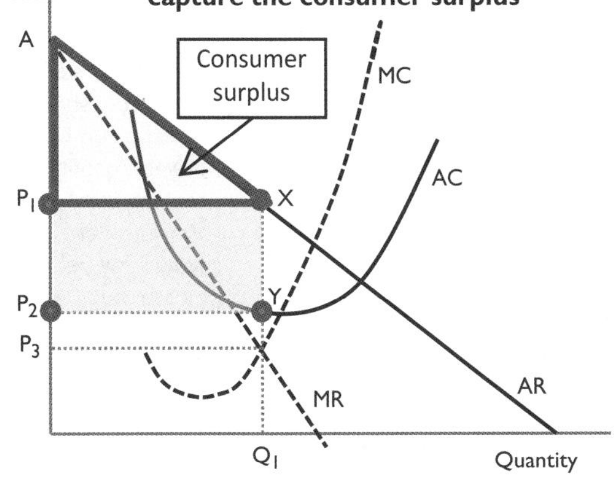

Figure 1. Monopolists try to capture the consumer surplus

To grab that consumer surplus the monopolist wants to charge some customers A for the service rather than P1. I could book a return train ticket to Manchester this Friday for £350 standard class. This is an 'open', flexible ticket to allow the business traveller to take any train there and back. An off-peak ticket costs £85 standard class. The business traveller is being discriminated against.

Grade B (ii) The beef (continued)

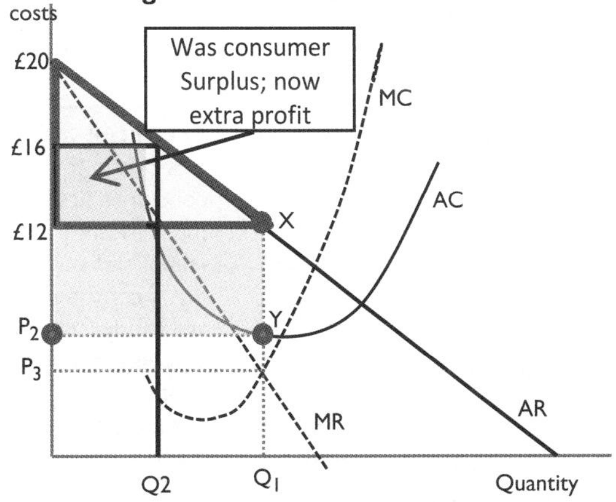

Figure 2. Price discrimination

Figure 2 shows a monopolist charging £12, from which a substantial supernormal profit is generated. The firm has identified a group of its customers willing to pay £16 (or more) for the service. That group numbers Q2 (about half of its regular customer total of Q1). By getting Q2 customers to pay £16, the firm receives £4 x Q1 extra revenue and profit. This comes from the consumer surplus.

Grade A* The critical perspective

When a University charges much higher fees to overseas students, price discrimination is taking place. Is it wrong, well perhaps not if those extra fees are used to give grants to less-well-off locals. But with many monopolies price discrimination is not a Robin Hood way to rob the rich to give to the poor. It's a way to take from customers to give to shareholders. Robin Hood never thought of that.

Necessary conditions:
- requires scope for separating different customer groups, e.g. over 65s
- the groups must have different price elasticities of demand
- must be impossible to trade the items between groups, which confines third degree discrimination to services, not goods.

Price discrimination is very frustrating if you are being discriminated against, but great if you are gaining. One Premier League club charges £499 for an adult season ticket, but £69 for under-16s. That parent is benefiting from the price discrimination. The single adult sitting in the next seat is the being discriminated against.

Exam tips: so, do you need to tell the examiner about 1st and 2nd degree discrimination? Not at all. 1st degree means charging a different price to every customer (not practical). 2nd degree means discriminating by quantity, as with bulk buying. For Edexcel only 3rd degree matters.

Costs & benefits of monopoly/natural monopoly

Grade C. What is it?

The main benefit of monopoly to firms, employees and suppliers is a quiet life. Even though suppliers face the monopsony (buying) power of the dominant or sole firm in an industry – at least that monopoly firm is not struggling to survive. So suppliers may have an easier life with a monopolist than with a firm in monopolistic competition trying to hang on to some supernormal profit. The main costs are faced by consumers, who will be paying higher prices, have less variety of brands/services on offer – and miss the innovativeness of firms in competitive markets.

Natural monopoly is based on physical factors that make it uneconomic to have more than one supplier. It's not realistic to have two sets of railway lines running from London to Newcastle – so there is a natural monopoly. The key question then is whether such a monopoly should ever be run by a private, profit-seeking firm? Shareholders would say yes please, but customers risk being exploited.

Grade B (i) Where's the beef?

The beef lies in the exceptions. The general rule is simple: unregulated monopolies overcharge customers – and are susceptible to x-inefficiencies that make costs rise and innovativeness fall. But generalisations work best if you know the exceptions. Japan Rail consists of 7 regional private sector railways that run monopoly services with stunning efficiency. The famous *shinkansen* superfast trains run to time and are much-loved by the Japanese. And the UK's NHS is much-criticised, but is one of the world's most efficient healthcare systems. So exceptions are possible.

Grade B (ii) Why it matters

A monopoly operates at a lower output/higher price equilibrium than a firm in a competitive market. So monopoly means lost jobs. Shareholders gain not only at the expense of consumers but also workers. Although the divorce of ownership and control is considered a bad thing, in this case it may help. Managers satisficing between profit and sales may produce and employ more than strictly needed.

Don't forget that barriers to entry can sometimes be disrupted, e.g. by new digital innovations from bright new firms.

Grade A The counter-argument

The main area for counter-argument is in relation to natural monopoly. It may be true that you can only have one railway line running from London to Newcastle, but there's no reason why you can't have competing services on the same lines. The 8.00 train could be run by company A and the 8.30 by company B; possibly that would create a competitive spirit to the benefit of passengers. Furthermore, the service to Newcastle also has competition from internal flights and the long drive. So there may be more competition around than 'natural monopoly' implies.

Exam tip: with monopoly, think consumer first and monopsony (suppliers) second. But if consumers are happy (think Google), beware of abstract attempts to dismantle something that works.

Grade A* The critical perspective

Economists and politicians rightly view monopolies with suspicion. But if something works well, it is foolish to tamper with it. Politician Chris Grayling decided to break up the UK's prisoner probation system and outsource it to private sector firms. It proved an expensive disaster and the service was re-nationalised in 2019.

Monopoly/natural monopoly: transmission mechanism (to top response level)

Chain 1. One of the easiest ways to attack monopoly power would be to dismantle laws on patents (1) ... but this might lead to big cutbacks in Research & Development (2) ... especially among pharmaceutical firms (3) ... meaning fewer medical breakthroughs (4) ... and a costlier NHS. (5)

Chain 2. Employees working in monopolies have secure jobs (1) ... that may make them complacent (2) ... or give a sense of purpose leading to greater involvement (3) ... and higher efficiency plus more creative participation (4)... leading to excellence in organisations such as the BBC or Japan Rail (5).

Monopsony

Grade C. What is it?

A monopsony exists when a firm's scale gives it power over its suppliers. There is no formal equivalent of the 25%+ market share figure that defines a monopoly, but it would be fair to assume that most firms with monopoly power also exert monopsony power. This power becomes close to absolute when a giant firm is able to pick and choose among small, rival suppliers. A good example would be Tesco, with its near-30% share of the UK grocery market and sales of over £50 billion a year, choosing whether to buy eggs from farmer A or farmer B.

Grade B (i) Where's the beef?

The beef comes from seeing monopsony power as another type of market failure that therefore causes a misallocation of resources. A bullying monopsonist could drive supply prices below their true market level, creating a potential consumer benefit in the short term. This could drive suppliers out of business and/or force them into mergers in order to increase their scale and force prices to rise. In other words a few big grocery buyers may soon lead to farmers coming together in huge, oligopolistic super-farms – to be able to fight toe-to-toe.

Grade B (ii) Why it matters

It matters because markets are supposed to be created by willing buyers and willing sellers. And from this position the invisible hand should guide supplier and consumer decisions to a stable market equilibrium price and quantity. Monopsony power implies scope for a bullying approach that distorts Adam Smith's vision of perfect competition.

Grade A The counter-argument

Although most economists view monopsony power negatively, some claim to see strengths. When Asda and Sainsbury attempted to merge, their argument was that their combined power over suppliers would push supply prices down. This would, in effect, reduce the suppliers' producer surplus, allowing Asda/Sainsbury to convert this into consumer surplus and pass savings on to consumers in the form of lower prices. Most economists followed the logic about cutting supply prices, but did not believe the lower costs would be passed on as lower consumer prices.

Grade A* The critical perspective

The job of a spokesperson for a firm is to argue for the firm's best interests. This is usually done by using a rational, objective-sounding argument that is highly selective. In other words it may be a version of the truth, but not the *whole* truth. In exams you often need to identify the weaknesses in such arguments.

Do remember that monopsony power can be cancelled out by the power of some suppliers. Tesco is huge, but not compared with the Coca-Cola corporation. Monopsony only means something if there are many small, weak(ish) suppliers.

Don't assume that a monopolist *must* also be a monopsonist. There may be only one pizza delivery outlet in a small town. It has a local monopoly. But it may be a small operation compared with its suppliers.

Exam tip: examiners like to think that, after two years' study, you are able to use economic terminology fluently. Not only think like an economist, but write like one. So appropriate use of 'monopsony' and 'producer surplus' always pays dividends.

Monopsony: transmission mechanism (to top response level)

Chain 1. A merger between two big retail chains (1) … could create a strong monopsony position (2) … putting small-scale suppliers in a perilous position (3). In the UK grocery sector a regulator protects suppliers' interests (4) … but in other sectors the suppliers have to fight to survive (5).

Chain 2. When the NHS buys cancer drugs its strong UK monopsony position (1) … allows it to purchase at significantly lower prices than individual hospitals in America's private sector health system (2). So UK taxpayers pay far less for healthcare than those in America (3) … at the cost of the suppliers' producer surplus (4). American politicians are very keen to stop this from happening (5).

Monopsony: costs and benefits

Grade C. What is it?

If a small supplier of vitamins managed to get stocked on the shelves of Boots The Chemist, it might wait 120 days to get paid. Boots is one of many large companies that takes 3-4 months to pay suppliers. Monopsony power is not just the ability to force small suppliers to give big discounts on price – it's also the ability to force harsh credit terms onto those suppliers. This, in turn, may force suppliers to take drastic action to protect their finances, such as employ staff on zero-hours contracts to turn fixed costs of employment into variable costs.

Grade B (i) Where's the beef?

An important monopsony power is over employees. If Virgin Rail is the only operator of high speed trains in the country, it is also the only employer of high speed train drivers. Therefore it has the power to force pay levels down – as there is no rival employer. Accordingly, the employees of monopsonists are highly likely to join trade unions to increase their bargaining power. This process of 'collective bargaining' provides **countervailing power** – to tackle the power of the employer.

Grade B (ii) Why it matters

We want to think of our country as a place where business operates on a level playing field – where there's a fair fight between competing firms. The managers at those firms think differently. They want to find an advantage that puts them above the fight (as in the famous Adam Smith quote about a 'contrivance to raise prices'). Using brute force to bully competitors (in monopoly conditions) or suppliers (in monopsony) is a market reality. In the UK grocery trade a regulator has been set up to allow suppliers to complain about the behaviour of the big grocery retailers. 'Ethical' retailers the Coop and Waitrose are on the list of poor performers.

Grade A The counter-argument

A monopsonist may be a tough customer, but also a huge one. So small firms that provide the right level of quality, reliability and price can grow almost infinitely to become huge suppliers. And whereas growing by finding more customers means more deliveries to a wider range of places, dealing with a single firm means hiring ever-bigger trucks, but only one driver. This can mean huge profit growth.

Grade A* The critical perspective

Putting Tesco and an organic farmer into negotiation is a bit like putting a super-heavyweight in a ring with a lightweight. No amount of refereeing/regulating will make this a fair fight. So organic farmers need to find a way to fight together against the big guys. That's what trade unions try to do for their members.

Do remember the term **counter-vailing power**. Used first by the economist J.K. Galbraith, it emphasises the importance in a modern economy of creating an ability to fight force with force. An individual employee or supplier is near-powerless when up against a giant monopsonist. Hence farm cooperatives and trade unions.

Don't assume that every monopsonist has to be a huge corporation. Power is relative and if a company has a 70% share of a £10 million market, it's not a big business, but it is a powerful one.

Exam tip: as long as your points and quotes are relevant, examiners love to see your knowledge of economists such as Adam Smith, J.K. Galbraith, Marx and Hayek.

Monopsony costs and benefits: transmission mechanism (to top response level)

Chain 1. If a monopsonist tries to force wages down (1) ... the natural response is to join a trade union to get collective power (2) ... and some legal protection from unfair dismissal (3). Free market economists regard unions with suspicion (4)...but Galbraith saw a need for countervailing power. (5).

Chain 2. The monopsonist is trying to boost its supernormal profit (1) ... by cutting input purchase costs and therefore its variable, marginal and average costs (2). The lower costs won't be passed on to customers (3) ... so the big monopsonist boosts its profit (4) ... at the cost of the small supplier (5).

Characteristics of contestable markets

Grade C. What is it?

A contestable market is one where barriers to entry and exit are low, no matter whether the market structure is freely competitive or oligopolistic. This theory runs counter to the standard ('neo-classical') approach which regards oligopoly markets as being protected by high barriers to entry and exit. Among the key characteristics of a contestable market would be:

- Free entry and exit, with no sunk costs (see right)
- The number of firms can vary, but there's no collusion
- Firms are short-run profit maximisers
- There is perfect knowledge among the firms in the market

As free entry to the market is inherent to the theory of freely and monopolistically competitive markets, the key thing about this theory is the different treatment of oligopolies.

Grade B (i) Where's the beef?

The beef is that whereas neo-classical theory says that oligopolies can maintain supernormal profits in the long run, this theory disagrees. Because of the low barriers to entry (and 'contestability'), even oligopolies can only enjoy super-normal profits in the short-term. In the long run they (just like monopolistically competitive firms) can make no more than normal profits. The constant threat of new competitors serves to keep firms efficient and innovative, and persuades them to use limit pricing to cut the attraction of the market for new entrants.

Grade B (ii) Why it matters

If markets are generally contestable, fears of oligopoly power/collusion and so on are exaggerated. Markets can be left alone, as the *threat* of competition works as effectively as the existence of competition. Government regulation is not needed as the threat of competition protects the consumer. Such a view also suggests that relatively few firms are making supernormal profits at any one time.

Grade A The counter-argument

The counter-argument today would be: look at the huge value of share buy-backs, i.e. firms giving cash away to shareholders. Between 2007 and 2018 the total for buy-backs in the USA was $4.5 trillion (according to JP Morgan); in the UK the figure has been rising fast. This suggests supernormal profits, not normal ones.

Grade A* The critical perspective

Aldi and Lidl's breakthrough into the UK grocery oligopoly shows that there may be no or low barriers to entry. But in the 6 months to April 2019 eleven entrants to the UK energy market went bust; contestability can't be taken for granted.

Sunk costs are those that have been invested but are irretrievable. By the time the Airbus A380 'superjumbo' plane went into production $25 billion had been sunk (invested) into the project. That could not be recovered by the time production ended. Examples of sunk costs include R&D, advertising and building a dedicated factory.

Perfect knowledge is quite an ask. Its importance in contestability is that all firms should have the same understand-ing of - and access to – technology, to create a level playing field. Patents and other I.P. (intellectual property) will get in the way of that.

Exam tip: the thing to remember is the importance of the *threat* of competition; that is the key idea within contestability.

Contestable markets (i): transmission mechanism (to top response level)

Chain 1. An oligopolist may feel safe behind barriers to entry (1) … but find newcomers eating away at its market share (2) … as plant-based 'meat' producers did in early 2019 (3) ... forcing Burger King and Unilever to react quickly (4)… to protect their market position from disastrous decline. (5).

Chain 2. Contestability can arise because oligopolists get slack (1) … perhaps as a result of complacency/x-inefficiency (2). As the barriers lower, entrepreneurs jump in (3) … but big corporate sleeping tigers can bite back (4) … causing the small business failures seen in the energy sector (5).

Implications of contestable markets

Grade C. What is it?

The implication for firms in a contestable market is that they must never relax on efficiency – and should at least consider limit pricing rather than pricing at the profit maximising point. With regard to efficiency, the constant threat of new competition forces the firm to operate where it's productively efficient. This is at the lowest point on its AC curve, which is where MC = AC. It will also seek to be allocatively efficient, which is where the marginal cost curve cuts average revenue (MC = AR). As you can see in the graph below, this will mean zero supernormal profit, which is the long-run expectation for a firm in a contestable market.

Grade B (i) Where's the beef?

Long-run equilibrium for a firm in a contestable market

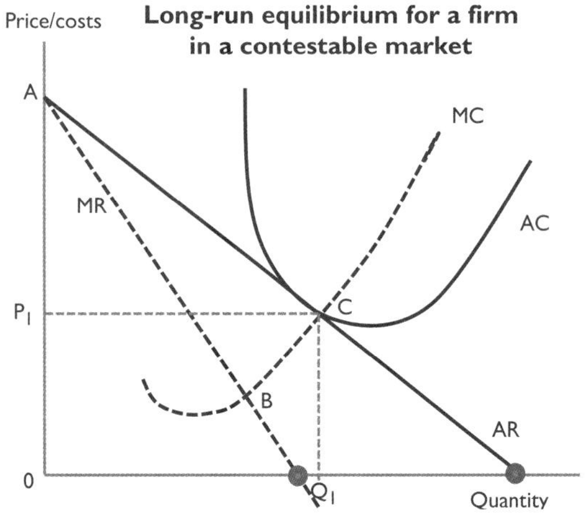

The graph shows the long-run position of a firm in a contestable market. The threat of competition forces it to keep prices down to where AR is no higher than AC – so no supernormal profits are being made. The graph shows MC cuts AC at its lowest point, so it's productively efficient; and MC = AR at Q1 output level, so it's also allocatively efficient.

Grade B (ii) Why it matters

It matters because if a marketplace is contestable, firms within the market will focus on keeping costs as low as possible to keep new entrants out. This will secure them a stable equilibrium based on normal profits. And consumers can enjoy the huge consumer surplus shown as A C P_1.

Grade A The counter-argument

But what if the assumed conditions of a contestable market are not fully met? Sunk costs are a fact in most markets, e.g. years of advertising spending behind brands such as Snickers or Pringles. These sunk costs give brands with small market shares the ability and power to stand up against new entrants.

Grade A* The critical perspective

The theory behind contestable markets is sound, given the assumptions built in. The implications for firms' behaviour are profound, as set out above, but only if all the underlying assumptions hold good. Perhaps there are too many for comfort.

Do think carefully about barriers to entry, as they are critical to the idea of contestability. Some are legally binding, such as patents (which can last 20 years). Others are threats rather than reality, such as the size and financial muscle of a huge incumbent such as Cadbury. And others are challenges, such as the strength of a brand such as Shreddies or Frosties.

Don't hesitate to question whether the business featured on the exam paper really conforms to all the assumptions that underpin the theory of contestability. As long as you have a one-sentence justification for your doubts, it works ever so well to express them.

Exam tip: the key implication is that supernormal profits are less common than usually assumed. You can question this, but don't forget it.

Contestable markets (ii): transmission mechanism (to top response level)

Chain 1. A complacent oligopolist might price high to gain super-normal profits in the short-run (1) … but have to cut prices after new entrants had jumped over the perhaps-low barriers to entry (2) … causing profits to sink to 'normal' (3) ... where MC = AR (4)… and AC = AR (5).

Chain 2. The worst scenario for a firm in a contestable market (1) … is new entrants with a more efficient production system (2) … and therefore a lower AC curve (3). Then the existing firm might have to price below its average costs (4) … causing short-run losses (5).

Barriers to market entry and exit

Grade C. What is it?

Barriers to market entry have changed in recent years. Brand names backed by advertising were difficult to overcome in years gone by, but now Boohoo.com + Love Island + celeb endorsement can mean not just market entry but huge success (Boohoo.com sales up 750% in the 5 years to February 2019). Yet new barriers have developed with new technology. The vast quantities of customer data owned by Facebook and Google create a major barrier to entry to their fields of social media and search.

Grade B (i) Where's the beef?

The key academic issue is sunk costs. Heavy past investments that are now un-recoverable give existing firms the ability to cut prices sharply, whenever they see a new competitor arriving. This makes it very hard for a new firm to enter, especially if they have to find the finance to sink into the same expensive capital (buying Airbus A350 planes at $200m each, perhaps). High sunk costs also make it expensive for existing firms to exit the market. So high sunk costs lead to passive stability within the market structure.

Grade B (ii) Why it matters

Barriers to entry matter as a source of protection to existing firms. Barriers to exit are at least as important, though, in relation to contestability. Getting out must be as easy and as cheap as getting in to a market, or else the market will lack the fluidity of competition implied by contestable market theory. A major barrier to exit can be 10-year leaseholds with landlords. I close my shop today, but have to pay £80,000 a year in rent for the next 10 years. Struggling Arcadia (owner of Topshop) has 2,500 UK stores. 2,500 x £80,000 x 10 is quite a barrier to exit.

Grade A The counter-argument

But not everyone faces exit barriers. Some online 'shops' carry no stock and therefore have no warehousing or other property costs. Customer orders are directed to manufacturers who produce and dispatch the goods. This type of online retailer can enter or exit the market at any time – and therefore opt out of the market temporarily if a price war was going on.

Grade A* The critical perspective

When an economic theory includes an assumption such as perfect knowledge, it is fair to raise an eyebrow. Existing firms accumulate huge amounts of numerical and other types of knowledge about the science and engineering of production and the attitudes and behaviours of customers. New market entrants cannot have that, so market knowledge can be a huge barrier to successful market entry.

Do remember these barriers to entry: capital costs such as machinery; sunk costs such as advertising; economies of scale, such as bulk buying plus technical economies; legal barriers such as patents; marketing barriers such as a powerful brand image (Apple? Nintendo?); and limit pricing – a way for existing firms to put off newcomers.

Don't forget the importance of collusion as a way existing firms can work together to repel newcomers. This is especially likely in commodity sectors such as cement and concrete production.

Exam tip: most students are expert on barriers to entry but oddly quiet about barriers to exit. It is well worth revising them with care.

Contestable markets (iii): transmission mechanism (to top response level)

Chain 1. Big, profitable firms with strong short-run supernormal profits (1) ... will work hard to maximise barriers to entry (2) ... to preserve their high profits for as long as possible (3). Airline 'loyalty' free-flight programmes are a good example (4)... of how to keep demand price inelastic (5).

Chain 2. It's hard to persuade new entrants into the market for nuclear power (1) ... because the barriers to exit are very high (2) ... as they involve waste that is radioactive for centuries (3) ... at costs that are vast, but highly uncertain (4). Nuclear power may be the least contestable market (5).

Sunk costs and degree of contestability

Grade C. What is it?

Sunk costs are an investment that is intended to create value (probably revenue) but doesn't involve or create a sellable asset. Buying the freehold to a shop is a real investment with significant residual value. But designing and building a quirky interior with unusual seats and tables might cost £250,000, but have no lasting value if the business closes down. That's a sunk cost. And sunk costs act as a barrier to market entry because they add to the cost of failure. An investment into freehold property can be turned into cash; sunk costs cannot.

Grade B (i) Degree of contestability

Uncontestable market ⟷ Moderately contestable market ⟷ Perfectly contestable market

Hugely high barriers to entry, e.g. patent walls	Low barriers to entry and exit; moderate sunk costs	No barriers to entry or exit; minimal sunk costs
One of the world's most expensive drugs is *Spinraza*, price: $750,000 per year per person	For example a firm in a retail market holding little stock and owning short leases on its shops	For example a 'virtual' online, stockless retailer run from a bedroom; or a 'pop-up' restaurant

Grade B (ii) Why it matters

The degree of contestability is a huge matter – giving scope for argument and debate. That's a good thing, because that gives the potential for high analysis and evaluation marks. These marks are helped by complexity not simplicity. Few firms operate in markets that are 'uncontestable' or 'perfectly contestable'. Most will be in the middle, competing with others in a similar situation. Just as you can have perfectly, highly or moderately price elastic products, so it's possible to have high or moderate contestability.

Grade A The counter-argument

Even if moderate contestability is a possibility, it may be no different in the long run than perfect contestability. If the barriers to entry are moderately high, they are likely to attract in enough competition to trample the barriers to the ground. Once ASOS broke through in online clothes retailing, it didn't take long for Boohoo and PrettyLittleThing to jump in.

Grade A* The critical perspective

Contestability may become a battleground between free market economists (who love the theory) and interventionists who see barriers to entry as a big problem.

Sunk costs are an important element in much of micro-economic theory. There are many sunk costs when starting a new firm or expanding an existing one:
1. The feasibility studies, market research and R&D costs.
2. Design, building and decorating costs that are personalised to the one business.
3. Promotional launch costs, e.g. advertising and web design.
By definition, if the firm goes under, the expenditure on these items has no lasting value.

Don't confuse 'sunk' with 'spent'. As long as there's something of residual, re-sellable value, it's not a sunk cost, e.g. a truck or company car.

Exam tip: contestable market theory can be contrasted with neo-classical, especially when considering oligopolies. The big difference is barriers to entry.

Contestable markets (iv): transmission mechanism (to top response level)

Chain 1. TV chef Jamie Oliver invested £1+ million to set up *Barbecoa* restaurant in London (1) ... almost all sunk costs, as he didn't own the property (2). This might have discouraged new entrants (3) ... but when the market turned difficult and the restaurant closed (4)... all the sunk costs were lost (5).

Chain 2. Patents eventually come to the end of their life, so a high barrier disappears overnight (1) ... forcing the firm to face contestability (2) ... and therefore focus hugely on minimising its AC curve (3). Drug prices can fall by 95% when patents lapse (4) ... causing an existential struggle for the firm (5).

Demand for labour

Grade C. What is it?

The price of labour is the wage a firm pays to its employees. So it should make sense that the demand for labour forms a downward sloping curve: the lower the wage rate the more staff firms are willing to employ. In addition to this common-sense approach, economists like to consider the marginal revenue product (MRP) of labour. This measures the marginal extra value of an employee's output, which can then be compared with the labour cost.

Grade B Where's the beef?

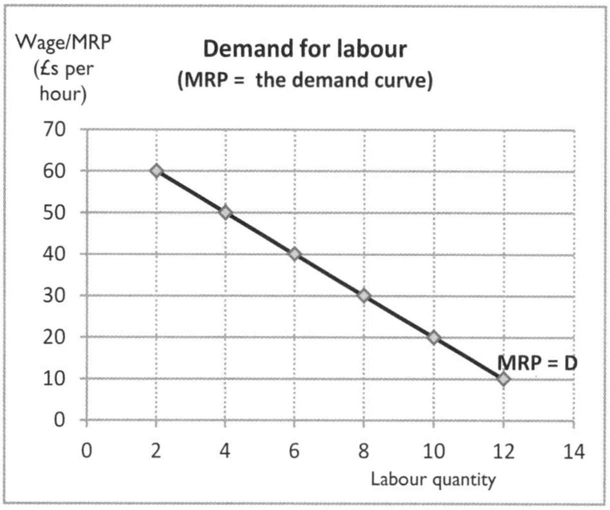

The diagram shows the demand for labour. If the wage rate is £60 an hour, it's not worth the firm's while to employ more than 2 staff. The MRP curve shows the most a firm will pay for an extra unit of a factor of product-ion, such as labour. So it is the demand curve for that factor.

Grade B (ii) Why it matters

The theory matters because of its impact on two important aspects of the labour market. The first is the national minimum wage (NMW). If the demand for labour is downward sloping, government action to protect low-wage earners will cut the demand for labour, causing unemployment. The second is the impact of unions; their efforts to increase members' pay will cause job losses and so be self-defeating

Grade A The counter-argument

The main factor in the demand for labour is demand for the goods & services of the firm in question: demand for labour is a derived demand. If Aldi opens more shops it needs more staff. So MRP theory may be less important than it seems.

Grade A* The critical perspective

All economics has political implications, but rarely so clearly as with the labour market. Free market economists hate regulation – except when applied to trade unions – and the fight for a minimum wage pitted government against economics.

Marginal revenue product (MRP) is based on the 'law' of diminishing returns. In the short run, if a business expands by taking on extra staff, diminishing returns will set in. The firm should go on hiring more staff until their MRP falls below the cost of labour. From then on, hiring more people cuts into profits.

Shifts in the labour demand curve are perfectly possible. An increase in labour productivity (efficiency) would shift the demand curve to the right. A fall would shift in leftwards.

Exam tip: the familiarity of the downward-sloping demand curve can make it easy to under-estimate labour market theory in general – and marginal revenue product in particular. Actually it's important to spend time revising MRP – so do take care over these pages.

Demand for labour: transmission mechanism (to get to the top response level)

Chain 1. A rise in market demand makes a firm want to boost production (1) … so, with other factors fixed in the short-run it hires more staff (2) … until their MRP starts to fall below their wage rate (3). From then on, only a boost in productivity (4) … makes it profitable to hire more people (5).

Chain 2. At Jaguar Land Rover, labour costs are less than 20% of total costs (1) … so meeting extra demand opportunities (2) ... may be more important than marginal revenue product (3)… to achieve sustained supernormal profit (4). In this case, balancing supply & demand may be the critical factor (5).

Supply of labour

Grade C. What is it?

Micro and macro success depends hugely on the labour market. The supply of labour to any individual firm needs to be of the right quality, with the right skills and at a price (the wage rate) that can allow the business to make profits. This seems simple but is not. It's hindered by market failures including geographical and occupational immobility. Membership of a trading bloc with free movement of labour was intended to help with this; at the time of writing the UK seems set to leave the E.U. and therefore make labour mobility significantly worse.

A backward-sloping labour supply curve is not just a theoretical possibility. A study of Canadian women found they became reluctant to supply extra labour once their hourly pay rate had risen beyond a certain level. Firms might take this as a reason not to pay high wages. Oddly, company directors never worry about higher pay in the Boardroom.

Grade B Where's the beef?

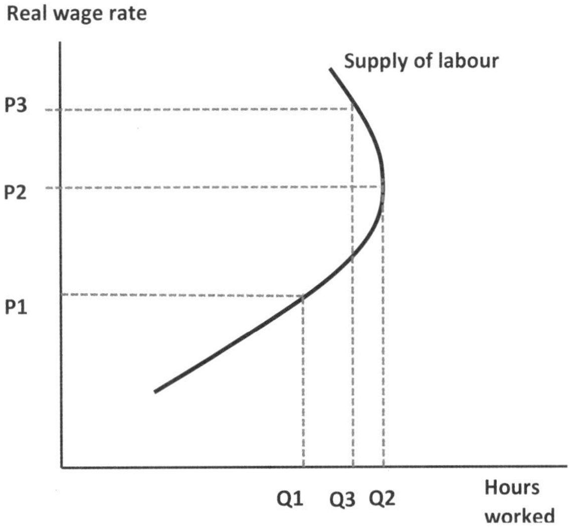

The diagram shows the supply labour. Up to and including P1Q1 the supply curve slopes upwards as you might expect. The higher the wage, the more I want to work. But the theory of the backward sloping supply curve suggests that once people are earning enough to meet their lifestyle, they're inclined to prefer time off to more work. See right.

Don't forget that labour supply can mean being torn between caring for kids or ageing parents – and earning the money needed to keep the household going. This is a tough trade-off.

Grade B (ii) Why it matters

The theory matters if it gives a realistic explanation of human behaviour. It doesn't work on super-rich footballers, who put in extra hours to make money from advertising. But for most of us it may be that an income effect works up to a point (I need more money, I must work more hours) and then a substitution effect takes over, with a trade-off between more income and more leisure time.

Exam tip: the idea of income and substitution effects from work is an interesting one. Nevertheless most people (even today) are full-time workers with regular hours. So the issue of the backward-sloping supply curve is not very relevant.

Grade A The counter-argument

The backwards-sloping labour supply curve may be a distraction; the more important part of the curve is unarguable: higher pay rates attract more labour.

Grade A* The critical perspective

For years firms have complained that the labour supply coming from the education system is ill-trained/ill-prepared. Perhaps firms should do more training themselves

Supply of labour: transmission mechanism (to get to the top response level)

Chain 1. A contestable market requires firms to move fluidly in and out of a market (1) … requiring labour supply that is highly flexible (2) … probably on zero-hours contracts – the ultimate in flexibility (3). This is great for the firm and potentially for consumers (4) … at the cost of workers' security (5).

Chain 2. Trade unions want employees to have more control over labour supply (1) … perhaps limiting it to full time, permanent jobs only (2). This would give workers more negotiating power over wages (3)… but fewer jobs on offer (4). Labour supply issues are always controversial (5).

Labour market equilibrium

Grade C. What is it?

The market for labour is a factor market, and therefore should behave like any other factor market, such as for capital. But of course it doesn't. It raises huge questions such as why are footballers paid more than surgeons? The diagram below shows the labour market within a well-paid industry, where wage rates are £30 an hour. Note, though, that employers are willing to pay £60 an hour to 2,000 staff (see below). A trade union would certainly take note, and negotiate a £30 minimum, but with extra pay 'increments' to take senior staff to that £60 mark.

Grade B Where's the beef?

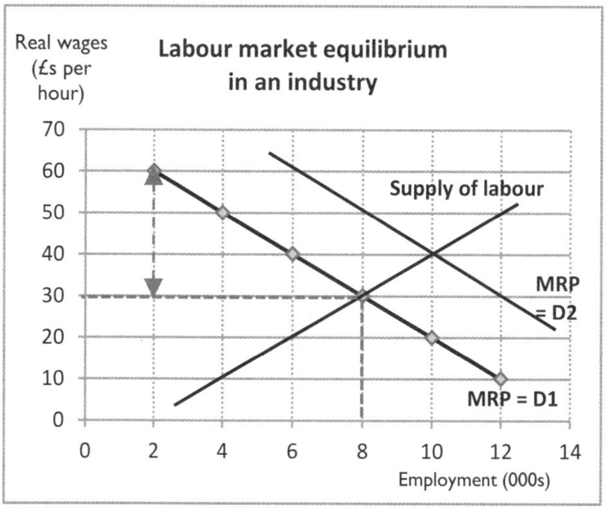

The diagram shows an equilibrium wage rate of £30 an hour, giving jobs to 8,000. The upward-sloping supply curve indicates a normal labour market. Another possibility is a horizontal labour supply curve. This occurs in a perfectly competitive factor market, where a huge pool of people offer the same skills.

Grade B (ii) Why it matters

Labour markets matter because the amount and type of pay has a huge effect on households. Those working for the minimum wage face a constant struggle with household bills, let alone saving. Free market economists want the labour market to be infinitely flexible, with every individual negotiating their own pay with their employer (and no legal minimum wage). Zero hours contracts fit perfectly into this thinking.

Grade A The counter-argument

In contrast with infinite flexibility, employees want good, predictable wage packets and job security. It's impossible to get a mortgage on a zero-hours contract.

Grade A* The critical perspective

Economics should be careful about proposing labour market conditions that force other people into conditions of poverty. Moral issues matter hugely in economics.

Questions 1-3 are based on MRP = D1.
1. Calculate the weekly wage bill in the industry, assuming an average working week of 40 hours.
2. Explain the effect of a trade union negotiating a real wage of £40 an hour.
3. Calculate the labour cost per unit if industry output is 50,000 units a week.
4. Explain the effect of a rise in productivity in the industry, shifting demand to D2.

Don't forget that the labour demand curve hinges on labour's MRP.

Answers:
1. £30 x 8,000 x 40 = £9,600,000.
2. A minimum wage of £40 an hour would mean 10,000 people wanting a job, but only 6,000 jobs on offer. 2000 would have lost their jobs.
3. £9,600,000 / 50,000 = £192 p.u.
4. A productivity rise would mean a new equilibrium of £40 and 10,000 staff

Labour market: transmission mechanism (to get to the top response level)

Chain 1. Ambitious firms in high-tech or creative industries pay *above* the prevailing industry wage rate (1) ... to hire the very best people (2) ... whose abilities generate high marginal revenue products (3)... and therefore repay their high wages (4). Hiring on the cheap rarely makes business sense (5).

Chain 2. The big issue in modern labour markets is zero hours contracts (1) ... which give employers the flexibility they desire (2) ... by turning labour from a fixed into a variable cost (3)... which may be necessary for delivery drivers (4) ... but may also be used by greedy firms that don't really need it (5).

Government intervention in the labour market

Grade C. What is it?

Governments may intervene in the wider labour market by setting maximum or minimum wage levels. Putting a ceiling on wages was tried in the 1970s as a way to limit wage-push inflation. It worked in the short-term, but at the cost of serious long-term consequences. Virtually no economist or politician would advocate this today – except possibly for very highly paid company directors. National minimum wages are now common in developed countries; governments have brought them in against widespread criticism from free market economists.

Grade B Where's the beef?

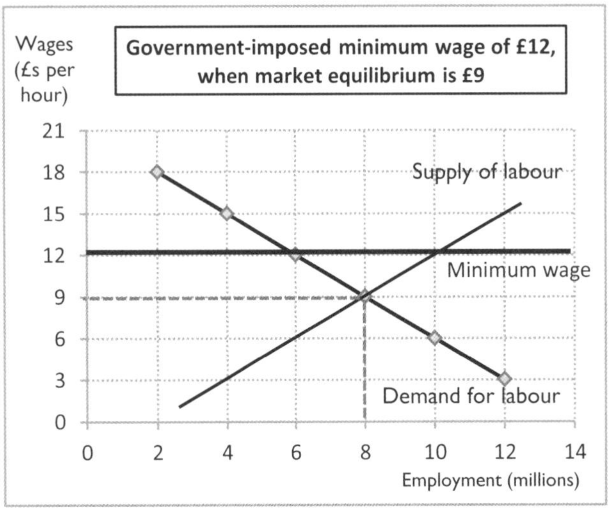

The beef lies in the gap between theory and reality. The theory is clear: a minimum wage of £12 cuts the demand for labour from 8 million to 6 million – pushing unemployment up by 2 million. But it's hard to find evidence for this in the real world: minimum wages have been brought in with no measurable effect on employment.

Grade B (ii) Why it matters

Government involvement in the labour market matters for two reasons: economic efficiency and economic equality/inequality. Setting a reasonably high minimum wage is an attempt to combat poverty – especially absolute poverty. This can help address a market failure: households being unable to pay their bills. To maximise efficiency, free market economists call for uber-flexibility, with minimal regulation.

Grade A The counter-argument

The counter to those wanting minimal regulation is to emphasise the need for higher skill levels within our labour market. Free market economists seem focused on labour being cheap; interventionists want better educated, better trained staff who can create higher marginal revenue product and therefore pay for themselves.

Grade A* The critical perspective

When writing about labour market issues, remember you're talking about people's jobs and household incomes. Yes, be objective; but then reflect on the implications.

Do remember that governments are major employers, i.e. a key element in demand for labour. When the austerity period began in 2010, the Chancellor placed a pay freeze on its 5.5 million staff. This would have had a knock-on effect on private-sector wage rates. If 5.5 million get zero pay rises, private companies feel less pressure to increase pay rates. The labour market 'softens'.

Don't forget that labour market flexibility needs geographically mobility. The UK housing market is dreadful for this, e.g. when Ford closed its factory in South Wales, many couldn't afford a move to London where there were more jobs. Governments need to address this problem.

Exam tip: Remember that despite much criticism, the UK's labour market is one of the world's most flexible.

Labour market (ii): transmission mechanism (to get to the top response level)

Chain 1. Boosting labour mobility requires a government re-think on housing policy (1) … to enable workers to move from low house price areas to high price ones (2) … because that's where the jobs are (3). This may require much bigger investment (4) …in publicly-owned, so-called 'social' housing (5)

Chain 2. A key objective among Brixiteer politicians (1) … is labour market deregulation (2) … to increase flexibility and, in effect, the market power of employers (3). They believe this will boost economic growth (4) … by making the UK economy more like the transatlantic/American model (5).

Labour market elasticities of demand and supply

Grade C. What is it?

The price elasticity of demand for labour is an important aspect of every sector's labour market. It is low when the employer is in great need of that particular skill. In modern markets that means the labour cannot easily be substituted by robots or other forms of capital investment. Even when hourly pay rates rise significantly, the employers keep hiring. Price elasticity of demand for labour is high, therefore, when the skill-level is low and can easily be substituted.

The price elasticity of supply for labour depends on many factors, including the flexibility of the labour market and the degree of freedom of movement between different countries. For firms within the E.U. the complete freedom of movement of labour is highly beneficial, as it almost guarantees high supply elasticity.

Do take a moment to understand the diagram. It shows an original (DL1, SL1) equilibrium wage of £30 an hour. Then a reduction in labour supply forces the wage level up to £42 an hour (a 40% wage increase!). But if the labour demand curve was more price elastic (DL2), the wage would only have needed to rise to £34.

Grade B Where's the beef?

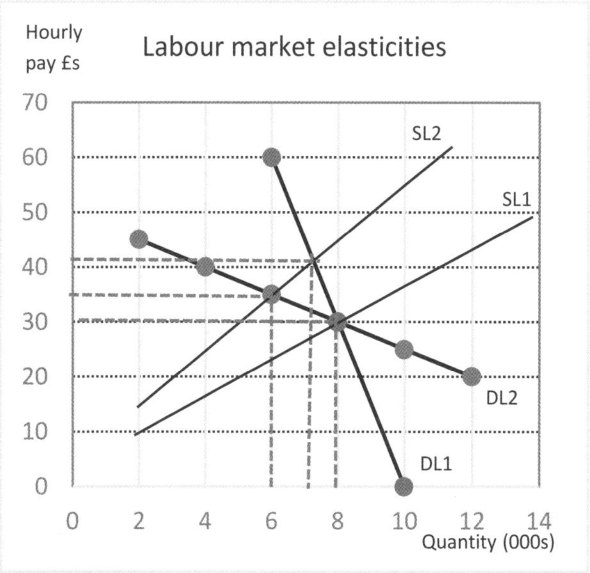

The diagram shows the importance of the elasticity of demand for labour when labour supply falls from SL1 to SL2. If demand for labour is price elastic (DL2), the equilibrium number of jobs falls from 8,000 to 6,000. If demand for labour is price inelastic (DL1), the number of jobs falls to 7,200. Implicitly this is the point of a university degree: to lower the price elasticity of <u>your</u> labour.

Don't ignore the power you have to affect the price elasticity of demand for your labour. OK, you're not Christiano Ronaldo, with an almost vertical labour demand curve. But think how to make yourself vital to your employer, e.g. the only one to speak Mandarin or the one who gets on best with the firm's clients.

Grade B (ii) Why it matters

In the employers' perfect world, the supply and demand for labour would both be price elastic. Then it would be easy and cheap to hire and fire. For many workers, this was a key argument for Brexit – to put a stop to free movement of labour and therefore lower the elasticity of supply of labour; and thereby boost wage rates.

Exam tip: the PES and PED of labour are tough Yr 13 topics – an excellent way to strengthen the analysis in an answer.

Grade A* The critical perspective

It's easy to focus your economic analysis on what's best for firms and therefore economic efficiency. But there's no reason to care about economics if it's not a way to care about people's welfare. So staff's needs matter just as much as firms'.

Labour market elasticities: transmission mechanism (to the top response level)

Chain 1. If labour supply is price inelastic (1) … modest pay rises will have little effect at drawing new employees into the sector (2) … so big pay rises might be necessary (3) ... to persuade people to switch jobs completely (4). So employers prefer price elasticity of labour supply to be high (5).

Chain 2. A firm can increase the price elasticity of its labour supply (1) … by tackling constraints such as geographical flexibility (2). The British School of Tokyo gives new staff a flat or house for at least a year (3)… to encourage teachers to come from Britain (4) … without having to offer high wages (5).

Government intervention to control mergers

Grade C. What is it?

In recent decades governments in America and the UK have tended *not* to intervene in takeovers or mergers. This 'laissez-faire' approach was surely a mistake when allowing Google to buy Youtube, Facebook to buy WhatsApp and Instagram and Tesco to buy hundreds of small shops when it bought T&S Stores. In the UK, this hands-off approach changed in 2018 when Andrew Tyrie became boss of the Competition & Markets Authority (CMA). One of Tyrie's first actions was to stop the planned merger between Sainsbury's and Asda, which would have given the combined group a market share of over 25%.

Grade B (i) Where's the beef?

The beef lies in the tension between the laissez faire instincts of free marketeers, who doubt the competence of government agencies to make a serious business decision. And on the other side are more interventionist economists who think: if the government doesn't stop the monopolisation of markets, who will?

Grade B (ii) Why it matters

It matters for two reasons: the first is the protection of the consumer from exploitation by an overly-dominant business. The key economic argument is wanting to avoid the market failure implied by a monopolist's ability to limit output, increase prices and hinder purchasing by those on low incomes. The second issue (argued by some E.U. governments) is that the ability to compete internationally may be helped by creating bigger business units through mergers.

Grade A The counter-argument

There is always a tension between the arguments: big is better and small is beautiful. But this argument is about economic efficiency and flexibility. If future politics gets dominated by environmental concerns, there may be pressure to focus on waste minimisation and sustainability, rather than unit costs. This may re-shape the debate over big v small – probably in favour of the latter.

Grade A* The critical perspective

It's completely fair to question whether politicians and civil servants are in any position to judge whether consumer and the wider public interest is served by a merger or takeover between two rival companies. But where governments can play a role is in the automatic assumption that mergers between rivals reduce competition and therefore stand in the way of efficiency and fair prices. Any firm wanting to defeat that position would need some amazingly strong arguments.

Do remember that research shows takeovers and (especially) mergers to be a flawed growth strategy – in so far as the majority create negative economic value. So a generally negative mindset by the CMA would be no bad thing – to help save the firms from their own managements.

Don't forget some of the losses made by the great takeover flops:

Daimler/Chrysler lost over $50bn

TimeWarner/AOL lost over $100bn

RBS/ABN Amro cost more than $50bn forced RBS Bank to beg for a UK government bail-out.

Exam tip: Don't assume that senior managements are acting in their firms' best interests. The divorce of owner-ship and control is especially acute with takeovers & mergers.

Government and mergers: transmission mechanism (to top response level)

Chain 1. The toughest government decision comes when two small-ish firms want to merge 'to give stronger competition for the market leader' (1). This sounds like a good thing for consumers (2) ... but only if big is beautiful (3). Why shouldn't two firms provide tougher competition (4) ... as each has to try its hardest to survive in tough market conditions. (5)

Chain 2. Farmers might merge to create a cooperative (or agri-firm) capable of standing up to Tesco (1) ... this could be justified as the only way to tackle a monopsonist (2). But government should be wary of allowing a monopoly supplier to develop (3) ... because even though it could combat the monopsony buyer (4)... it still seems probable that consumers will lose out due to higher prices (5).

Government intervention to control monopolies

Grade C. What is it?

Government action to control a monopoly could be through price regulation, profit regulation, quality and performance standards. These would all be covered by a regulator. There has also been special action in the past to set extra taxes on exceptionally profitable North Sea oil producers. As shown below, an extra tax would increase the monopolist's effective average costs, eating into the firm's supernormal profit. In the diagram, supernormal profit is approximately halved to P1, X, Z, P4 – with the remainder going to the government.

Grade B (i) Where's the beef?

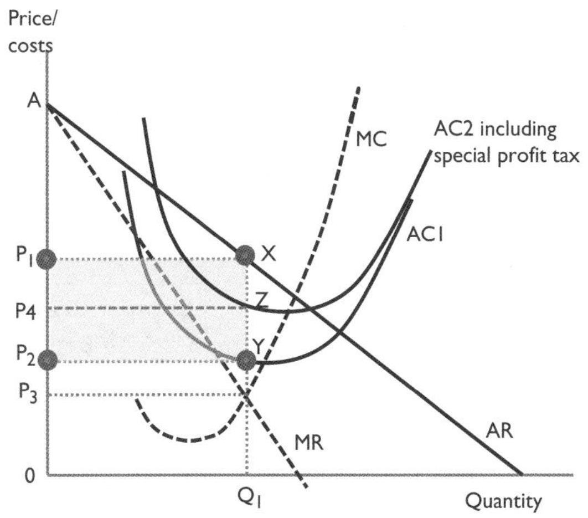

Other interventions:

1. Price regulation might set maximum prices, e.g. a price of P4, which would work as effectively as the profit tax shown.
2. Profit regulation might limit return on capital to perhaps 6%. The problem is that this removes the firm's incentive to be as cost-efficient as possible.
3 Regulating quality or performance targets risks excess bureaucracy, thereby causing government failure.

Grade B (ii) Why it matters

Government intervention matters because consumers (pretty much by definition) have nowhere to go to avoid monopoly power. I must have running water in my house, so I have to buy from Thames Water. I might prefer Welsh Water, but it's not available in London. That's important with water, and perhaps even more important with a life-changing drug (*Zolegensma* by Novatis is priced at $2.1m).

Grade A The counter-argument

Pure free-marketeers mistrust any government intervention. They believe that market responses can be trusted. If a drug is priced at $2.1m, even if its patent cannot be broken, ingenious people will be lured by the supernormal profits to find a way around the patent – and the monopoly will be broken.

Grade A* The critical perspective

A key issue is the problem of regulatory capture. Government-appointed 'independent' regulators are too often in thrall to the interests of the industry, not the consumer. A solution is appoint independent academics, not industry insiders.

Do remember that all government interventions suffer from asymmetric information. The monopoly firm knows more about its business than the government. So the firm may persuade the regulator to agree maximum prices or profit levels that are actually quite easy to achieve.

Don't have too much faith in quality or performance targets. The targets set for UK water and rail regional monopolies have regularly been missed. Trains arrive late and water leakages remain far too high – and the fines paid by the firms are too small to change their behaviour.

Exam tip
Most examiners agree that monopolies should be prevented, but if they exist, need regulation. None would doubt that effective regulation is hard to get right.

Government and monopolies: transmission mechanism (to top response level)

Chain 1. Government regulation of monopolies suffers because the firm's consistent objective is to minimise the effect of the rules (1) ... whereas political parties have shifting policies (2). So the firm outlasts the political will (3) .. weakening the regulator's resolve (4) ... at the cost of the consumer. (5)
Chain 2. There's a strong case for extra taxes on monopoly profits (1) ... perhaps allowing the firm to make its own, unregulated decisions (2) ... but making sure of a social dividend (3) ... from the taxpayer's share of the supernormal monopoly profits (4). The NHS & schools could use the money (5).

Government intervention to promote competition

Grade C. What is it?

To promote competition and contestability, governments can use four measures: promoting small business/entrepreneurship to boost competition; deregulation; competitive tendering for government contracts; and privatisation. Recent governments have tried all four, with varying degrees of success. Perhaps the most consistently promoted has been deregulation – both in the UK and in the United States.

Grade B (i) Where's the beef?

The graph below shows how to turn a boost to competition into a valid diagram. Building an answer around this would make it relatively easy to generate high marks for Knowledge, Application and Analysis.

Grade B (ii) How it's shown

Figure 1. A firm with monopoly power faces competition from new small firms.

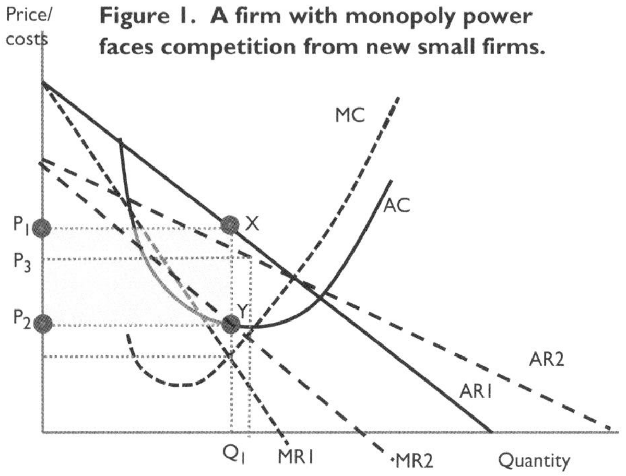

The graph shows the effect of successfully attracting new small firms to enter a monopolistic market. The firm with monopoly power finds its demand curve flattening (from AR1 to AR2) as competition increases the price elasticity of its products/services. So price slips back from P1 to P3, cutting super-normal profit to the benefit of consumers.

Grade A The counter-argument

Past governments and some economists have ended up being confused over their thinking and motives. Instead of focusing on the need to boost competition and ease of market access (to help contestability), policy has focused on transferring assets from the public to the private sector. This simply exposes consumers to the potential for private monopolies to take advantage of their market power.

Grade A* The critical perspective

If it's hard to boost competition, it's even harder to promote contestability. The latter needs fast-moving, flexible firms to push past low barriers to entry and exit. A bold government would shorten the legal life of patents, perhaps to 15 years – but that would require overcoming industrial lobbying, especially from America.

Privatisation means transferring or selling a public sector asset to the private sector. This might open up a monopoly market to competition, as in the case of telephony. Or it might mean switching a state monopoly into a private sector (profit-maximising) monopoly, as with UK water supply.

Competitive tendering was designed to stop the monopoly supply of public services by public sector (often unionised) workforces. Unfortunately, the winning bid goes to the firm promising the lowest prices. This may lead to underpaid staff and a poor quality service.

Deregulation: governments can encourage parliament to repeal laws in the name of removing 'red tape', i.e. bureaucracy.

Government intervention (iii): transmission mechanism (to top response level)

Chain 1. Firms want a flexible labour market (1)... to increase their price elasticity of supply (2). Governments see the importance of this, to increase market contestability (3)... and to help push the LRAS curve to the right (4). Hence the pressure on government to deregulate labour markets. (5)

Chain 2. The worst treatment of customers, such as people in care (1) ... tend to come with public-private partnerships (2) ... where responsibility for customer care falls between the two sectors (3). So it may be best to rely either on full privatisation (4) ... or keeping services in the state's hands. (5)

Government protection of suppliers/employees

Grade C. What is it?

Governments have a great deal of power to help suppliers and employees against the power of monopsonists. For the most part, they choose not to use those powers. Only in the UK grocery sector is there a concerted effort to tackle monopsony. That began in 2013 with the Grocery Code Adjudicator Act. Since then the head adjudicator, Christine Tacon, has acted boldly and independently. No suggestion here of regulatory capture. For example in 2019 the Coop was criticised severely for its failure to warn suppliers they were at risk of being 'de-listed' from the stores. This caused unnecessary damage to small business finances.

Grade B (i) Where's the beef?

The beef lies in the reluctance of governments to take meaningful action. Whistle-blowers in the NHS have received far too little support from government ministers; the same is true of small firms complaining of late payment by monopsonists such as WH Smith and Holland & Barrett. The latter was blamed for a 'purposeful culture of poor payment practices', but no action was taken to help the small firms. Only farmers interest politicians; other small suppliers get talk, not action.

Grade B (ii) Why it matters

It matters because allocative efficiency and contestability are best served by market structures based on rivalry among plenty of small firms. Monopsonists risk pushing small firms out of business – through excessively tough negotiations on price, credit terms and delivery conditions. The potential result is markets dominated by big companies talking to each other – and the consumer losing out.

Grade A The counter-argument

An alternative approach would be to nationalise industries with excessive market and monopsony power. This would mean the government buying out the share-holders – turning the business into a state-owned enterprise. In theory the removal of the profit motive might lead to better behaviour towards suppliers and staff. In fact the track record of state-run industries is little better than private sector firms when it comes to diversity in the workplace, or fairness to suppliers.

Grade A* The critical perspective

Governments have huge powers and great responsibilities. They have an important part to play in the awkward interface between business and society in markets such as cigarettes, alcohol, gambling and the environment. But perhaps they need to be more modest about their expertise and reach. With suppliers in particular, honesty over the limits of intervention might be helpful. Let the supplier beware.

Do remember the need to protect the staff of monopsonists. They are at risk of being exploited because they have no rival employer to go to. So 'whistleblowing' needs special, legal support. If systematic discrimination or bullying takes place at work, staff need to know they will be protected if they tell senior staff (or the media) who is to blame. In fact many whistle-blowers have received too little protection – and lost their jobs/careers. Governments need to do more.

Don't forget that nationalisation has resurfaced. In 2019 a Conservative government renationalised the prisoner probation service. And the sky didn't fall in.

Exam tip: an exam answer on this topic should take a free market v interventionist perspective.

Government protection: transmission mechanism (to top response level)

Chain 1. Monopsonists such as WH Smith have such power over small suppliers (1) ... that there's an irresistible temptation to push down input prices and push up the time taken to pay (2). This could be addressed by a regulator as powerful as in the grocery trade (3) ... but only if politicians and the media showed interest and concern (4). Perhaps there are more important things to focus on (5).

Chain 2. Where government focus would be valuable is in supporting whistle-blowers (1) who call-out discrimination and bullying (2) ... to force changes to firms' practices and culture (3). This can be transformational, as recently at the BBC (4) ...but politicians must give 100% legal & moral support (5)

The impact of government intervention

Grade C. What is it?

This section covers the impact of government intervention on prices, profit, efficiency, quality and choice. For free-marketeers, the impacts are entirely negative, with consumers being hard-hit, as is macro-economic growth, via falling efficiency. This viewpoint is easier to assert than to prove, however, as the UK's awful productivity performance since 2009 has coincided with sustained attempts by government to deregulate and to privatise.

Grade B (i) Where's the beef?

Fig 1. Effect on a firm of heavy government intervention

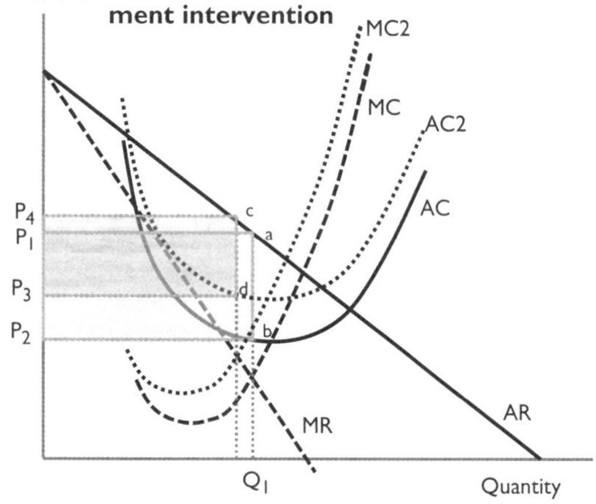

The graph shows a firm's marginal costs and average costs rising due to heavy regulation – as in the financial sector after the 2007-2009 financial crash. A firm in a monopoly (or a short-run monopolistically competitive) market position sees its super-normal profits cut from P1,a,b,P2 to P4,c,d,P3. The firm would complain about the hit to its global competitiveness, but consumers (and taxpayers) may benefit from tighter rules.

Fig 1. On this graph, the effect of government regulation would be to push prices up from P1 to P4; to cut profits sharply; to increase costs per unit and therefore cut efficiency and possibly to force firms to cut their product range and therefore reduce consumer choice. All this might be worthwhile to improve the quality received by consumers – and avoid the £1,000 billion support bill paid by taxpayers to keep the banking system afloat in 2007-2010.

Grade B (ii) Why it matters

Economists urge governments to use market-based methods to boost demand for merit goods or to cut demand for those with negative externalities. A market-based method might use taxes to force consumers to think harder about whether they *really* want Coca-Cola rather than water. This still leaves the consumer able to judge the utility of the can of Coke, i.e. if they're desperate for a Coke, they can pay the higher price. Government regulation, by contrast, can force firms to follow rules that restrict supply in a more drastic way, as in the diagram below.

Fig 2. Negative production externality diagram

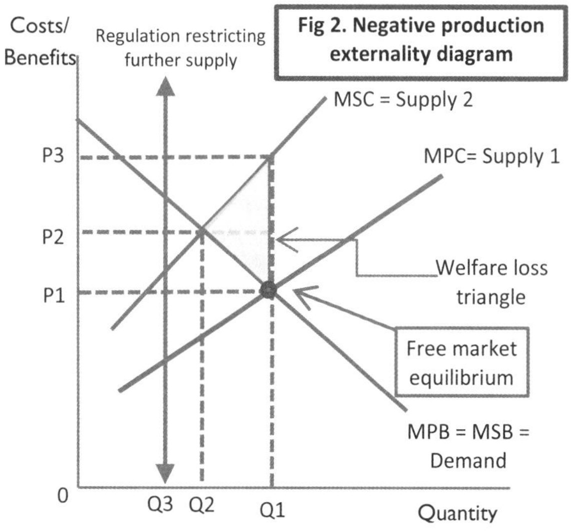

On the left you can see the downside of certain types of government involvement. If the state chooses to tax the item, it pushes the supply curve leftwards, cutting the sales volume from Q1 to Q2. Prices rise (to P2) but thirsty customers can get their bottle of Coke. Regulation can have a more drastic effect, cutting allowable supply to below the level of demand, thereby affecting consumer choice.

Fig 2. could be showing gambling in an untaxed state, where Q1 customers are being put at risk of gambling addiction.

Exam tip

On a graph such as Figure 2 it's easy to forget what is meant by 'welfare loss triangle'. In fact, as drawn there's a case for labelling it 'welfare gain triangle' as it represents the gain to social welfare of taxing the good with negative externalities. It's only a welfare loss if the absence of state intervention means public consumption is at Q1.

The impact of government intervention (ii)

Grade B. Why it matters (ii)

Some government attempts to introduce competition into markets have been failures. Before 2003 'directory enquiries' was a monopoly service offered by BT. It cost 40p and received 600 million calls a year. Then it was deregulated, with lots of different businesses and in 2018 regulator Ofcom said charges were as high as £20 for a 90-second call. To get their numbers recognised firms spent hugely on TV advertising – and then charged high prices to try to cover their costs.

Grade B (i) Where's the beef? – profit controls

Fig 3. Effect on a firm of profit controls encouraging x-inefficiency

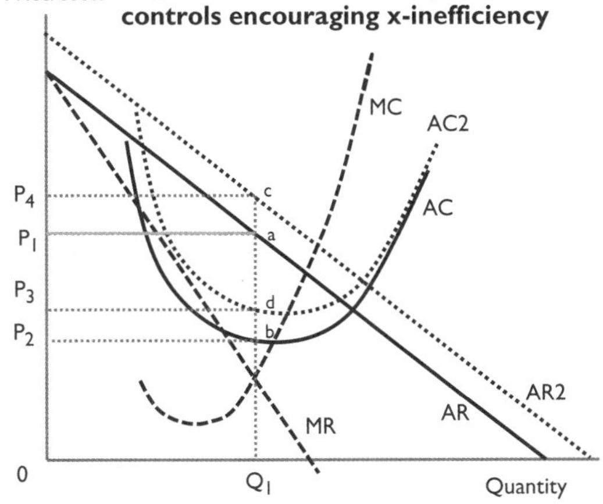

As a way to regulate natural monopolies, governments have insisted that some privatised companies must work within a profit ceiling. This is usually set in relative terms, e.g. as a % of sales or a % of capital employed. Just as Sainsbury and Tesco work for a profit margin of less than 4% of sales revenue, a ceiling of 4% could be set for a monopoly provider of water or electricity. That would appear to protect consumers from a 'rip-off'.

The problem is that a profit ceiling can make a firm complacent about its costs. X-inefficiencies grow and the rising costs are passed on to consumers as rising prices – while the firm carries on making its 4%. So the profit target creates rather than solves a problem.

Grade A The counter-argument

The impact of government intervention can be flawed or disappointing. In some cases there is little excuse. Economists warned against privatising natural monopolies such as water supply and regional railways – but governments went ahead. And then allowed weak regulators to be outwitted and perhaps captured by the main firms in the industry. But in other cases governments feel compelled to act because of moral or environmental pressures or pressure groups. Firms will always find arguments to defend laissez-faire; sometimes governments need the courage to see through the self-interest involved when business leaders' protest.

Grade A* The critical perspective

Politicians and their economic advisors find comfort in using economic theory to justify actions such as using competitive tendering to dismantle an existing, state-salaried workforce. The new private companies running the service offer worse terms and conditions for staff, but the service is provided more cheaply (in the short-run). The rise of populism in the west may partly be due to the mistrust and bitterness felt by staff whose interests have been ignored in this process. They once had secure, well-paid jobs with a career structure. Now they have a zero-hours contract. Economics without moral considerations is 'the dismal science'.

Fig 3 Do remember that you first identify the profit maximising point where MC = MR. Then you continue a vertical line from the horizontal axis up to the AR curve. Then you can identify super-normal profit as the vertical difference between AR and AC multiplied by Q1. In Figure 1, the super-normal profit after cost increases have pushed the AR curve to the right (prices have risen) is the rectangle P4, c,d,P3.

Don't allow this section of the specification to lull you into the view that markets are static and therefore easy to control. In reality markets are changing constantly and both firms and governments struggle to keep up with the changes.

Exam tip
When answering a high-mark question beware of losing track of the question. It happens all the time in exams. The rule is: 'after every paragraph, re-read the exam question'.

Impact of government: regulatory capture

Grade C. What is it?

Governments often set up regulatory agencies to look after stakeholder interests in the face of a firm or firms with significant monopoly power. The regulator's primary concern should be the interests of consumers, but industry efforts to 'capture' the regulator can have a significant effect. Regulatory capture occurs when the regulator is (probably unconsciously) acting to support the interests of the firms rather than the consumer. The lobbying efforts of the firms have been so successful that the regulator absorbs the firms' arguments, not the consumers.

Grade B (i) Where's the beef?

The beef lies with the idea that regulatory capture can be framed as an example of government failure. The state is spending taxpayers' money to correct a market failure – the overcharging of consumers due to manipulation of an overly-strong market position. So if the government's efforts make things no better (or even make them worse), the wasted spending must represent government failure.

Grade B (ii) Why it matters

It matters because most of the regulated industries were previously in the state sector – and were often natural monopolies. Under state ownership the industries may have been relatively inefficient and certainly were under-capitalised, but they were rarely if ever exploitative in a conscious way. So the privatising of these relatively benign institutions created a call for protection of the consumer interests – the regulator.

Grade A The counter-argument

Some might argue that the regulator needs full understanding of the industry – and therefore should have regular, close contacts with industry experts. In pursuing this, the regulator might be won over to the industry's views – on purely rational, objective grounds. Siding with suppliers might not be evidence of 'capture'.

Grade A* The critical perspective

Since the wave of privatisations in the 1980s, sectors such as water and energy have struggled to find a fair balance between the interests of shareholders and the consumer. Regulators Ofwat and Ofgem allowed remarkable feats of financial engineering as many of the individual firms were bought by overseas or private equity firms. After 30 years regulating the water industry, only in 2017 did Ofwat demand lower payouts to shareholders – and more investment in cleaner water and fewer leaks.

Do be aware that regulators have been exposed accepting regular, lavish restaurant meals and 'corporate hospitality' to Wimbledon and Henley. These are called bribes by some, but are more fairly seen as a failure to understand the regulator's need to be – and seen to be – independent.

Don't forget that government failure is not just an abstract concept. There will be costs in running the regulator, then further costs for civil servants who are liaising between politicians and the regulator. These costs eat into the sums available for social care or disability payments.

Exam tip: your examiners care about competition and the consumers' best interests – so they care a lot about regulatory capture.

Regulatory capture: transmission mechanism (to top response level)

Chain 1. For a former state-run utility, focus on customers can slip into focus on shareholders (1) ... and market power over price inelastic essentials such as water (2) … can translate into huge profits (3). So it makes sense for the firm to get involved, pressing the regulator to employ its staff on secondment (4) … perhaps creating a revolving-door effect of staff slipping from regular to regulated and back (5).

Chain 2. A captured regulator could set easy-to-meet targets for maximum costs and maximum profit (1) … possibly ignoring that a major firm has been bought by a private equity fund (2) … that has loaded massive debts on the business (3) ... cutting profits artificially because of huge interest payments (4)… that may also mean no corporation tax is due in the UK. Thames Water was set up this way (5).

Government and asymmetric information

Grade C. What is it?

Asymmetric information is at the heart of many market failures. In many cases, these failures have had lethal consequences, such as the thousands of smokers who under-estimated the risks of their habit. In other cases families have had their finances undermined for life by making a wrong financial decision – perhaps bamboozled by a clever (and more knowledgeable) salesperson. So it is understandable that governments may feel a responsibility to close the most important asymmetries. The problem then can be that the government itself lacks the expertise held within the firms/industry – making it easy to make mistakes.

Grade B (i) Where's the beef?

The beef lies with the clash of philosophy between those who see state intervention as inherently undesirable and those who think *someone* has to look after public welfare – and that has to be an agency of government. It is another example of the intellectual battle between free market and interventionist economics.

Grade B (ii) Why it matters

It matters because if one accepts that the state sometimes has to address asymmetries, it follows that the state must accumulate the expertise to enable wise decisions to be made. Recent years have seen a hollowing out of civil service expertise, with governments outsourcing decisions to management consultancies. These firms may also work for large companies in the industry under scrutiny (e.g. gambling), leaving the government lacking in truly independent expertise.

Grade A The counter-argument

The free market economists' view is summed up in one phrase: 'caveat emptor', or 'let the buyer beware'. They believe the state should not get involved. It is for consumers to take full responsibility for their decisions. Implicitly they see the answer to information asymmetry to be that consumers should work harder to learn and understand the implications of every decision they make.

Grade A* The critical perspective

It is easy to agree with the idea that consumers should take responsibility for their decisions. Unfortunately asymmetric failure may have excessive consequences. A mistaken financial decision aged 22 might drain the family finances for the next 30 years – more like a jail sentence than a penalty for a sloppy decision. Or a bit of fun with gambling might turn into an addiction. So even if it's right that the state does as little as possible, there are times when intervention seems unavoidable.

Do remember the term 'moral hazard'. Economists worry that government action to protect consumers leads to a lazy approach to big decisions, trusting that they'll get their money back. The moral hazard occurs when consumers make reckless decisions – with others having to pay the bills. No government wants this to occur when tackling asymmetric information

Don't forget that information asymmetry may not just be due to lack of research by the consumer – it may be partly due to a conspiracy by the seller – deliberately putting critical factors in print too small to be read in comfort.

Exam tip: accept that information asymmetries are especially likely when government gets involved in high-tech markets.

Asymmetric information: transmission mechanism (to top response level)

Chain 1. When making multi-£billion decisions on building new motorways or railways (1) ... the government needs the in-house expertise to know if building a bridge should cost £40m or £60m (2) ... because they are spending our (taxpayers') money (3). Without that expertise there's a risk of a major information asymmetry (4) ... where private sector suppliers exploit government ignorance (5).

Chain 2. If the government sponsored new laws to protect passengers from airline bankruptcies (1) it might encourage people to book with newer, less financially stable airlines (2) ... safe in the knowledge that the government will arrange their flight home (3). This would create a moral hazard in which travellers become less careful (4) ... and their losses are paid-for by taxpayers or other travellers (5).

Appendix A: Answers to Maths Questions

1.2.3a) Price elasticity

Q1a) Price elastic

Q1b) Price inelastic (-0.8)

Q2a) Revenue per flight

A 15% price rise will change demand by 15% x - 0.2 = -3%.

So sales revenue rises from 200 x £4 = £800

to 194 jars x £460 = £892.40

ANS: revenue rises by £92.40

Q3a) Galaxy PED = % ch in Q (= +40%) / % ch in P (= -10%)

ANS = *minus* 4.

3b) Galaxy sales revenue rises from 80 x £0.60 = £48

to 112 bars x £0.54 = £64.80

ANS: revenue rises by £16.80

Q4a) To boost sales from 40,000 to 50,000 means a 25% sales increase. If PED is -0.625 the calculation is +25% / ? = -0.625. Plus 25% / -0.625 = - 40%, i.e. £1.20 **ANS**

Q4b) PEDs change over time, rising if a product has become less fashionable. Perhaps the product is less trendy now than it was the last time its PED was estimated.

1.2.5b) Price elasticity of supply

Q1a) Supply price elastic

Q1b) Supply price inelastic

Q1c) Unitary price elasticity of supply

2a) This 50% increase in price doubles the desired supply quantity (from 5 to 10). So the PES is +100% / +50% = +2 **ANS**

2b) This 50% price increase increases desired supply by 66.6%, so PES is +1.33 **ANS**

2c) The price rise from £12 to £14 pushes desired supply up by 20% from 25 to 30 units. So a £2 / £12 x 100 = 16.66% price rise increases demand by 20%, making a PES of 20% / 16.66% = +1.2 **ANS**

3. A.I. robots could work 24/7 with the intelligence to make sure that the right stock was made, delivered and shelf-stacked to make sure that customers were always 100% sure of finding a fresh ready-meal of the right type.

1.2.6b) Use of supply and demand diagrams

Q1. New equilibrium is H. (Supply shifts left due to higher costs)

Q2. New equilibrium is K. (Demand shifts left due to higher sales of a rival)

Q3. New equilibrium is B. Demand for choc falls; so does supply price of cocoa

Q4. New equilibrium is H. Cost of the tax makes supply more expensive

Q5. New equilibrium is C. Supply curve shifts rightwards due to lower costs

Q6. New equilibrium is L. Demand for choc rises; demand curve shifts rightwards

Q7. New equilibrium is J. Demand for Quality Street rises; but supply costs rise

Q8. New equilibrium is H. Supply curve shifts leftwards

Q9. New equilibrium is C. Supply curve shifts rightwards due to lower costs

Q10. New equilibrium is L. Demand for Quality Street rises; demand shifts right

Do make sure to set out the formula you're using to answer maths questions. It helps the examiner, but much more importantly it helps you structure your answer. That makes mistakes much less likely.

Don't forget that price elasticity of demand is always negative and price elasticity of supply always positive. Whereas income elasticity and cross price elasticity can be positive **or** negative. So you have to take especial care over YED and XED.

Exam tip: maths-y questions will be 20% of the marks on each exam paper. This is a hugely important 20%. If you're good at them, 20/20 is a serious possibility. While others will be getting 0/20. That makes maths questions a big swing factor in getting top grades.

Appendix B: Quantitative skills in Economics

QS1. Calculate, use and understand ratios and fractions

1a) A firm invests £4.8m into capital equipment and £7.2m into Research & Development (R&D). Ai) Calculate its capital spend: R&D ratio. Aii) Calculate its R&D spend as a fraction of its total investment spending.

1b) If the firm's new investment budget was £15m, what would be the new R&D budget if the ratio was unchanged?

QS2. Calculate and use percentage change and % point change

In 2018 the UK current account deficit was 3.9% of GDP, up from 3.3% in 2017 (ONS data). 2a) Calculate the % change in the deficit between 2017 and 2018.

2b) Calculate the % point change in the deficit between 2017 and 2018.

2c) Explain why the difference matters between these two results.

QS3. Understand & use the terms mean, median and quartiles.

Median earnings for full-time workers are £580; mean average earnings are £720.

3a) Explain the meaning of each term

3b) Which is the more useful indicator of ordinary workers' earnings, and why?

3c) Weekly mean earnings in the bottom quartile are £185. What does that mean?

QS4 is construct & interpret graphs (not covered). **QS5** covered on next page.

QS6 Calculate cost, revenue, profit (marginal, average & total)

Sales (units)	Revenue	Total variable costs	Total fixed costs	Total costs
0	0	0	£2500	£2500
200	£6000	£4000	£2500	£6500
400	£12000	£8000	£2500	£10500

Use the above table to calculate: 6a) Profit if 400 units are sold. 6b) Average costs at 200 and at 400 units of output. 6c) The selling price. 6d) Variable costs per unit.

QS7 Convert from money terms to real terms

7a) In the past 12 months average earnings have risen by 3.5%. Inflation has been 1.9%. Calculate the % change in real incomes.

7b) In the past year the rate of interest has been 0.5% while inflation has been 1.9%. Calculate the real interest rate.

QS8 & 9 are covered elsewhere in this book

QS10 Distinguish between change in level & the rate of change

Sales (units)	Sales (Product A)	Sales (Product B)
2 years' ago	168,000	427,000
Last year	174,000	438,000
This year	183,000	447,000

10a) Calculate the sales growth for Product A and Product B over the past 2 years

10b) Calculate the rate of change in sales for A and B over the past 2 years.

QS11 & 12 will be covered in Book 2 on Macro-economics, out in 2020

Answers Q1-3

1ai. 1:1.5

1aii. 6/10ths

1b. £9m

2a) A 15.4% deterioration in the UK's current account

2b) A decline of 0.6 percentage points.

2c) Opposition politicians will point to the 15.4% deterioration as evidence of economic decline. The government will say no, the fall is only 0.6 of a % point

3ai) Median is the mid-point in a range of everyone's earnings. 3aii) Mean is total earnings divided by total employees. 3b) Median is better, because it isn't distorted by the vast earnings of the super-rich. 3c) That among the lowest-paid quarter of full-time workers, their average pay is £185.

Answers Q6-10

6a) £1,500

6b) £32.50 at 200, £26.25 at 400.

6c) £30

6d) £20

7a) 3.5-1.9=1.6%

7b) *Minus* 1.4% (negative real interest rates)

10a) A = +15,000 B = +20,000

10b) A = + 8.9%

Appendix C: Index numbers in Micro-economics

Brief explanation

Indexing data means taking a data series and relating it to a base period set at 100. The method is used widely in micro and macro-economics.

Do recognise that indexed data is great for comparing apples and oranges, e.g. sales (in units) compared with total variable and/or total unit costs. As the base period will be set in the same year and the data values start at 100, a direct comparison can be made based on trends.

Making date easier to interpret at-a-glance.

A firm wants to relocate and has shortlisted two cities: Manchester and Coventry. Among many other comparisons, the managers want to look at wage rates in each city. They are known to be about 10% higher in Manchester, but this 'time series' data is uncovered:

	Hourly wage Manchester		Hourly wage Coventry	
3 years' ago	£14.50		£12.76	
2 years' ago	£14.70		£12.95	
Last year	£14.92		£13.21	
This year	£15.08		£13.39	

This data can usefully be shown as an index, with the figure for 3 years' ago acting as the base year. Calculate the Coventry figures and write in the boxes.

	Hourly wage Manchester	Wage index 3yrs' ago=100	Hourly wage Coventry	Wage index 3yrs' ago=100
3 years' ago	£14.50	100	£12.76	100
2 years' ago	£14.70	101.4	£12.95	
Last year	£14.92	102.9	£13.21	
This year	£15.08	104.0	£13.39	

Workings and Answers

Coventry wage index:

2 yrs ago: £12.95/£12.76 x 100 = 101.5

Last yr: £13.21/£12.76 x 100 = 103.5

This yr: £13.39/£12.76 x 100 = 104.9

So even though wages are lower in Coventry, they're rising faster.

Aiding comparisons between data sets at a different scale

A firm has two products. One sells around 700,000 units a year; the other sells just under 90,000. The left-hand graph shows the raw sales figures, but trends are impossible to compare. Far more useful is the indexed data on the right.

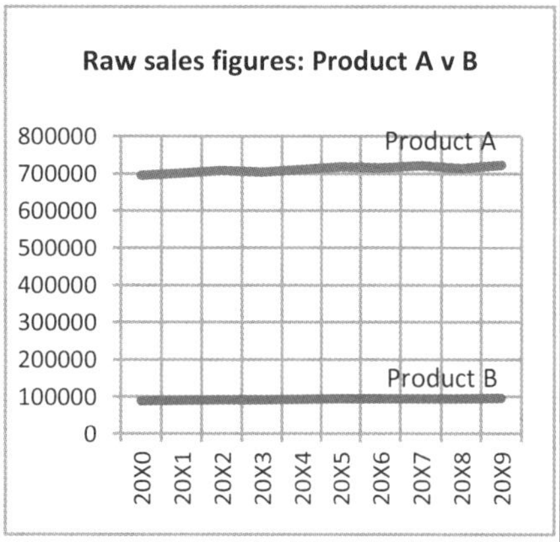

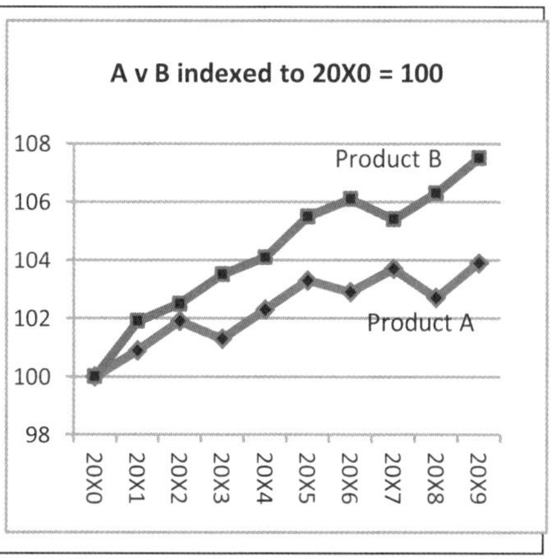

In the right-hand graph, product B's sales go from an index of 106.3 in 20X8 to 107.5 in 20X9. Examiners like to ask for the % change between 20X8 and 20X9, expecting that some will answer +1.2%. In fact the answer is 107.5-106.3/106.3 x100 = +1.1%. year.

Exam tip: with indexed time series, ask yourself why a particular year was chosen as the base period. Is it because it flatters the firm's performance – or makes one manager look more successful than another? When consuming statistics – just as when buying an expensive item – caveat emptor – let the buyer beware.